DANCE TEACHING AND LEARNING:
Shaping Practice

Second Edition

Edited by
Lorna Sanders

Youth Dance England

Edition © Lorna Sanders 2013

Preface © Linda Jasper 2013

Individual chapters © Janet Briggs (14); Sue Davies (19, 20); Linda Jasper (22); Veronica Jobbins (13); Maggie Killingbeck (4); Christina Kostoula (7); Anna Leatherdale (18); Helen Linsell (25); Jo Rhodes (28); Linda Rolfe (8); Jeanette Siddall (11, 12, 17); Lorna Sanders (1, 2, 5, 9, 15, 16, 21, 23, 26); Alysoun Tomkins (3, 6, 10, 24, 27).

All rights reserved. No reproduction, copy or transmission of this publication may be made without written permission from the publisher.

First published 2012 by
Youth Dance England
Unit 7G2, The Leathermarket, Weston Street, London SE1 3ER

Second Edition - 2013
Youth Dance England
Unit A402A, The Biscuit Factory, 100 Clements Road, London SE16 4DG

Youth Dance England is the national organisation that champions excellence in dance for and with children and young people. www.yde.org.uk

Charity registration: 1105635
Company registration: 5033279

ISBN 978-0-9573112-1-3

Designed by Youth Dance England.

Front cover: Taha Ghauri (front), Chaeyoung Chang (left), Joey Latimer (right). Photographer: Brian Slater

Printed and bound in the United Kingdom.

Contents

Preface		5
Acknowledgements		7
Notes on the Contributors		8
Editor's Introduction		10

UNIT 1 TEACHING AND LEARNING IN DANCE — 13

1	Learning Theories (Part 1): Overview *Lorna Sanders*	14
2	Learning Theories (Part 2): Motor Learning Theory and Dance Teaching *Lorna Sanders*	25
3	Teaching Styles *Alysoun Tomkins*	35
4	Movement Analysis in Dance *Maggie Killingbeck*	44
5	Session Planning (Part 1): Breaking Down Individual Tasks *Lorna Sanders*	57
6	Session Planning (Part 2 – macro level issues): A Planning Framework *Alysoun Tomkins*	66
7	Inclusive Dance Practice: Barriers to Learning *Christina Kostoula*	75
8	Fostering Creativity in Dance Education *Linda Rolfe*	83
9	Assessment in Dance *Lorna Sanders*	93
10	Evaluation of Dance Teaching Practice *Alysoun Tomkins*	102

UNIT 2 PROFESSIONAL KNOWLEDGE OF DANCE TEACHING — 113

11	Youth Dance Contexts (part 1): Arts, Culture and Sports Contexts *Jeanette Siddall*	114
12	Youth Dance Contexts (part 2): Health and Youth Justice *Jeanette Siddall*	122
13	Dance in the Formal Education System *Veronica Jobbins*	130
14	Dance Training (part 1): Anatomy and Child Development *Janet Briggs*	136
15	Dance Training (part 2): Training Principles, Hydration, Nutrition *Lorna Sanders*	146
16	Dance Training (part 3): Safe Practice *Lorna Sanders*	153

17	The Legislative Framework (Part 1) *Jeanette Siddall*	162
18	The Legislative Framework (Part 2). Legal Requirements for Dance Practitioners *Anna Leatherdale*	167
19	The Professional Context (Part 1): Working Well with Others *Sue Davies*	174
20	The Professional Context (part 2): You and Your Career *Sue Davies*	184

UNIT 3 CRITICAL REFLECTION ON DANCE TEACHING — 195

21	Critique not Criticism: Observing Teaching *Lorna Sanders*	196
22	Good Practice in Dance Teaching *Linda Jasper*	206
23	Models of Good Teaching *Lorna Sanders*	216

UNIT 4 DANCE TEACHING IN PRACTICE — 227

24	The Reflective Journal *Alysoun Tomkins*	228
25	Behaviour Management and Communication in Practice *Helen Linsell*	236
26	Presenting a Detailed Lesson Plan *Lorna Sanders*	247
27	Preparing for the Viva Voce *Alysoun Tomkins*	253
28	Rehearsing a Lesson for Assessment *Jo Rhodes*	256

Preface

This publication aims to support dance artists, leaders, practitioners and teachers who work with children and young people, to reflect on their practice and learn from others working in dance education, youth dance and wider education and community contexts beyond statutory education.

There is a growing demand by children and young people to dance and an increasing number of dance professionals who wish to progress their skills and knowledge in teaching and leading. Youth Dance England, the national organisation that champions and supports young people's dance, has produced this publication as part of its work in developing the qualification, Diploma in Dance Teaching and Learning (Children and Young People), as a member of the Dance Training and Accreditation Partnership (DTAP). DTAP is a consortium of leading national dance organisations in England created as a result of action taken by the sector to address long standing issues concerning standards of teaching / leading – beyond statutory education and the private dance sector. Trinity College London was commissioned by DTAP to produce this new dance teaching qualification, working closely with its members. Youth Dance England (YDE) led on this development on behalf of DTAP and identified the need to create resources to support dance practitioners wishing to take the qualification.

DTAP has also created The Dance Register (led by the Council for Dance Education and Training) that is the first register of its kind, to help people from across the UK find suitably trained and/ or experienced dance teachers, leaders and artists in their area. Another new development from DTAP is the Foundation for Community Dance's series of leaflets on the National Occupational Standards in Dance Leadership - one for dance artists, one for dance employers and one for providers of continuing professional development. More information is available at:
www.dtap.org.uk

The publication covers a wide range of areas that are relevant to practitioners. Although it is written for those who mainly work in extra-curricular, community, recreational and youth contexts in dance, it is also relevant to a wide range of people including: independent dance artists / practitioners; employees in dance organisations; agencies and companies; students enrolled on courses at Higher Education Institutions and other training and education establishments offering undergraduate courses in dance education; postgraduate students training in applied areas such as teaching / dance development; PGCE students; undergraduate and postgraduate students within Europe and elsewhere.

The publication provides the following:
- a tool for learning by giving an overview, applied specifically to dance, of key theories, concepts and frameworks that can be applied practically by practitioners as a means to critically analyse their own practice and that of others
- an articulation of the field of enquiry and introduction to its knowledge base and skills to those who may be / will be unfamiliar with it
- information for practitioners on the range of theories, concepts, research in the field to ensure that they know where to seek relevant material to support their study and practice
- illustrations of the range of practice that takes place within various contexts in which practitioners work with young people

- a new dance resource that scopes a field of practice that is not represented in other publications.

As there is a recognised shortage of material that adapts learning theories, concepts and frameworks specifically to dance and for the different contexts in which the artists / practitioners work with children and young people, YDE commissioned contributions from 12 leading experts in the field, edited by Lorna Sanders (an eminent dance educationalist, academic and writer) to create this publication.

The publication was originally produced with funding from the Paul Hamlyn Foundation who supported YDE to deliver a two-year research project to test out different training and mentoring models to support practitioners to take the qualification.

Linda Jasper
Director, Youth Dance England

Linda Jasper is Chair of the Dance Training and Accreditation Partnership's Qualification Working Group and she also directed the Qualification Research Group's work, funded through the Paul Hamlyn Foundation, to test methodologies for delivering training / mentoring schemes associated with the Diploma in Dance Teaching and Learning (Children and Young People).

Acknowledgements

I wish to thank all the contributors who so generously gave up their time to write their chapters at short notice. And a particular word of thanks to Lucy Zidour for designing the book and especially to Linda Jasper for her unstinting support.

Lorna Sanders

Notes on the Contributors

Dr Lorna Sanders (Editor) taught in schools and community contexts for over 20 years. She lectures on Masters courses in Holland and Malta and is course leader for Ballet Education Practice, a teacher training course run by The Royal Ballet School / Royal Opera House Education. The author of numerous resources for teachers and two books, on Henri Oguike and Akram Khan, she co-edited a new edition of *Fifty Contemporary Choreographers* (Routledge 2011). She is Professional Development Manager (Education and Community Programme) at Trinity Laban and an assessor for DDTAL.

Janet Briggs MSc MCSP is a dance physiotherapist, working for the Royal Ballet School and RBS Associate Programme for 19 years. She also works with Laban CAT Students. Other posts have included: Royal Ballet Company, the Remedial Dance Clinic and the Australian Ballet School. Paediatric work includes Royal Manchester Childrens Hospital and Great Ormond Street. She is joint author of 2 papers on 'Hypermobility in Dancers' (Rheumatology 2004 and 2009) and has presented at IADMS conferences in both the USA and UK.

Sue Davies MA, PGC Business Psych, B.ED provides learning and development services tailor made for dance artists & organisations. Her career coaching practice is person centred and helps individuals make their own career decisions. Sue also offers research, evaluation and training. She has been working in dance for over thirty years in a range of capacities. Her breadth of experience provides a sound base for her strategic knowledge about dance organisations and how people can work well together.

Linda Jasper MBE, MA, Cert.Ed is Director of Youth Dance England. Trained as a dancer and a teacher of dance, before starting YDE she was Director of South East Dance and Senior Professional Training Tutor for the University of Surrey's Department of Dance Studies. Working as the first Dance Development Officer for Berkshire during the 1980s she initiated a county-wide dance programme. She writes for many publications and co-edited *Managing Dance: current issues and future strategies*, with Jeanette Siddall

Veronica Jobbins is Head of Professional and Community Studies at Trinity Laban where she directs the Education and Community Programme and lectures in Dance Education and Teaching Studies. She trained as a specialist dance teacher before teaching for 20 years in London secondary schools and further education colleges, including time as an advisory teacher with the ILEA PE Inspectorate. Veronica has taken an active interest in promoting and developing dance in schools throughout her career and was instrumental in the formation of the National Dance Teachers' Association in 1988, of which she was Chair until 2008.

Maggie Killingbeck M.Phil is a Principal Lecturer at the University of Bedfordshire where she leads the PGCE Dance course, is Head of Dance on the undergraduate Physical Education programme and an Employability Fellow. Maggie has taught dance at all levels from primary through to higher education in addition to dance inset courses. Maggie is a member of the Lisa Ullmann Travelling Scholarship Fund Management Committee and a moderator for GCSE Dance.

Dr Christina Kostoula trained as an inclusive arts practitioner and became an outreach member of Chicken Shed Theatre Co. She was artistic leader of a children's theatre group in East London and her PhD thesis offered a Critique of Inclusive Dance Education and Performance. She has been a visiting lecturer at Goldsmiths College, Middlesex University and University of Surrey. She is currently a research leave cover, lecturing in Dance at Roehampton University.

Anna Leatherdale studied contemporary dance at the Laban Centre where she obtained her Master's degree before going on to work with the Council for Dance Education and Training and the National Campaign for the Arts. She currently works for Trinity College London, and the Foundation for Community Dance, and continues to teach and perform in a variety of community contexts throughout the UK and Europe.

Helen Linsell has worked extensively as a community and education dance practitioner in a range of settings across the UK and internationally and is now Artistic Director of Dance United Yorkshire. Helen has delivered five years of intensive contemporary dance projects with young offenders and young people from challenging circumstances and is now leading Dance United's development in the Yorkshire region. Helen is also a mentor on the DDTAL course with Yorkshire Dance.

Jo Rhodes has created professional work and been commissioned to choreograph for various youth dance companies, performing across the UK. She was the producer / choreographer of a dance and film project screened nationally and internationally. Jo has worked extensively as a freelance artist in community, education and university settings, forging cross-sector partnerships. She authored 'Raising Choreographic Standards', YDE and 'Dance Active', DanceXchange. Jo undertook the DDTAL qualification as a pilot student in 2011.

Linda Rolfe worked in schools, directed youth dance companies and was an advisory teacher. As senior lecturer at the Graduate School of Education, University of Exeter, she lead the Secondary PGCE Dance and Masters in Creative Arts courses. Linda was an Ofsted inspector for dance and a lead assessor for the CDET. Her publications included books and articles on dance education. She was editor of the international journal *Research in Dance Education*.*

Jeanette Siddall is a freelance consultant, previously Director of Dance for Arts Council England and Director of Dance UK. She has worked with the Department for Education's Music and Dance Scheme on the development of Centres for Advanced Training (CATs) and evaluated Youth Dance England's pilot School Dance Coordinators programme. She co-edited *Managing Dance* with Linda Jasper and wrote *Dance In and Beyond Schools* (2010).

Alysoun Tomkins taught in schools, theatre-in-education and community contexts for 20 years. Following this she lectured in community dance at Trinity Laban and was subsequently appointed as Head of Community Dance and One Year Programmes. She has also lectured at London Contemporary Dance School, University of Surrey, Roehampton and taught in Madrid, Hong Kong, South Korea, Italy and Taiwan. Alysoun currently delivers the DDTAL qualification at Swindon Dance and is a DDTAL assessor.

---

* In early 2012, Linda Rolfe sadly passed away before publication of this book. Her knowledge, expertise and enthusiasm for dance will be sorely missed.

Introduction
Lorna Sanders

This edited collection of twenty eight chapters offers new ways of investigating how frameworks from diverse disciplines such as aesthetics, psychology, education, youth and community, safe and effective dance practice can be applied to the teaching of children and young people. It does not replicate publications that are 'how to teach' text books but is written to stimulate debate about good practice and to provide support for practitioners in planning, delivering and evaluating their own practice.

Provision of enjoyable, high quality dance experiences for children and young people requires teachers and leaders who are knowledgeable and passionate about their subject. Whether you are experienced or embarking on a career, this book offers information and guidance to help improve your practice, and practitioners undertaking a variety of dance teaching qualifications will find the content useful.

Chapters are organised into four sections, corresponding to the units of study required for the Diploma in Dance Teaching and Learning (Children and Young People), referred to as DDTAL:

- Teaching and Learning in Dance
- Professional Knowledge of Dance Teaching
- Critical Reflection on Dance Teaching
- Dance Teaching in Practice

The aim is not to provide narrowly focused DDTAL assessment advice, rather the book offers insight into key theories, knowledge, methods and processes in order to develop broader understanding.

How to use the book: each chapter introduces a topic and provides an overview, with case studies, reflective questions and a bibliography. Where chapter content cross references with that of another chapter, this is indicated.

Learning is more effective when the content is actively responded to, so be as interactive as possible and approach each chapter as a learning opportunity. Use a note book to keep a record of thoughts and questions.

Case Studies are provided to help application of the information to individual practice. It is important to engage in considering these fully, as and when they arise. Use a note book to keep a record of the responses to the case studies and to track developments in thinking.

Reflection sections provide guidance questions to encourage reflection on the whole topic and to point to further applications in practice. Respond to each question in turn to assist a deepening and enrichment of understanding before moving on to the next chapter.

Bibliographies at the end of each chapter not only list the sources used but also function as further reading to follow up. This will deepen research and understanding since key texts for the topic are included.

Standard use of terminology and concepts, aligned with that used in the current DDTAL syllabus, is maintained wherever possible across all chapters. The terms and concepts are broadly in line with those used more widely within the education sector and where other sources might refer to these differently an attempt is made to identify this.

Details of the DDTAL qualification can be found on the following website: www.trinitycollege.co.uk/ddtal

For this second edition I have updated many of the chapters and bibliographies to indicate the position, as far as possible, of current legal requirements, new government policies, new research and new initiatives by dance organisations.

UNIT 1

TEACHING AND LEARNING IN DANCE

Chapter 1
Learning Theories (part 1): Overview
Lorna Sanders

Introduction

We all have a personal notion, whether we know it or not, of what learning is, how it takes place and how we know that we have learned something. This is a learning theory.

Consideration of how we learn is a huge field, and since no single theory has yet accounted for all its aspects the information in this chapter is intended as an introduction.

A definition of learning is that it is 'the process whereby knowledge is created through the transformation of experience' (Kolb, 1984, p. 38). From our experience of raw reality we discriminate between the critical attributes of different objects, we identify types and eventually form categories of things. In turn, these develop into the broad concepts with which we learn to function in the world and eventually we express our understanding of experience using abstract representations (for example words or mathematical symbols).

Concept formation, the result of our assimilation and accommodation of experience, is a way of understanding the world and our place within it. This points to the fact that the process of learning is generally thought of as needing an active engagement and this notion underpins most current theories.

> Learning occurs when we take in information, think about it, make sense of it, and fit it in with what we already know. This may mean changing what we already know, or may confirm our previous knowledge. Learning also requires that we can see how to apply new information and where to apply it.
>
> (Diploma in Dance Teaching and Learning, Syllabus, p.12)

Learning theories fall into four categories based around slightly different assumptions about the place of experience and how human beings function in relation to it.

1. Behavioural Learning Theories

In the early years of the 20th century, change in behaviour was seen as the immediate response to external stimuli. For example, **Pavlov** discovered that dogs would salivate when offered food and that they would also do this when an associated cue (stimulus), such as a sound, was heard. The dogs learned to salivate (a conditioned response) and expect food to appear just from hearing the sound alone (conditioned stimulus). This was termed classical conditioning. The learning process is one of association and the response becomes stronger with each reinforcement of the stimulus-response activity.

Skinner developed a theory of operant conditioning by experimenting with rats. They learned to press levers to gain food and their trial and error activity quickly became intentional. The desired behaviour needed to be followed by an almost immediate reward, but once established the learned tendency would continue with only intermittent reinforcement. Under these theories, behaviour is adapted in response to a stimulus and learning is seen to have taken place. Behaviour modification was considered to be possible through a systematic application of the conditioning processes.

2. Cognitive Learning Theories

Piaget provided a hugely influential theory of cognitive development. He aimed 'to discover, by analysing performance and verbal introspections, the quality and nature of children's concept attainment at a particular time in their lives' (Child, 1995, p.157).

According to Piaget, children's thinking evolves through a series of predetermined biological phases. To mature is to progress through all of these in chronological order and when meeting new information adults may return to an earlier stage in order to begin to process it. This cognitive approach also has reflex action and behaviour at its base. Piaget describes how we learn through forming sensori-motor action schemas. Babies respond to the environment using reflex activity and this begins to develop purpose. For example, the grasp reflex is adapted to grip objects that come into reach: this becomes an extended reflex. Memory begins to develop rudimentary thinking skills, seen when a baby is surprised when a grasped object does not behave quite like last time, such as when a dropped object disappears. A schema develops in which the toddler / baby adapts the extended reflex to similar situations and learns to modify it to meet new demands, for example holding a spoon to scoop up food.

This requires active learning, in which play and imitation are essential. When sensori-motor action schemas are replaced by symbols (words) the child is able to represent the world mentally – they have internalised and assimilated experience. This means that through language, objects can be represented in their absence and that for Piaget thought is a form of internalised action. Symbolic language frees us from the need to manipulate raw reality in order to form new schema.

- We can eventually move into manipulating thinking operations (or thought processes) rather than just being at the whim of what happens in the real world.
- We can undertake mental operations and operate in the realm of abstract thinking.
- We begin to move from concrete experience to abstraction.
- We can deal with increasing complexity.

Piaget's developmental stages are outlined in Chapter 14 and will not be repeated here. An excellent source for understanding the theory and for further information about the application of the stages is Fontana (1995).

Piaget's work has been criticised for its dependence on language-based evidence, its ignoring of the importance of cultural factors and for overemphasising a strict age-related chronology of development. His theories have influenced many others however. Kohlberg, for example, although retaining the notion of biological stages, considers that age is less important in this and that 'people's conceptual level contains a mixture of different stages of development' (Jarvis *et al*, 2005, p.35).

Vygotsky places more emphasis on social influences. He considered 'it is the reality and the relations between a child and reality that are missed in his [Piaget] theory (Vygotsky, in Jarvis *et al*, 2005, p. 36). Vygotsky suggests that culture, its symbolic representations and tools have an impact on how concepts are structured in the first place. He also points out that children begin to recognise superficial relationships between similar things and can often *appear* to understand the labels that adults give to concepts before they have full understanding of these; they develop pseudo-concepts (Child, 1995). Hence, concepts and verbal acquisition need to be built together. Vygotsky (1978) also introduced the useful notion that there are two levels in the learning process: the actual developmental level reached, and what he terms the Zone of Proximal Development (ZPD). This ZPD is the gap between the level that the individual can demonstrate on their own and the increased achievement they can master when supported by adults or when collaborating with peers of higher ability. This challenges views that consider learning as a mainly individual process and highlights the importance of its social character. Whereas for Piaget cognitive development precedes learning, the significant point for Vygotsky is that 'developmental processes do not coincide with learning progression. Rather the developmental process lags behind the learning process' (Jarvis *et al*, 2005, p.37). For Vygotsky, learning precedes cognitive development.

> **Zone of Proximal Development**
>
> Skills that are too difficult to master can be accomplished with the provision of scaffolding

What is known ──────────▶ What is not known

The provision of appropriate assistance and guidance / scaffolding, is important in order to boost learning to the next level. Once the student has accomplished the task, the scaffolding can be removed so that they will then be able to complete the task again on their own. The teacher or peer providing support is there as a facilitator until the learner becomes independent. Under this view, group members should have different levels of ability so more advanced peers can help the less advanced. It needs differentiated and individualised instruction, and scaffolding can take many forms.

Case Study 1

Identify an occurrence when you learned something complex and new. Was scaffolding involved? How were you guided or supported? Did your peers assist?

Vygotsky considered that children undergo conceptual development more effectively through social interaction and when involved within their ZPD. Key to success is identifying the area just beyond a child's capability, but not too challenging.

Bruner (1966) looked at how learners transform information. He considered there were three modes of representation: Enactive, which does not use imagery or words but operates through action (learning by doing); Iconic, which employs imagery to form a conception (picturing the information); and Symbolic, which uses language and similar abstract modes, in reflective thinking. For example, Fontana (1995) offers the following example of a stranger asking for the way. You can accompany him to show him the route (Enactive), or you can draw a map (Iconic), or you can give him verbal instructions (Symbolic). Bruner considers that children develop through these three modes (a development approach similar to Piaget).

Bruner's work encouraged discovery learning. Conceptualisation is seen as 'an active process in which the learner infers principles and rules and then tests them out' (Fontana, 1995, p.145). The significance of the learner's own knowledge, their personal characteristics and behaviour is highlighted and he considers that there are three major cognitive processes:

- Acquisition of information.
- Transformation or manipulation of this information.
- Testing and checking the adequacy of this information.

(Bruner, in Fontana, 1995, p. 165)

Scaffolding (different forms of guidance) is again important. The teacher needs to keep a clear eye on the learning objectives while providing support by using different means to suit the level of conceptual ability of children. Although it is important for learners to discover facts for themselves, discovery learning should not be a hit and miss affair but needs a clear presentation of principles, simulation and problem solving processes. In particular, Bruner's work points to the personal layers involved in transforming experience:

> by filtering it into [...] the categories he or she already has for understanding the world [...] [the stimulus] becomes a personal thing, which individuals interpret (or misinterpret) and transform in their own fashion dependent upon their previous experiences, thoughts and aspirations.

(Fontana, 1995, pp. 144-145)

3. Social Learning Theories

Bandura (1977) builds on socialisation theory. People do not just react to external circumstances. There is a continual process of social interaction between cognition, behaviour, and the environment. This is less hierarchical and more cyclical than Piaget's view. The communicative aspects of learning generate expectations about projected outcomes which in turn alter behaviour and subsequent expectations (Jarvis et al, 2005). If expectations are met this strengthens the behaviour; if they are not, this weakens it.

Bandura points to the importance of imitation and mimicry in the learning process with children watching others model behaviour and social expectations. He conducted a famous piece of research in which young children shown a film of aggressive behaviour in adults repeated this without any further reinforcement. Of particular interest is the notion of tolerance limits, in which responses can be strengthened or weakened, and the idea that children adapt or inhibit their behaviour accordingly. 'For example, if children see a certain kind of behaviour go unpunished which they previously regarded as punishable, they are less likely to inhibit their behaviour' (Child, 1995, p. 108).

The theory argues that individuals are more likely to emulate that which is modelled if it matches behaviour already in their repertoire, or if the role model is admired, or the behaviour is perceived to have functional value. Bandura observes that 'it is evident from informal observation that vicarious learning experience and response guidance procedures involving symbolic and live models are utilised extensively in social learning to short-circuit the acquisition process' (Bandura, in Child, 1995, p. 109).

4. Experiential Learning Theories

These offer the notion of a whole person: 'the cognitive, the physical, the emotional and the spiritual: that is, the individual's knowledge, skills, attitudes, values, beliefs, emotions and senses' (Jarvis et al, 2005, p. 55).

In this broad category experience is seen as the foundation and the stimulus:

- Learners actively construct their own experience.
- Learning is holistic.
- Learning is socially and culturally constructed.
- Learning is influenced by the socio-economic context within which it occurs.

(Miller and Boud, 1996, in Jarvis et al, 2005, p. 56)

Kolb considered how experience is translated into concepts. In this he was influenced by Lewin's experiential model. See *Figure 1*.

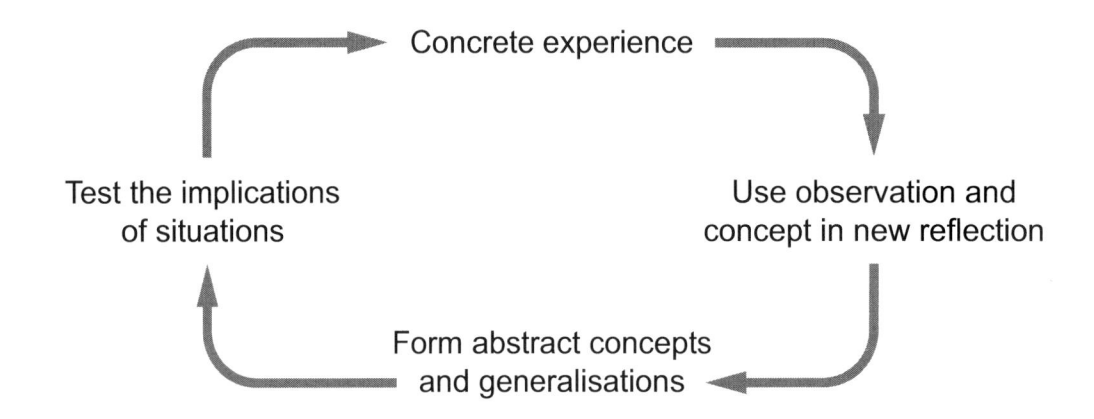

Figure 1: Lewin's Experiential Model, adapted from Kolb (1984)

Kolb developed Lewin's four aspects. 'Four different kinds of abilities...correspond to the four stages of his learning cycle...any individual will have strengths in particular parts of them...and will need to develop the skills to operate along the full range (Boud et al, 1994, pp. 12-13). These abilities are: Concrete-Experience (CE); Reflective-Observation (RO); Abstract-Conceptualisation (AC); and Active-Experimentation (AE).

Learners must be able to:

- Involve themselves fully, openly, and without bias in new experiences (CE).
- Reflect on and observe their experiences from many perspectives (RO).
- Create concepts that integrate their observations in logically sound theories (AC).
- Use these to make decisions and solve problems (AE).

(Kolb, 1984, p. 30)

Kolb saw these as generating personal preferences in ways we perceive and process information. See *Figure 2*.

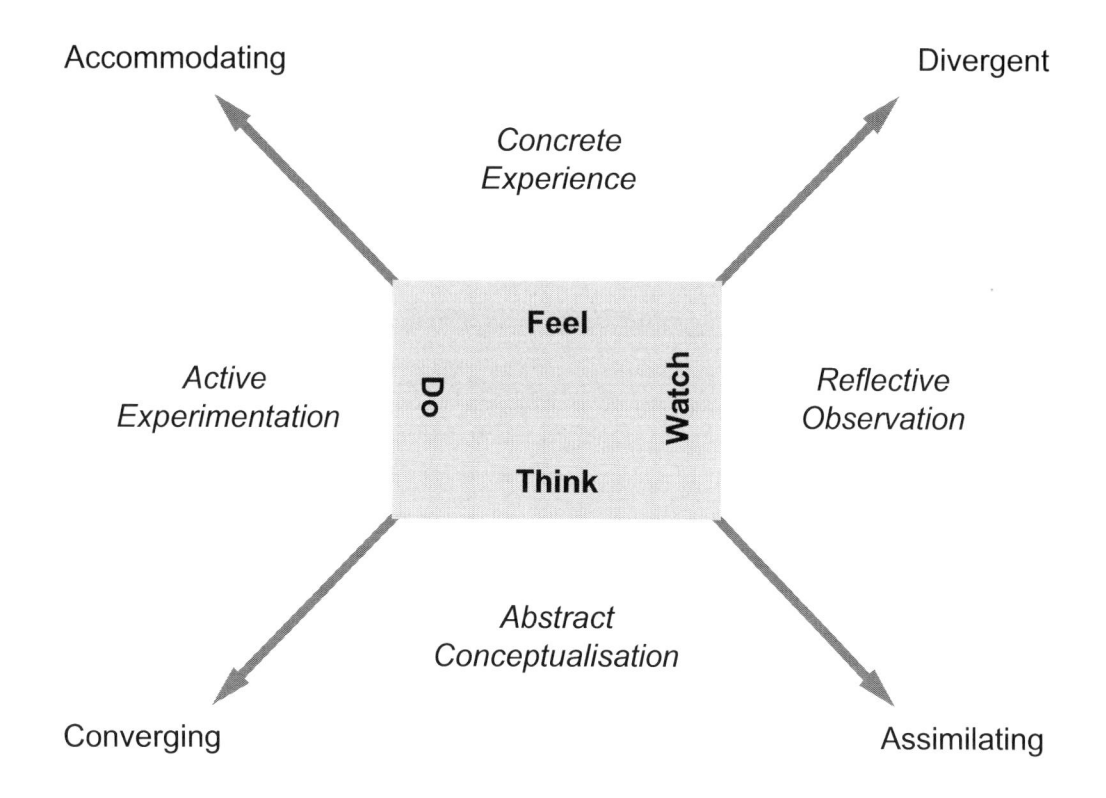

```
Accommodating                          Divergent
         ↖         Concrete         ↗
                  Experience
              ┌─────────────┐
              │    Feel     │
   Active     │             │   Reflective
Experimentation│ Do    Watch │   Observation
              │    Think    │
              └─────────────┘
                  Abstract
         ↙    Conceptualisation    ↘
Converging                           Assimilating
```

Figure 2: Adapted from Kolb and Fry (1975)

- Divergent thinkers are strong in imaginative ability, good at generating ideas and seeing things from different perspectives. They like to ask 'why'.
- Assimilators have strong ability to create theoretical models, enjoy inductive reasoning and abstract concepts. They like to ask 'what' and have the most cognitive approach.
- Convergers prefer the practical application of ideas, they like reasoning based on specific problems (forming and then testing a hypothesis). They like to ask 'how'.
- Accommodators enjoy reacting to circumstances and solving problems intuitively. They like a hands-on approach, and prefer doing. They like to ask 'what if?'.

(Source: http://changingminds.org)

Case Study 2

Do any of these descriptions match you and your preferences when learning? Do you have a propensity to feel, to do, to watch or to think?

Honey and Mumford (1995) developed a typology of learning styles associated with the stages in Kolb's learning cycle. See *Figure 3* on the next page.

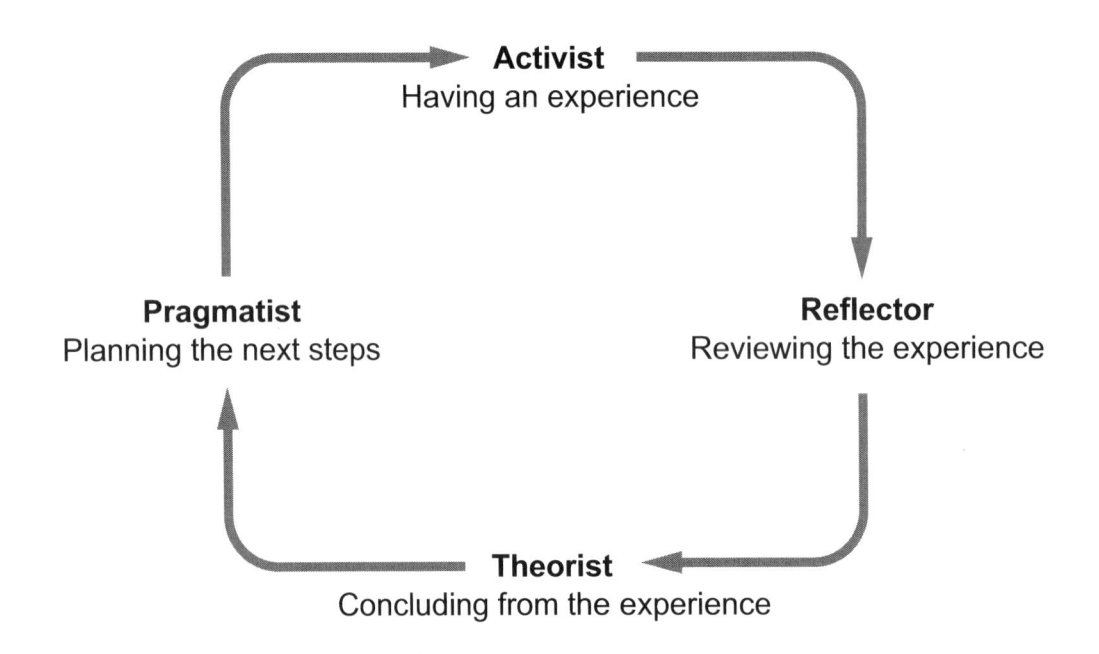

```
         Activist
   Having an experience

Pragmatist              Reflector
Planning the next steps  Reviewing the experience

         Theorist
   Concluding from the experience
```

Figure 3: Learning cycle and styles adapted from Honey and Mumford (1995) p. 13.

- Activists learn best from shorter here-and-now tasks involving active learning, structured team work, games; they learn least well when listening or in a passive role.
- Reflectors learn best from activities where they can stand back and observe or listen and where they can collect information and think about it; they learn least well when rushed into things without time to plan.
- Theorists learn best when they review a concept, a theory or a model, and are interested in quite abstract ideas; they learn less well from activities presented without theory.
- Pragmatists learn best when there is a link between the content to be learned and a real-life problem, and where strategies / techniques can be applied to their immediate circumstances; they learn less well when activities do not have immediate relevance.

(Honey and Mumford, 1995)

For further information, see www.learningandteaching.info

Fleming and VARK

VARK (Visual, Aural, Read / write, Kinaesthetic) are categories of instructional preferences which 'are focused on the different ways we take in and give out information' (Fleming, 2006, p. 1). Often it is forgotten that these are modes, based on perceptual preferences. For example, the idea that visual learners learn best from watching dance is overly simplistic. A description of the four types is given below. All the information quoted is from Fleming (2006).

Visual: these learners are more aware of their immediate environment and their place in space. They respond to charts, diagrams, symbolic patterned information which represents concepts and words (p. 1). This category does not include pictures, movies, videos and animated websites (simulation) that belong with kinaesthetic.

Aural: have a preference for spoken / heard information. They respond to discussion, oral feedback and tutorials (p. 2).

Read / write: have a preference for information displayed as words. They respond well to quotations, lists, texts (p. 2).

Kinaesthetic: have a preference for using experience and practice, whether simulated or real. They respond well when connected to reality: 'some theorists believe that movement is important for this mode but it is the reality of the situation that appeals most' (p. 2). They respond well to example, practice and simulation.

Multimodal: there is no clear preference or an equally strong preference for two, three or four modes is present. Any mode will suffice and the danger here is that when different modes repeat the same information they get bored.

One further clarification is needed. These preferences are not static because learning and experience is a dynamic relationship. We also need to develop the full range for effective learning and familiarisation with all modes is important. Preferences will vary across different contexts, purposes, age and culture for example, and all are teachable/can be learned.

Howard Gardner's Multiple Intelligences Theory

Gardner developed his theory as 'a way of conceptualising the human intellect' (1999, p. 3). He considers that intelligence is not one single capacity but is multiple. Initially, he identified linguistic, logical, musical, spatial, kinaesthetic, interpersonal and intrapersonal (Gardner, 1983). In 1999 he added naturalistic, spiritual, existential and moral. The theory, although it caused widespread interest, remains contentious and many theorists do not agree with it. They see intelligence not as a range of discrete capacities but as forms of intelligent behaviour.

Linguistic intelligence is associated with the auditory sense. It appears as an appreciation of differences in the subtle shades of meaning of words, for example, as in spilling the ink "intentionally" or "deliberately". Perception is alert to word order, quality of their sounds, rhythms, emphases, and also to the different functions of language, for example, its potential to move, to argue, or to convey facts.

Musical intelligence, also connected to the auditory sense, begins to emerge by age two or three. Like linguistic intelligence with which it seems associated, it shows itself in the ability to appreciate pitch, tone and rhythm.

Logical / Mathematical intelligence deals with ideas and concepts. Although understanding of mathematics emerges through experimentation and play in the manipulation of objects, volumes and numbers for example, the expression of this intelligence is within concepts and abstract thought. This includes the ability to create and relate abstract thoughts and translate concrete objects into symbols and concepts, which can be manipulated mentally without a concrete model.

Bodily / Kinaesthetic intelligence is defined as the ability to control bodily motions and to manipulate objects skilfully. It has been criticised for not addressing embodiment and motor learning issues. This intelligence is reflected however in the dancer's ability to mimic movement, to be able to transform a dynamic visual image into physical action for example, or to hear directions and translate these into movement.

Although Gardner differentiates between performing and creating music in his description of musical intelligence, he ignores this type of difference in bodily / kinaesthetic. He does not consider the contrast between dancing the moves others have created and creating choreography for others to perform.

Spatial intelligence is connected with the visual sense. Spatial characteristics are evident in the capacity to accurately perceive the visual world, to be able to manipulate mentally the forms that have been perceived, and to produce new forms in the imagination.

Interpersonal intelligence is the ability to make distinctions among individuals, particularly being sensitive to their motivations, intentions, moods and personal temperaments. Having good people skills is evidence of this intelligence.

Intrapersonal intelligence is the ability to think deeply about ideas and concepts, to have the capacity to discern your feelings and to use them to understand and guide your behaviour. To be in touch with your inner self is a simple way of understanding this.

Those are the seven intelligences originally described in Gardner's 1983 book. In 1999 new intelligences were added. They are: a **Naturalist** intelligence which is the ability to discriminate among things and to be able to classify that information; and **Existential**, **Spiritual** and **Moral** intelligences, which are characterised by interest in questions of a spiritual or transcendent nature.

Maslow's Hierarchy of Needs

Before leaving this area it is useful to understand what barriers there might be to learning. Maslow's Hierarchy of Needs indicates how an individual's physiological and psychological needs must be met before effective learning can begin.

1. Trancendent Needs
   – altruism, helping others

2. Self-Actualisation
   – self-fulfilment, personal achievement

3. Aesthetic Needs
   – order, beauty

4. Cognitive Needs
   – understanding, knowing, exploring

5. Esteem Needs
   – approval, recognition

6. Belonging Needs
   – acceptance by others

7. Safety Needs
   – safeguarding, feeling safe

8. Bodily Needs
   – hunger, thirst, sleep

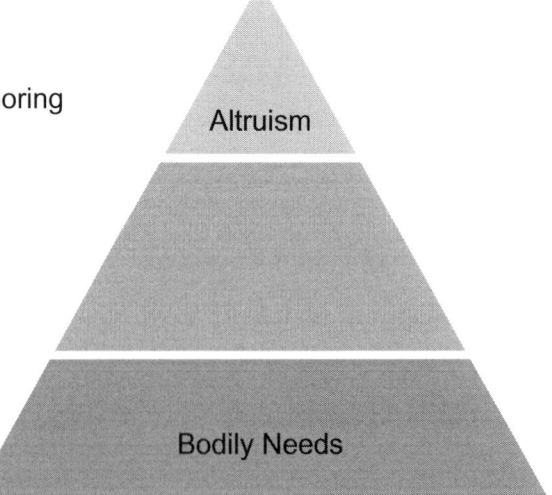

Maslow gives the image of a pyramid to indicate the amount of each need and its importance

Source: Orlich *et al* (2004) p. 202

Maslow indicates that for intellectual development to be effective the first four stages (numbered 5-8 above) need to be in place. From this it is clear that there is a need to create a learning environment that considers welfare, promotes self esteem, group cohesion, and takes account of children's feelings for example. It may be that some needs are difficult to meet due to external forces (for example problems at home).

> **Case Study 3**
>
> How might you apply the hierarchy in your teaching? Take each of the stages in turn. For example: Bodily Needs - ensure participants basic needs are met such as toilet access, water breaks; identify suitable snacks they can bring; give advice about what meal to have before they come to an evening workshop; ensure a good temperature in the room.

REFLECTION

If you are studying DDTAL you need to begin writing your Reflective Journal while you are undertaking Unit 1. If you are approaching study from a different perspective, journals are a significant way of reinforcing your own self-directed learning. You will find details on use of Reflective Journals in Chapter 24. All the reflections indicated below offer a good place to start.

1. David Kolb's Experiential Learning Theory seems to be applicable in dance.

> Learning dance is more a cyclical experience than a linear one, in terms of progression. Material should be revisited, concepts reintroduced, skills re-encountered in order to give students the opportunity to reinforce understanding and to widen and deepen their knowledge.
>
> (Gough, M. 1999 Knowing Dance: A guide for creative teaching. London: Dance Books, p. 29)

Consider this cyclical learning experience in the dance class. How do you experience this as a participant or teach this kind of structure? Sketch out the stages in one class you remember.

2. Can you find examples in your experience of today where you used Bruner's three modes (Enactive, Iconic, and Symbolic).

3. Look at the descriptions of Honey and Mumford's learning styles. Do you recognise yourself there? How would you teach a new dance step or phrase to a child or young person with the same style?

Bibliography

Bandura, A. 1977 *Social Learning Theory*. Englewood Cliffs: Prentice Hall.

Boud, D. Keogh, R. and Walker, D. (eds) 1994 *Reflection: Turning experience into Learning*. Abingdon: Routledge Falmer.

Bruner, J. S. 1966 *Toward a Theory of Instruction*. New York: Norton.

Child, D. 1995 *Psychology and the Teacher*. [5th edition] London: Cassell.

Fleming, N. 2006 *Teaching and Learning Styles*. [2nd edition] VARK Strategies.

Fontana, D. 1995 *Psychology for Teachers*. [3rd Edition] Basingstoke: Palgrave Macmillan.

Gardner, H. 1983 *Frames of Mind*. London: Fontana.

Gardner, H. 1999 *Intelligence Reframed: Multiple Intelligences for the 21st Century*. New York: Perseus / Basic Books.

Honey, P. and Mumford, A. 1995 *Effective Learning*. London: Institute of Personnel and Development.

Jarvis, P. Holford, J. & Griffin, C. 2005 *The Theory and Practice of Learning*. Abingdon: Routledge Falmer.

Kolb. D. & Fry, R. 1975 Toward an applied theory of experiential learning, in Cooper, C. (ed.) *Theories of Group Processes*. London: Wiley.

Kolb, D. 1984 *Experiential Learning: experience as the source of learning and development*. Chapter 2 free to download: http://learningfromexperience.com/media/2010/08/process-of-experiential-learning.pdf

Miller, N. & Boud, D. (eds) 1996 *Working with Experience*. London and New York: Routledge.

Orlich, D. Harder, R. Callahan, R. *et al*. 2004 *Teaching Strategies*. [7th edition] Boston: Houghton Mifflin.

Vygotsky, L. 1978 *Mind in Society*. Cambridge, MA: Harvard University Press.

Vygotsky, L. 1986 *Thought and Language*. Cambridge, MA: MIT.

Chapter 2

Learning Theories (Part 2): Motor Learning Theory and Dance Teaching

Lorna Sanders

Introduction

In this chapter, you will be introduced to an area of theory which helps to explain how we build on our inborn kinaesthetic and perceptual capacities in order to learn how to dance. Learning *how to learn* in one sense is the first step. This area is complex and is the subject of continued research and debate. What follows here, therefore, summarises the key concepts and opens up the issues that seem most applicable to dance. It will enable you to approach the more in-depth reading which is identified in the Bibliography and will assist you in further research.

We are born with genetically determined biological structures and abilities and a propensity for movement. Eventually we learn to control and co-ordinate our bodies by developing automatic responses (habits). The system, which is immature in its functioning for several years (and herein lies the difficulty of teaching children), remains open so that we can learn new habits, new movements and we can recall, even years later, a particular way of doing something. Memory and its structures play their part in all learning. How do they operate?

Memory Cycles

Our brain is a highly complex organ and thus there are many theories that might be discussed. An information-processing model of memory is explored here because of its usefulness in explaining how one learns dance skills. The different stages in the cycle protect us from information overload. The brain would quickly be in crisis if we remembered every stimulus of which we become aware, so forgetting is actually an inbuilt benefit. In the table below, the relationship between short term and long term memory is illustrated. Read it from the bottom, up.

Long-term memory	Codified and stored for use
Attended to as important through repetition, recall, rehearsal	**Remembered**
Short-term memory	Remembered temporarily. Short span.
Stimulus or signal is paid attention to in some way	**Forgotten**
Stimulus or Signal	Momentarily noticed
Information received from the environment / body; noticed only subliminally	**Forgotten**

(Model adapted from Child, 1993, p. 126)

Short-term memory (STM) is a temporary store of limited information which in adults is thought to be capable of holding approximately seven *random* items (children less). This is assisted by chunking / grouping information together so that bigger amounts can be learned. The content and subject specific aspects connect us to other networks of thoughts and this assists retention, as does recognition that the material is important in some way. Links between new information, context and prior knowledge can ensure the input is *not random*. New information lasts for perhaps 20-30 seconds (on average) so further processing and repetition is needed to maintain it in the STM (Magill, 2011). Short-term *motor* memory has a longer duration of around one to two days in adults, depending on their experience. This is maturational, in that it is less in children.

> **Case Study 1**
>
> Out of you sight, ask someone to put around 20 random objects onto a tray. Look at the objects for 20 seconds only – use a stop watch. Remove the tray and see how many you can instantly recall.

If you remember many more than seven it is often because you made links between some of the objects and they were not random to you.

Information disappears relatively quickly unless it is worked on to store it in the long-term memory (LTM). Repetition and rehearsal replay the information back through the STM loop until it is remembered by being codified, organised and integrated into existing memories. Meaning is made here because information is linked with other understandings during this structuring, hence the importance of ensuring participants have a clear understanding of the purpose (Magill, 2011). This is the stage when applying deliberate recall strategies can be useful. See Buzan (2002) for a range of ideas. He states that 'your brain is better than you think' (p. 20). LTM integration and storage always takes time, but relearning becomes easier with each subsequent revisiting. Forgetting, once in the LTM, is often resolved by active recall (i.e. needs a cue).

LTM storage is affected by:
- Prior knowledge.
- Amount of information and its complexity.
- Opportunity for the initial learning being optimal.
- Opportunities for revisiting the information in different ways.
- Individual age and ability.
- Degree of motivation or the need to remember.

Memory Retrieval

Once information is in the LTM, a cue or clue or a conscious effort (as in searching for a fact) might be needed in order to retrieve it or bring it to the surface.

For example, dance cues could be:
- Verbal.
- Musical.
- A marked demonstration of part of it.

- Imagery.
- Feelings.

Depending on how the information has been personally structured the cue might need to be quite individual. Motivation and self esteem also play a part (Fontana, 1995).

As with physical systems, memory also tires and reaches overload. After new information is taken in, too many instantly repeated efforts at recall are usually counterproductive and memory is often better after a short lapse of time. Reinforcement needs to be interspersed with brief rest intervals (distributed practice) and information revisited regularly, and in different ways, rather than compressing opportunities for learning into small periods of time. Child (1993) points out that the process of recalling, because it requires an active condition, in itself is also tiring and that clues which aid recognition should be used.

Habit and Forgetting

A correlation exists between STM and LTM and the adaptation of movement habits. We are designed to create habits as we will see when we examine motor learning theory in more detail, but when learning new material or trying to correct a habitual error, it is useful to know that short term *motor* memory declines after approximately two days and then returns. For example, participants may appear to perform poorly during class but this seems to improve later without any further reinforcement.

This 'diminution [and] rebound effect' (Peretz, in Clarkson and Skrinar, 1988, p. 284) illustrates how inhibition is thought to build up during the overlaying of new information in the muscles, interfering with their functioning and making it difficult to learn the new habit. However, a period of rest disperses the effect and performance improves (sometimes to be lost again later). This also explains why overcoming habits is difficult; fully embedded in the LTM, they continually reassert themselves.

The Senses

We pick up signals / stimuli from our environment (and internally from our bodies) because we have sense receptors which convey this information, via the nervous system, to the brain. Sight, hearing, taste and touch are perhaps obvious but in soft tissues such as ligaments, muscles, tendons and joint capsules we have small groups of cells and nerve endings responsible for the sense of proprioception: our body sense or body awareness. This is how we know where the different parts of our body are located in relation to all the others. These receptors underpin our kinaesthetic awareness and help us in controlling co-ordination. We can see the first impacts of proprioceptive learning when we watch babies. Their early explorations are often concerned with establishing a sense of their body: its limits, its relationship to the space, and the range of movement in the limbs for example. At the same time they are also developing their perceptual abilities by beginning to discern that space has depth. See Cratty (1979) for details.

The Fundamental Motor Skills

As dance teachers we build on the sets of fundamental movement skills and perceptual abilities that young children bring to the lessons: we teach them the specialised skills of dance, they bring their movement with them. Balyi (2001) cites these basic skills as running, jumping, hopping, bounding, throwing; for example, at a basic level you do not teach children to do these actions, they teach themselves and you might supply the opportunity for practice. Watch toddlers learning to walk for instance: they learn by mimicry, trial and error. A parent might hold a child's hand to assist balance but they are not teaching the child *how* to walk. A ballet teacher might train the pointing of the foot but the walk is, in effect, already there and this is developed and adapted in the training.

To these basic actions, Balyi adds generic skills: agility, balance, co-ordination, speed, kinaesthetic awareness, gliding, buoyancy and striking. Although there is wide variation and chronological age is not always a good indicator, typically the generic motor and perceptual skills are in basic functional form around the age of five to six years and early childhood is important in facilitating skill development. The system however remains immature until around ten to twelve years of age. Skrinar (in Clarkson and Skrinar, 1988) cites the importance of hand-eye co-ordination, and adds 'rhythm, spatial and visual discrimination' (p.271) to the list of generic skills which are acquired elsewhere, for example through play, and which are then utilised and further developed within dance education. Côté-Laurence (2000) also indicates the importance of rhythm as fundamental in acquiring ballet skills (rather than the reverse).

Writing in 2003, Kimmerle and Côté-Laurence consider that 'any attempt to make a comprehensive and exhaustive list of what to include under the label of "dance skills" may be futile' (p. 13), but they offer the following fundamental *movement skills*: control of centre; changing base (by which they mean transference of body weight); control of limbs; rotation; elevation; locomotion; and basic perceptual ability within time, space and force relationships (these categories link to Laban's framework – see Chapter 4).

They suggest it is useful to screen beginner dancers (of all ages) to assess their ability in these fundamental movement structures so that issues can be addressed.

Case Study 2

How might you adapt warm-up activities, for example, to make a quick diagnostic assessment of these fundamental movement skills which participants bring to learning?

You might have come across notions of reading readiness. What we have here is a notion of dancing readiness: for example, if a child is not yet equipped with the ability to elevate (as in the fundamentals listed above) it is not possible to teach them a split leap. The more complex dance action relies on the basic fundamental skill being present. In general, from a motor learning perspective, when a child's nervous and perceptual systems are mature and fully functioning at around the age of ten to twelve, if they are a beginner dancer what they will lack is experience on which to develop. Like all skills, however, we have an inborn capacity and children do not all develop equal levels of basic competence. Although experience can and does affect this, some may never develop fully.

A word of warning: research indicates that hypermobile dancers (a condition of extreme natural flexibility) can have nervous systems which provide them with poor or inefficient proprioceptive feedback (McCormack, 2010). Special care is needed in their training to help them with kinaesthetic understanding. It is now thought that Hypermobility Syndrome makes dancers particularly susceptible to a range of aspects such fatigue, digestive problems, concentration lapses and sequential learning challenges (Knight, 2011).

A list of perceptual skills related to dance is provided in the table below. List some dance examples to illustrate your uses of these in teaching. You will have been developing and using these perceptual abilities even if you were unaware of this.

Case Study 3		
Perceptual Skills Related to Dance:		
Kinaesthetic	• Body Schema (the internal image we carry of our body in our head). • Laterality (not right or left dominance but the ability to perceive right and left – e.g. stroke victims sometimes 'forget' one side). • Inter-limb co-ordination.	
Spatial	• Directionality / spatial mapping. • Mental rotation (reversing an image in your head). • Ability to visualise abstract spatial patterns (in your head).	
Temporal	• Perceive tempo – slow / fast. • Identify and reproduce rhythm. • Respond to / synchronize with an external pulse.	
Perceptual Integration is seen when a dancer can:	• Demonstrate integration of visual and auditory cues. • Co-ordinate spatial, temporal and force elements in dance phrases. • Adapt movement in space and time to another dancer.	

(adapted from Kimmerle and Côté-Laurence, 2003, p.101)

A Motor Learning Model

This information processing model is outlined from Kimmerle and Côté-Laurence (2003). See also Cratty (1973); Magill (2011); and Schmidt and Wrisberg (2008). A hierarchical, three-staged approach to skill acquisition, involves kinaesthetic, perceptual, social, emotional and cognitive aspects. A new skill is introduced and the end product is a consistent, accurate reproduction. This might take many years of course.

The Attempting Stage	
The process involved:	The challenge for learners:
1. You pick up relevant cues. (might be visual and verbal)	• Knowing what is relevant to notice. • Teacher's first demonstration is vital. • Ability to pay attention to multiple layers of information (experience / maturation).
2. You form an abstract mental image of the skill. (you have a rough idea of it)	• Transference of information (adapting teacher's demonstration into useable proprioceptive information). • Obtaining an all-round view of the skill. • Having all the appropriate details.
3. You construct or retrieve a motor plan. (depends on prior learning and is usually an unconscious process – the brain automatically prepares neural pathways in the nervous system and muscles based on the mental image)	• Ability to access accurate proprioceptive information. • Needs accurate mental image for effective preparation of motor plan. • Prior learning provides a range of plans to tap into (brain recognises something familiar and tries the closest fit).
4. You execute the skill. (making a first attempt is vital, or you cannot move to the next stage)	• If the mental image is inaccurate, the first performance of the skill is poor. • If the attempt is poor, the brain has less effective information on which to re-programme the motor plan. • Psychological and social skills – needs confidence and motivation. • Need to consider yourself as a successful learner and understand performance is unlikely to be perfect at this stage.

(Adapted from Kimmerle and Côté-Laurence, 2003, p. 54)

During this stage, the process involved is generally unconscious. Much of the brain's activity in preparing the motor plan and muscle response is not directly under conscious control: for example, thinking about getting up from the chair triggers your brain to sequence and prepare the motor plan, so you can do the action almost immediately.

Ask participants to focus on the intended outcome rather than the movement and to think about what the new movement reminds them of before they attempt the skill (Magill, 2011). The closer this fits, the more effective the muscular patterning will be. Inexperience and youth slows information processing and makes the first attempt less effective, as does giving too much aural information simultaneous with the early visual demonstrations. Frustration can set in; social and emotional aspects can intervene. If participants lack confidence, they are less willing to have a go (Buckroyd, 2000).

An interesting outcome of image-making, that reveals its importance, occurs when the teacher inadvertently makes an error in the early demonstrations. When the teacher demonstrates the corrected version, the participants still seem slower than expected to produce their first attempt. The demonstrations confused them. The first demonstration needs to be accurate because the brain has already planned its response to this.

> **Case Study 4**
>
> Consider how you introduce new material.
> - What have you noticed about the way that the participants pick up new material?
> - Is there any information above that makes you see this in a new light?
> - How might you adapt what you do?

The Correcting Stage	
During this process accuracy is aimed at:	The challenge for learners:
1. You monitor the first execution of the skill, externally* / internally. * crucial where there is no experience of the correct feeling yet.	• Maturity of proprioceptive skills – needs body awareness and ability to 'listen' to the body (children are at a disadvantage). • Dependent on quality of teacher / external feedback and demonstration.
2. You assess and re-programme the motor plan. (you match your execution against your original rough idea)	• You may need to reform the mental image – in whole or in part. • You may need to construct or retrieve a new motor plan. • With lack of confidence / experience / poor body awareness, you might evaluate the execution ineffectively and re-programme inefficiently or even unnecessarily.
3. You attempt the corrected skill. (the second attempt allows checking against the rough idea, the first execution of it and the reprogrammed motor plan)	• You match your execution against the previous attempt (whatever its quality). • Reliant on monitoring – external and internal ('correct' feeling is usually not in place yet).
4. You engage in error detection. (involves teacher and learner)	• Children cannot attend to internal and external input simultaneously. • Children and inexperienced dancers process more slowly and reach information overload more quickly. • Relies on effective evaluation of attempted skill and proprioceptive ability to begin to 'feel' the correct version.

(Adapted from Kimmerle and Côté-Laurence, 2003, p. 58)

Achieving the correct feeling (when the mind maps the body and assesses it as achieving the image in the mind) can take some time and use of imagery is important. During the second and third attempts, aspects of the original motor plan are adapted; the difference between the executed action and the mental image is unconsciously related to the felt aspects of space, time or force for example. Sometimes big changes in performance occur as very different motor plans are tried and felt to be widely out of kilter. Integration can also come suddenly as the brain interprets the information and constructs an appropriate way to achieve the result. If self-monitoring or proprioception is ineffective, 'correlation between what students believe they have performed and their actual performance' may be lacking (Lodewyk *et al*, 2009, p. 3). In this case they may re-programme the motor plan unnecessarily and subsequent performances become increasingly poor.

The duration spent in the Correcting Stage, to produce what might be termed a good enough working reproduction, depends on prior experience, age and maturation, motivation, the effectiveness of the original image-making, the ability to recruit effective motor plans, and the evaluation and feedback being efficient. Making the learning strategies conscious can assist. Experience and practice in how to attend to the cues means skill reproduction can become more precise. Learning how to learn is not only important for self-reliance and confidence, it improves motor learning capacity.

In general, avoid describing or demonstrating what not to do (Magill, 2011). Effective error detection and external feedback to learners requires use of holistic imagery that enhances and integrates the automatic, organic responses of the body; vocalising (counting, correcting, praising etc.) needs to be selective to give learners time for the physical information to be fully sensed / felt; and use of the mirror needs to be intermittent, not constant (Batson, 2008). With young children, their inability to rotate the visual image in their head means that the mirror can confuse, rather than clarify.

> **Case Study 5**
>
> Consider how you usually aide learners at this point:
> - What type of imagery do you use and what is its effect? Does it work for all of them?
> - How do you typically use the mirror and what impact might this have?

The Perfecting Stage	
This is the ongoing refining process:	The challenge for learners:
1. Practice with ongoing monitoring. (thoughtful engagement in rehearsal and adequate time needed)	• Internal feedback becomes increasingly important. • The teacher must be relied on to identify habits which might infiltrate from other embedded skills. • Too much teacher demonstration now can disrupt the internal image of the skill.
2. Revise and improve performance. (gradual refinement is undertaken)	• Need a range of learning strategies to call upon – eg careful use of mirror; rehearsal with different purposes in mind (the rhythm, the expression, the arrival points, the initiation of breath etc.). • Needs good proprioceptive evaluation.
3. Produce skilled movement. (the correct schema - body / mind image, correct feeling and associated motor plan - is internalised now)	• A new habit has been formed in the LTM - the motor plan and revised image in the brain are integrated. This can temporarily interfere with other learned skills. • If the habit practised contains unnoticed errors these are also embedded.

4. Combine skills with other skills.	• The new skill must be tested and further integrated by making links, adjustments and preparations to embed it with other skills in sequences and dance phrases.
5. Self correction now	• Gains in refinement are smaller and improvements are less marked now – so needs patience, persistence, continual application. • Cannot achieve this until the nervous system is mature and proprioception fully developed.

(Kimmerle and Côté-Laurence, 2003, p. 59)

Teacher demonstration is increasingly less needed during the Perfecting Stage and can be confusing. Students should be taught to error detect and correct their own errors. To fully internalise the information, persistence is needed. It is important to identify what learning stage a student is operating in so that demonstration and feedback is given in the most effective way and at appropriate times. The younger or more inexperienced the dancer is, the more likely they are to be performing within the Correcting Stage for longer.

> **Case Study 6**
>
> Consider how you assist them during the Perfecting Stage.
> - How do you know what their learning needs are?
> - Do you address the different stages that they might be within?
> - How do you encourage self-correction?
> - How do you know when to demonstrate and when not to?

REFLECTION

1. Identify an experience when you learned something new in a dance lesson. How did you learn this? Do you know what your own learning strategies are? Attend a lesson where you will be sure of learning something unfamiliar and notice what it is that you do.

2. Identify an experience when you taught unfamiliar material to participants. Was the opportunity optimal? What might make for optimum conditions? Refer to Chapter 1: Maslow's Hierarchy of Needs.

3. What motivated you to learn to dance? Your participants might have very different reasons. How might you tap into what motivates them?

4. It was stated that immediate repetition with rest intervals (distributed practice) is needed for STM maintenance if the system is not to tire too quickly. Consider how you address these needs. (Understand that the point here does not refer to strength development or endurance exercises – although these too also need distributed practice). How might you adapt what you do to take account of adolescent bodies? See IADMS Education Committee 2000 (free resource).

5. Make a list of five of the fundamental actions or generic skills and consider what you do to provide opportunity for participants to practise and revisit these.

Bibliography

Balyi, I. 2001 Sport system building and long-term athlete development in Canada. *Coaches Report*, 8, Summer, pp. 25-28.

Batson, G. 2008 Proprioception. *International Association of Dance Medicine and Science*, Resource Paper, www.iadms.org

Buckroyd, J. 2000 *The Student Dancer*. London: Dance Books.

Buzan, T. 2002 *Use Your Head*. London: BBC.

Child, D. 1993 *Psychology and the Teacher*. [5th edition] London: Cassell.

Clarkson, P. M. and Skrinar, M. (eds) 1988 *Science of Dance Training*. Champaign, Illinois: Human Kinetics.

Côté-Laurence, P. 2000 The Role of Rhythm in Ballet Training. *Research in Dance Education*, 2, 1, pp. 173-192.

Cratty, B. 1979 *Perceptual and Motor Development in Infants and Children*. [2nd edition] London: Prentice Hall.

Fontana, D. 1995 *Psychology for Teachers*. [3rd edition] Basingstoke: Palgrave Macmillan.

Kimmerle, M. and Côté-Laurence, P. 2003 *Teaching Dance Skills: A Motor Learning and Development Approach*. USA: J. Michael Ryan.

Knight, I. 2011 *A Guide to Living with Hypermobility*. Singing Dragon Books.

Lodewyk, K. Winne, P. and Jamieson-Noel, D. 2009 Implications of task structure on self-regulated learning and achievement. *Educational Psychology*, 29, 1, pp. 1-25.

Magill, R, 2011 *Motor Learning and Control*. New York: McGraw-Hill International.

McCormack, M. 2010 Teaching the Hypermobile Dancer. *IADMS Bulletin for Teachers*, 2, 1, pp. 5-8. http://www.iadms.org/displaycommon.cfm?an=1&subarticlenbr=186

Schmidt, R and Wrisberg, C. 2008 *Motor Learning and Performance*. [4th edition] Champaign, Illinois: Human Kinetics.

Wilmerding, V. and Krasnow, D. 2009 Motor Learning and Teaching Dance. *International Association of Dance Medicine and Science*, Resource Paper, www.iadms.org

Chapter 3
Teaching Styles
Alysoun Tomkins

Introduction

The terms 'Teaching Styles' and 'Teaching Strategies' are often used synonymously and interchangeably. This chapter will differentiate between the two but demonstrate how a Teaching Style may be enhanced by the inclusion of one or more Teaching Strategies and hence how the two are linked. The word 'teacher' is used generically to include dance practitioners, dance artists and any dancer who may teach or lead as part of their career.

It is important to reflect upon what teaching is and why we do it. Central to teaching is the learner and yet teachers often plan sessions based on the material they wish to teach rather than the people they are teaching. Within the informal sector this becomes even more relevant as teachers are not required to adhere to any particular syllabus or curriculum. There might well be themes or topics chosen by either the teacher or presented by a partner within a project, but how these themes or topics are expressed through dance is the decision of the teacher. Therefore the choices that are made about what and how we teach are governed by our knowledge and expertise, certainly, but also the needs of the learners with whom we are working and the context in which we work.

In dance teaching we have the advantage of working with the physical, intellectual and emotional components of a learner as dance is not only a physical activity but also an art form. Sometimes, in our keenness to address the technical needs of our students, the physical aspects of the session are the main focus, so we must find ways to redress the balance and include the intellectual and emotional aspects of our learners through asking questions, discussing outcomes, presenting opportunities for creative exploration and allowing expressive qualities to emerge and develop. This may then define both how we plan the presentation of our sessions and the reason we teach: to observe the development and growth of the young people before us is rewarding and it is gratifying to know that we as teachers have a part to play. If we deny the young learners the chance to be actively engaged in their learning process then we are not addressing the whole person. In order to achieve this we need to be creative and take risks with our teaching in the same way as we expect learners to be creative risk takers.

Good teaching practice is concerned with encouraging and facilitating learning with the learners as active rather than passive members of the group, sharing responsibility for both their learning and progress. In the chart below it is suggested that the roles of both teacher and learner change during the course of a session according to the teaching styles being used. For example, the teacher may alternate between instructor, guide and facilitator with the learner's role moving between observer / copier, investigator and selector. Using a variety of teaching styles and adopting different roles as a teacher may take you out of your comfort zone, but effective teaching is not reliant on the teacher's preferred methods but on the needs of the learners. Gough says:

> Each one of us has a particular way of teaching […] that reflects our personality, skills and beliefs. Whilst retaining this, one's repertoire should include a variety of styles and strategies to enable young people to learn more effectively and for the work to be of good quality.
>
> (1993, p.30)

Teaching Styles

In the following chart, Hayden-Davies and Whitehead (2010) expand upon Mosston and Ashworth's (2002) definitions of Teaching Styles by describing the role of both the teacher and learner in each style. The chart also indicates the type of learner, according to VARK (Fleming, 2001), who would respond best to each teaching style. For further information on learning theory see Chapter 1.

TEACHING STYLE	WHAT IS IT?	TEACHER'S ROLE	LEARNER'S ROLE	RELATING TO WHICH LEARNING STYLE
Command / didactic / demonstration	Teacher has all the knowledge, ideas and makes all the decisions – learners are passive.	Instructor	Observing and copying.	Visual Kinaesthetic
Practice	Learners carry out teacher prescribed tasks – rehearse whilst teacher gives feedback and encouragement.	Establishing	Rehearsing / repeating and improving	Kinaesthetic
Guided discovery / problem solving – convergent discovery (one outcome)	Allows the learner to go beyond the known. Teacher sets task with one outcome based on previously learnt knowledge. Learners find their own way to achieve the learning outcome.	Guiding	Investigating	Auditory Kinaesthetic
Guided discovery / problem solving – divergent discovery (many outcomes)	Allows the learner to go beyond the known. Teacher sets task based on previously learnt knowledge but this time there are various solutions which learner can then evaluate.	Prompting	Creative	Auditory Kinaesthetic
Reciprocal	Learners in pairs giving peer feedback and evaluation according to teacher's guidelines.	Supporting	Peer assessing	Visual Auditory Kinaesthetic

Learner designed / participant-led	Allowing learners to lead eg warm up exercise or set a task.	Advising	Initiating	Visual Auditory Kinaesthetic
Self-check	Learners evaluate own performance of task in collaboration with teacher and against criteria.	Mentor	Self critiquing	Visual Auditory Kinaesthetic Read / write
Inclusion	Learners select from teacher's variety of tasks which is most relevant to their ability / requirements.	Facilitating	Selecting	Visual Auditory Kinaesthetic Read / write

Gough's Teaching Styles

Gough (1993) identifies the uses and outcomes of four different teaching styles.

1. Demonstration (Do as I do): in order to achieve the best outcome for all the learners Gough advises demonstrating the whole sequence before breaking it down into smaller sections, providing feedback, repetition and clarification when necessary.

- Gives teacher control of scope, content and pace of session.
- Good demonstration by the teacher is essential.
- Demands total concentration from the learner.
- Allows for clarity of objectives.
- Outcome is the same for everyone.
- Requires young person to observe and translate movement into their own body.
- Ability of learners to accurately describe their observations is essential.

2. Self-evaluation: if a teacher is requiring the learner to be self-critical then:

- The content and movement quality of the task set should be clear in order that the learner has criteria against which they can assess their performance.
- The teacher may be required to give guidance.
- The learner must be competent in working alone.
- The learner is given responsibility for their improvement.

The teacher may wish to extend this style by placing the learners in pairs or groups to enable peer feedback.

3. Problem solving: related to Mosston and Ashworth's divergent style.

- Teacher poses questions or tasks for learner to solve.
- Task is open ended.
- Learning outcome is different for each learner.

4. Collaboration: Gough suggests this method invites co-operative learning rather than rivalry and competition. Learners need to develop negotiation and organisational skills, and tolerance of others. They also develop critical yet positive attitudes to one another's work.

- Teacher has ensured that the learners have movement material upon which they can draw.

- The task is clearly structured.
- A time limit for completion is set.
- Advisable to ensure learners do not work with the same individuals so as to encourage social skills.

By incorporating a range of the teaching styles mentioned above in each session, the teacher is addressing the different learning styles of the participants; allowing for ownership of material by the learner; encouraging the learners to be responsible for their learning; and providing structures for creative responses.

Teaching Strategies

If a teaching style is the method we chose to deliver our classes, then a teaching strategy is the manner in which we enhance that delivery to ensure quality in both our teaching and in the responses of the learner.

Strategies may be employed to encourage the following:

- Engagement in the session.
- Quality of the movement achieved.
- Understanding of the movement or given task.
- Dynamic variances.
- Good behaviour.
- Class management.
- Musicality and phrasing.
- Movement memory.
- Performance skills.
- Team work.

The following chart identifies some, although by no means an exhaustive list, of the teaching strategies which can be used to ensure the best possible outcome.

AIM	POSSIBLE TEACHING STRATEGY	MY STRATEGIES – identify strategies you use to address each aim.
Encourage engagement in the session	<ul><li>Ask questions to both the group and individuals.</li><li>Move around the space / change front.</li><li>Set individual tasks.</li><li>Set individual learning plans.</li><li>Support struggling individuals.</li></ul>	• Q/A throughout session • Drawing back to tasks/aims

Quality of movement achieved	• Use imagery to achieve required dynamic. • Use pictures / film / props. • Perform good quality demonstrations. • Give feedback and encouragement • Use video and playback to group.	
Understanding of movement or given task	• Explain the task in a variety of ways changing the language used. • Ask questions. • Give verbal or physical examples. • Ask individuals to demonstrate.	
Dynamic variances	• Use voice dynamically. • Add dynamically appropriate accompaniment. • Use imagery. • Perform effective demonstrations. • Ask 'HOW' will you do that?	
Good behaviour	• Learn names. • Acknowledge all individuals. • Use encouragement and praise when deserved. • Ensure material is challenging but achievable. • Discuss and agree code of conduct.	
Class management	• Give clear instructions. • Employ control mechanisms. • Employ clear strategies for getting into pairs / groups.	
Musicality & phrasing	• Use phrasing – rhythm and accent in the voice. • Choose appropriate accompaniment. • Count in using both time signature and / or vocal sounds.	
Movement Memory	• Allow repetition. • Recall work from session to session.	
Performance skills	• Give performance opportunities – to each other. • Use stage / performance space terminology. • Check focus.	
Team work	• Change partners or groups frequently.	

Motivation

If we as teachers consider the learner to be an active member of the dance class and encourage and value their contributions, then it is essential that the individuals are motivated. In a class where the learners are passively receiving information from the teacher it is difficult to judge whether they are, or are not, motivated. If they are required to copy the teacher's movements for the whole session it is very difficult to assess whether they are 'going through the motions' or are really engaged and motivated. Incorporating teaching styles which require a more active approach from the learner can motivate them to want to be engaged.

Gough (1999, pp. 16-18) discusses the factors which can encourage or discourage learners' motivation and identifies three areas which may impact upon the success of motivating students:

1. The material or content of the session.
2. The learner's role within the session.
3. The environment in which the learning takes place.

When planning a session the following questions need to be asked:

Material:
- Is the material relevant to the group?
- Will the level of material and tasks given stimulate and challenge the group?
- Does the material meet the needs of the group at this time?

Learner's Role:
- Will they be actively involved?
- Will they be part of the process and feel ownership of a finished product?
- Will they be given responsibility for decision making?
- Will their input be acknowledged, valued and respected?

Environment:
- Do I create a positive, welcoming learning environment?
- Is the space too large, too small, too dirty, too cold or hot?
- Is the flooring conducive to dance?
- Are the numbers in the group too large, too small?
- Do I create social cohesion in my session?

Gough points out that young people attend dance classes, particularly in the informal sector, for various reasons. It may be that they require technical training, an outlet for creative expression, a way of keeping fit or that they look upon their dance class as a social event. Whatever it is that motivates them to attend must be recognised and in order to maintain attendance it is partly the teacher's role to keep their interest and enthusiasm and also to develop it.

Case Studies

In the following three case studies, the group and context is identified. The reasons for the choices of teaching styles and teaching strategies are given. These are not meant to be definitive but used to illustrate how one might justify those choices given the group and context and to demonstrate how teaching strategies can enhance the chosen teaching style. Think these through carefully.

Case Study 1

CONTEXT: A group of pre-school children attending a playgroup or nursery. The children will know each other.

TEACHING STYLE	TEACHING STRATEGY	REASON FOR CHOICES
Command	• Clear demonstrations. • Use voice dynamically, rhythmically. • Use of language that will support learning- spatial directions; body parts; numbers; colours. • Use imagery.	At this age they are learning through imitation. The children are moving from parallel play to loosely organised cooperative play and would find working with a partner or group challenging.

Guided Discovery – convergent and divergent	• Ask questions:
	  - Can you stretch your arms to the ceiling?
	  - Can you show me how you would splash in a puddle?
	• Choose children to demonstrate their solutions.
		Allows children opportunity to find their own solutions to problems.
		Builds self esteem.
		Children can observe each other and start to critique each other's work.

Self-check	• Ask questions: - Are your fingers stretched?	Gives opportunity for children to take responsibility.

Case Study 2

CONTEXT: Male Street Dance company – not interested in being taught material but want a place to rehearse and need mentoring.

TEACHING STYLE	TEACHING STRATEGY	REASON FOR CHOICES
Practice	• Give encouragement. • Give feedback.	Allows group to rehearse and improve.
Self check	• Offer individual guidance. • Film and watch video with group.	Allows individuals to be critical of performance against criteria.
Inclusion	• Offer suggestions on, for example, choreographic aspects of work.	Allows group to select and make choices on choreographic aspects of work.

Case Study 3

CONTEXT: After-school club for 11-14 year olds. Want to broaden their knowledge of dance styles.
Style chosen: Lindy Hop.

TEACHING STYLE	TEACHING STRATEGY	REASON FOR CHOICES
Command	• Good clear demonstration. • Verbal instructions. • Use voice to give rhythm.	• To teach set sequence in the Lindy Hop style. • Develop observational skills. • Through demonstration, stylistic qualities can be observed.
Guided Discovery - convergent	• Observe and give feedback.	• Set task of working out sequence on left side.
Practice	• Observe and give feedback. • Provide musical accompaniment appropriate to the style of dance and the era it was popular.	• Ensure that students have embodied material. • Encourage movement memory.
Guided Discovery - divergent	• Set tasks with many outcomes. • Give individual assistance and feedback.	• Students begin to make own choices in developing the material.
Reciprocal	• Encourage critical feedback between peers on given criteria.	• Develop critical skills. • Develop performance skills.
Learner designed	• Set tasks to develop material. • Provide opportunity for individuals to teach peers.	• Developing choreographic skills within a framework.
Self check	• Video group and watch. • Lead discussion and encourage self criticism.	• Develop observational skills. • Develop critical skills.

REFLECTION

In order to challenge yourself as a teacher and to develop your own practice, it might be useful to consider the following questions. Depending upon the answers to the questions, you can take those risks referred to earlier and try new ways of leading your sessions.

1. What kind of learner am I? Does this influence the way I teach?

2. Which are my preferred teaching styles and why?

3. Which of the teaching styles above do I least use and why?

4. Which of the above teaching styles will I incorporate into my teaching and with which groups?

5. Which teaching strategies do I use to address:
    - Engagement in the session.
    - Quality of the movement achieved.
    - Understanding of the movement or given task.
    - Dynamic variances.
    - Good behaviour.
    - Class management.
    - Musicality and phrasing.
    - Movement memory.
    - Performance skills.
    - Team work.

Bibliography

Fleming, N. D. 2001 *Teaching and Learning Styles: VARK Strategies*. Honolulu: VARK – Learn.

Gough, M. 1993 *in touch with dance*. Lancaster: Whitethorn.

Gough, M. 1999 *Knowing dance: A Guide to Creative Teaching*. London: Dance Books.

Hayden Davies, D. & Whitehead, M. 2010 www.physical-literacy.org.uk/Teaching-Styles.pdf

Mosston, M. & Ashworth, S. 2002 *Teaching physical education.* [5th edition] San Francisco: Benjamin Cummings.

Chapter 4
Movement Analysis in Dance
Maggie Killingbeck

Introduction

This chapter considers movement and dance analysis. It reviews three existing models, noting the link between movement and meaning and identifying the relevance of dance and movement analysis for dancing, performing, creating and watching (Siddall 2010).

In her model of dance analysis, Adshead notes that 'the movement component [...] is perhaps the most important' (1988, p. 111). Movement analysis, she suggests is the foundation upon which a fuller dance analysis builds (p. 110). Hence movement components can be said to be at the heart of dance analysis. Making a similar point, Smith-Autard goes on to suggest that 'movement principles' should inform performing, creating and watching dance experiences (2002, pp. 177-8). The movement principles to which Smith-Autard and Adshead refer come from a model of movement analysis established by Rudolf Laban.

Model 1: Laban's Analytical Framework

Like Schönberg, Kandinsky and other artists working during the late nineteenth / early twentieth century, Laban challenged the status quo (Bradley, 2008). In an attempt to discover an approach to dance that identified with man's lived experience both internal and external, Laban worked with Mary Wigman 'to derive a curriculum for training dancers' (Bradley, 2008, p. 12). They based their approach on the movement of the body in space and time 'in order to clarify steps and techniques and in order to move beyond dance steps into meaningful movement' (p. 12).

Laban analysed movement into four categories: action, space, dynamics / effort and relationships. Below is a précis of the basic features of his movement analysis with examples (from Bounce's 2009 *Insane in the Brain*) to clarify the character of each component. For more detailed understanding of the comprehensive nature of the analysis and its potential for complexity refer to Laban (2011) and Newlove (2004).

1. BODY / ACTION - is concerned with WHAT the body does.

In other words if you ask the question, 'What are the dancers doing?' the answer is likely to be concerned with actions. 'The dancers are running and stopping, waving their arms, looking from side to side and falling to the floor.' In other words, action words are doing words (verbs). Action is probably the easiest place to start teaching or analysing insofar as everyone will know what they are required to do (balance, fall).

Laban identified the following framework for action:

- Bend, stretch and twist as the fundamental actions underpinning all movement.
- Six different kinds of action: travel, turn, transfer weight, stillness, gesture and elevation.

- In action, body parts could:
    - → be used simultaneously (as in a pivot turn) or successively (as in a body ripple)
    - → be isolated (the only part of the body moving or still)
    - → be emphasised such that attention is focused on that body part regardless of what other actions are being performed
    - → lead movements (a push with the heel of the hand which leads into a lunge).

It is important that whilst in action, dancers should be helped to sense the actions of the body in terms of mastery and expression. It is worth noting that Laban's analysis offers a framework for progression insofar as simple movement material using single actions can be used with very young children, whilst older / experienced groups can combine four different *kinds* of action simultaneously, layered with additional demands of body parts.

Action: What does the body do?	Examples
Bend, stretch, twist – underpin all movements. Travel (locomotion) – movements from one point in the dance space to another (arriving at a new place).	Running from one side of the stage to the other.
Turn – movements involving a change of front.	Quarter turn; dancers change front from Stage Right to Down Stage.
Gesture – movements of non weight-bearing body parts.	Body popping / locking movement of torso and arms.
Elevation – movements in which the body is jumping / fighting gravity / without support. There are five basic variations of footwork: 　one foot to the same foot 　one foot to the other foot 　one foot to two feet 　two feet to one foot 　two feet to two feet	e.g. hop e.g. leap e.g. assemblé e.g. sissonne e.g. changement
Weight transference (stepping) – movements in which support transfers from one part of the body to another	Breakdance six step and spins.
Stillness – movements in which the body is intentionally still	Breakdance freezes.
Body – During the execution of the types of action listed above: • Any part of the body can lead, be emphasised or isolated. • Body parts can be deployed successively or simultaneously.	• Arms and legs emphasised in body popping / locking phrases. • Arms and legs move simultaneously in striding travel material.

Figure 1

> **Case Study 1**
>
> **1.** Create a notebook in which you have separate pages for each of Laban's six different kinds of actions. Use the following to start; run, stop, wave, look, fall, pirouette, ripple, lunge, leap, spin, freeze, spring. Keep updating your action vocabulary.
>
> **2.** Use your vocabulary notebook to create an action task. Use an action word from each of the different categories of action (depending on the age of the group you teach these could be required successively or simultaneously and layered with specific demands of body parts). Alternatively create the material yourself in the style in which you work and teach it to your group articulating the action / body demands.
>
> **3.** Watch a professional dance work: describe the use of the body in the six different kinds of action.

2. SPACE - is concerned with WHERE movements are located.

This concerns the orientation of movement in space. It is concerned with the environment in which the dancer works and also describes the spatial features of body actions. In other words if you ask the question, 'Where are the dancers moving?' the answer is likely to involve spatial language. 'The dancers are on the floor, in the air, all over the stage, facing the front / diagonal'. In other words spatial words locate the dancers' whereabouts in the performance space, the direction of travel, facings, pathways etc.

Attention to the spatial aspects of movement involves:

- Personal space / the extent you can reach (kinaesphere), general space / space available in the studio.
- Levels - high medium and low.
- Size of the movements.
- Pathways - linear or curving (floor and air).
- Directions - forwards, backwards, sideways, upwards, downwards, diagonal.
- Planes (two dimensional) – door / transverse plane: uses height and width (up / down and side to side); wheel / saggital plane: uses height and depth (up / down and forward / backward); table / horizontal plane: uses depth and width (side to side and forward / backward).
- Planes (three dimensional) - diagonals which use height, width and depth e.g. high, forward and slightly sideways to the left.
- Shape of the body – e.g. curved, wide, narrow, linear, symmetrical.

Again kinaesthetic awareness is required to develop the technical expertise to be precise and controlled in space and to be aware of the expressive potential of these aspects.

Spatial awareness can be developed progressively from a simple requirement to change level with young children, to demands requiring dancers to switch their dimensional orientation, changing the movement's size and working in spatial opposition to a partner.

Chart Summarising Space	
Space: Where is the action located?	**Examples**
General / Personal space – the extent to which movements extend into space more generally or are contained within the dancers' kinaesphere.	Running and jumping movements use the whole of the stage space, breakdance and body popping / locking uses more personal space.
Size – the amount of space movements require for execution; degree of extension.	Big movements using a lot of space, some small finger waggling.
Proximity – movements close to / far from the body; near and far.	Arms hug tummy.
Pathways – curved / serpentine, straight / angular, on the floor, in the air.	Mostly linear / angular pathways on the floor and curved air patterns with arms.
Levels – low, medium, high.	High: dancers jump and use each other / the set to gain height, medium: travelling and hip hop moves, low: breakdance moves, rolling, sliding.
Directions, dimensions, planes.	Movements largely travel forwards towards centre front.
Facings – direction in which the body faces.	The dancers all face the side.
Body design / shape – includes element of wide, narrow, twisted, curved and linear.	Breakdance freezes; combination of wide, small and twisted body shapes.
Symmetry and asymmetry.	Symmetrical shapes in balletic second position; asymmetrical movements in body popping / locking material.
Transitions – different points in space can be linked centrally (coming in close to the body); peripherally (carried around the edge of the kinaesphere).	Movements are balletic, mostly carried around the edge of the periphery from one position to the next.

Figure 2

Case Study 2

1. In your notebook add separate pages to record spatial words. Use the following to start: the floor / low level, in the air / high level, all over the stage / general space, diagonal, backward, peripheral, curving. Keep updating your space vocabulary.

2. Use your vocabulary notebook to create a spatial task which involves a number of spatial variations (depending on the age of the group you teach these could be simple, eg movements in one direction followed by the next; or more complex, eg movements in several different directions at the same time layered with specific size / pathway requirements). Alternatively create the material yourself in the style in which you work and teach it to your group articulating the spatial demands.

3. Whilst observing another dance teacher, list all of the spatial vocabulary used during the session.

3. EFFORT / DYNAMICS - is concerned with HOW the body moves.

Effort / dynamic qualities colour the execution of actions in terms of the energy used. In other words if you ask the question, 'How are the dancers moving?' the answer is likely to involve dynamics. 'The dancers are moving quickly, slowly, softly, hesitantly, strongly'. In other words, dynamic words describe how the action words are being performed (adverbs).

Attention to the dynamic aspects of movements involves the dancers' use of:

- Weight qualities / body tension - ranging from moments of maximum tension (firmness, strength, force) to moments of minimal tension (lightness, softness, delicacy), or indeed, moments of no tension (completely relaxed).

- Time qualities - the duration / speed of movements ranging from sudden (quick, swift, fast, staccato) to sustained (slow, lingering, prolonged, legato); time qualities include acceleration and deceleration.

- Flow qualities - ranging from free flow that is difficult to stop (ongoing, fluid, continuous) to bound flow that is easily arrested (controlled, careful, stoppable).

- Spatial qualities - the dancer's attitude to space ranging from indulgent (plastic, indirect, multidirectional) to restricted (direct, focused).

It should be noted that each of the above is a continuum in that movements will be coloured by qualities between the extremes, as well as at the extremes. The dynamic content of a series of movements may change within an individual movement or from movement to movement, and in this way dynamic rhythm develops.

Laban also identified three different phrase shapes:

- Impulse (dynamic accent at the beginning of the movement / phrase).
- Swing (dynamic accent in the middle of the movement / phrase).
- Impact (dynamic accent at the end of the movement / phrase).

Effort / dynamic awareness can be developed progressively. Simple requirements with young children could change the time (speed) quality within their dance. More complex demands might combine weight, time and flow qualities simultaneously, sequencing them with gradual, less gradual, and abrupt transitions whilst including an impulse, impact or swing characteristic to the overall phrase.

Chart Summarising Effort / Dynamics	
Dynamics: How the body moves	**Examples**
Time – the length of time taken to execute body action(s); duration.	Movements rapid / sudden / staccato.
Weight – the amount of tension required in the execution of body action(s).	Movements mostly quite firm / strong / tense throughout.
Space – the focus given to body action(s).	Some movements very multi directional.
Flow – the type of energy flow.	Movements mostly quite bound / easily arrested.
Rhythm – variations in time, force and flow.	Patterning of time / force coincides with metric rhythm.
Phrasing – use of impulse, impact, swing.	Movements performed with a swing.

Figure 3

> **Case Study 3**
>
> **1.** In your notebook add separate pages to record words associated with weight qualities / dynamics. Use the following to start: rapid, sudden, staccato, tense, firm, strong, plastic, multi-directional, bound, easily arrested. Keep updating your space vocabulary.
>
> **2.** Use your vocabulary notebook to create a task which uses dynamic words from each of the different categories ie weight, space, time, flow (depending on the age of the group you teach these could be required successively or simultaneously and layered with specific demands in relation to phrasing). Alternatively create the material yourself in the style in which you work and teach it to your group articulating the dynamic demands.
>
> **3.** Whilst watching a dance film, relate the dynamics to the dance idea.

4. RELATIONSHIPS - are concerned with, WITH WHOM OR WHAT the dancer dances.

In other words if you ask the question, 'With whom / what are the dancers dancing?' the answer is likely to be concerned with relationships. 'The dancers are following each other, in pairs (duets), bouncing on beds, in permanent contact.' Relationship words identify the nature of the dancers' interaction. Relationships can also be found within attitudes to spatial and timing aspects.

Attention to relationships involves consideration of the many and varied ways dancers can work with:

- A partner: copy (exactly the same); mirror (exactly the same but using opposite sides of the body as in a mirror image); lead - follow, (not necessarily in a line); meet – part; pass - avoid; action – reaction (sometimes called question and answer); unison (at the same time); canon (sequentially); contrast / opposition (different); and contact / weight taking (weight relationship). A partner allows the possibility of further spatial relationships: for example, one over the other, through spaces created by the other, around each other, under each other's body parts.

- A group: the partner relationships identified above can be replicated in a group, for example, three dancers turn, lunge and look, in response five dancers run forward and turn away (action – reaction). Larger numbers reinforce the relationships by virtue of their replication on a larger scale, for example 'around' a partner can become 'surround' in a group setting. Larger numbers offer different numerical variations (four dancers can dance as four soloists, a soloist with trio, two duets, and as a quartet) and group formations (semi circle, diagonal line, scattered group, solid block, V shape, circle etc.)

Kinaesthetic engagement is again essential for mastery since the dancer has to be aware of their own body whilst sensitive to others and peripherally alert. In addition dancers need to be conscious of the expressivity of the way they work with others.

A sound understanding of relationships enables progression. For example, simple movement material, dancing independently / all together with the teacher, can be used with very young children whilst older / experienced groups can combine four different kinds of relationship within a phrase of movement simultaneously layered with additional demands regarding group formations.

Chart Summarising Relationships	
Relationships: WITH WHOM or WHAT the dancer moves	**Examples** (from Bounce's 2009 *Insane in the Brain*)
Partner – copy, mirror, lead, follow, meet, pass, part, action, reaction, unison, canon, opposition (space and time relationships); under, over, around, through (spatial relationships).	Action / reaction 'doctor' – 'patient' conversation, copying movements on the beds, travelling and passing across the stage, 'patients' over / under / around each other.
Group – as for a partner plus numerical variations, inter group relationships and group formations eg line, circle, wedge, block, V shape, scattered, random.	Random groups of varying numbers interacting in a range of relationships, fragments of formations come and go.
Contact – lift, lean, lower, counter balance / tension, support.	Lots of contact as 'doctors' support / control 'patients' / 'patients' interact with each other.

Figure 4

Case Study 4

1. In your notebook record words associated with relationships. Use the following to start: question / answer, surround, split, thread through, clump, scatter, follow, mirror, canon. Keep updating your relationship vocabulary.

2. Use your vocabulary notebook to create a task which uses relationship words from the partner list (depending on the age of the group you teach, fewer or more relationships could be required over a longer / shorter movement phrase. Older / more experienced participants could be required to convert more complex duet material for larger groups). Alternatively create the material yourself in the style in which you work and teach it to your group articulating the relationship demands.

3. In your notebook identify a dance idea with which you have not worked before; list the relationships suggested by the dance idea.

From the above *Figures* it can be seen that any component / principle in the left-hand column can be addressed as a single focus with younger participants, or combined with increasing sophistication to ensure progressive development in technical mastery and *feelingful* movement in the context of dancing, performing, creating and watching. Central to Laban's analysis of movement is that the dance participant is aware of / attends to: what, where, how and with whom / what he or she is moving. If the movement intention is clear, meaningful communication is likely to be facilitated.

Case Study 5

Consider a short phrase of movement that you have taught recently. Create a table similar to *Figures 1-4* above which analyses this into action, space, dynamics and relationship content. Complete your own examples of each of Laban's four movement aspects in the right hand column.

In the context of dancing, performing, creating and watching, Laban's analysis:

- Has relevance for all movement regardless of the genre or style.
- Allows dance practitioners to share a common language.
- Allows practitioners to use a language that is accessible to beginners who are not familiar with codified, technical terms.
- Enables dance participants to make links across different dance genres.
- Provides a structure that can be used by dance practitioners to articulate progression from simple tasks, involving single movement components from a single category, to complex tasks requiring attention to a number of components from each category.

REFLECTION

1. Review your teaching experiences to date. Reflect on the extent to which you address all four aspects of movement when you teach.

2. To what extent are you conscious of progression in your teaching? Can you use Laban's analysis to articulate your progressive expectations in performance, composition or appreciation across a given age range?

3. To what extent do you make reference to the inherent meaningfulness of movement?

Model 2: Dance Analysis

Writing at a time when dance was only just beginning to be studied as an academic discipline in secondary and higher education, Adshead considered that the theoretical foundations for dance were 'shaky' (1988, p. 5). She felt that:

> a newly emerging discipline inevitably, and rightly, faces the challenge of identifying its central concerns, demonstrating its methods of procedure and clarifying how achievement in the subject is to be judged.
>
> (Adshead, 1988, p. 5)

In order to meet this need, Adshead identified a comprehensive approach to analysing dance. Her conceptual framework, based in Laban's account, points to 'the nature and range of knowledge which is necessary both for understanding the meaning and appreciating the value of the dance' (p. 109). She represents her conceptual framework as a chart which 'allows the spectator to note the selection from the total possible range of components which constitute a dance' (p. 109).

Since accessing meaning and attributing worth involve interpreting and evaluating the perceptible features of the dance, Adshead's chart identifies the 'concepts which are necessary for making sense of that which is discerned, that is, for attributing to the features character, quality, meaning and value' (p.110).

Figure 5 is a précis of the basic features of Adshead's chart with examples (from Hofesh Shechter's 2011 *Political Mother: The Choreographer's Cut*) to clarify the character of each interpretive stage. For more detailed understanding of the nature of the analysis and its potential for complexity refer to Adshead (1988).

Stage 1 Describing the components of the dance	
This stage makes reference to:	**Examples**
Movement content (the body in action, its spatial orientation and dynamic texture).	Hunched travelling across the diagonal (DSL to USR) with a shuffling but urgent step, waving both arms with impactive flicks to the diagonals.
The dancers (number, gender).	16 dancers, 9 men and 7 women.
Visual setting (performance arena, lighting, costumes, props).	Bright rays of light / dark shadows identify location of dance / sound within the proscenium arch stage, all dancers wearing casual / combat trousers and T-Shirt, live band on three levels at the back of the stage.
Aural setting.	20 musicians on stage; very lively, very loud rock music.
Stage 2 Describing the dance form	
This stage makes reference to relationships:	**Examples**
Between the components of the dance described in Stage 1 above (at given points in time, through time and in relation to each other)	Pedestrian / folk / physical theatre content with overt dynamic texture / rhythm, repeated in unison in seemingly casual groupings; as dancers accumulate, repetition became stronger and accompaniment louder; similar highlights are repeated at important points throughout the loosely narrative episodes.

CHAPTER 4: MOVEMENT ANALYSIS IN DANCE

Stage 3 Interpreting the dance	
This stage makes reference to:	**Examples**
The contextual information which will inform the viewer's interpretation (socio-cultural context, purpose, genre, subject matter).	Post-modern dance genre, pedestrian / folk / physical theatre movements used to communicate idea concerned with political obedience / repression; feeling central to creation of exciting / visceral audio / physical dance event (rock / dance gig likely to appeal to wider audience).
The features of the dance which will inform that interpretation (the character of the dance, its qualities and the meanings that arise).	Exciting / dramatic dance concerned with episodes of oppression / liberation / subservience / celebration; images abstracted and organised episodically, sampled content; dancers appear to be moving at the behest of a political dictator with reluctance / enthusiasm. |//

Stage 4 Evaluating the dance	
This stage makes reference to:	**Examples**
The concept of value generally and the value attributable to the specific dance	Conforms to expectations for post modern dance as art, powerful physical / audio images communicate paradox of title, movement and sound powerfully engage throughout, dynamic richness sustains repetition (mostly), style and genre wholly appropriate for dance idea, the total commitment of performers is hypnotic.

Figure 5 (includes material from www.hofesh.co.uk)

It is worth noting that although Adshead's dance analysis was written in the context of higher education, the broad headings are appropriate more widely and the appreciation requirements of a number of accredited courses in dance echo these, notably the GCE A Level. Although Adshead's framework was designed to facilitate the study of dance and in particular dance appreciation, the four stages of her chart can also inform the choreographer and the performer as s/he goes about her / his work and also the practitioner and participants involved in feeding back on creative work. The chart thus provides structures for analysis and awareness of the complexity of dance and can enrich understanding of both creating and performing.

In other words knowledge, skills and understanding in relation to components, form, interpretation and evaluation will inform the work of the dance participant learning to create / perform dances, as well as appreciate the work of others.

REFLECTION

1. Review your teaching experiences to date. Reflect on the extent to which you generally address movement content, form, interpretation and evaluation.

2. Create a table similar to *Figure 5* above. Consider a section from a dance performance that you have attended recently or which you have on DVD. Complete your own examples of each of Adshead's four stages in the right hand column.

3. Set yourself a target for including a more enriched appreciation discussion in a lesson. This could be after participants have engaged in a showing and sharing experience. For example, when someone offers the opinion that they "liked" what they saw, prompt more in-depth interpretation.

Model 3: Strategies for Dance Analysis

Smith-Autard (2002) develops tools / strategies to enable participants to engage fully in their dance experiences. This requires dance analysis strategies that integrate dance performance, composition and appreciation. Central to this approach is that performing, creating and watching inform each other.

For example, in order to help young people to analyse why dances mean what they do and why they might be enjoyable, disconcerting, uplifting etc. she provides integrated performance, composition and appreciation tasks in relation to:

- *Sensory qualities* - the qualities with which the movements are performed, e.g. softly, smoothly, purposefully, suddenly.
- *Expressive qualities* - the meanings that the movements appear to suggest, e.g. caring, self-concern, cruelty, playfulness etc.
- *Formal qualities* - the patterns / structural elements in the dance, e.g. accumulating dancers, repetitive rhythms, contrasting motifs etc.

Importantly, in describing the qualities we perceive in a dance, we might not have the words to describe what we see. Importantly, we might not notice aspects for which we have no descriptive terms! As a result, in teaching dancing, performing, creating and watching, Smith-Autard encourages dance teachers / leaders to:

- Use the widest range of vocabulary possible.
- Use metaphors, e.g. a slicing gesture to convey the straight, clean precise, sharp, divisive quality of the gesture.
- Use similes, e.g. land like a butterfly to suggest the delicate, gentle, soft, secure, careful quality of the landing.

In teaching, use of a rich analytical vocabulary, which includes references to images with which dance participants are familiar, can only advantage the quality of their dancing, performing, creating and watching. Below is a précis of the basic features of Smith-Autard's model, with examples to clarify, from Lea Anderson's 1991 *Cross Channel*. For more detailed understanding of aesthetic qualities please refer to Smith-Autard (2002).

Sensory qualities are concerned with:	Example
How movements are performed / the dynamic quality of movements as perceived by the senses, particularly sight and sound (whilst the dynamic qualities of the movements will be of the greatest significance, the action content, spatial orientation and relationships will also have an impact on the sensory qualities of dance movements).	The precision, languidness, feeling of unhurried, contemplative, relaxed, sustainment of the arm and leg gestures (as the dancers are lying in linear formation on their sun beds moving within their personal space in perfect unison).

Expressive qualities are concerned with:	Example
The feeling / meaning that is communicated to the viewer as a result of the sensory qualities identified above.	Time to spare, indulgence, relaxation, holiday, communal confidence, self awareness / obsession, oblivion, carefree.
Formal qualities are concerned with:	**Example**
The form of the dance (both the micro and the macro form), the structural elements, the organisation of the dance content in and through time, the features of the dance that confer a sense of shape to the dance as a whole.	Repetition in and through time, contrast (trampolining / magazine reading) / complementary (magazine reading), canon (suitcases), narrative episodes, sense of unity, proportion, fragmentation, formation.

Figure 6

In building on Adshead's framework for dance analysis, Smith-Autard supplies the dance teacher with an integrative framework and interactive strategies for learning and teaching in dance. She states that,

> in all the performing, creating and viewing experiences involved in producing the dance outcome [...] the children should be encouraged to perceive the feelings embodied in the movements. They should practise performing to gain a kinaesthetic feeling of the sensory qualities [...] In most instances talking about their kinaesthetic feelings and perceptions of aesthetic sensory and expressive qualities will help children to become more aware of them.
>
> (Smith-Autard, 2002, p. 93)

In other words dance analysis can make a significant contribution to the likelihood that dance participants will have high quality dance experiences. The approach will be found useful to dancing, performing, creating and watching.

Dancing the Lindy Hop, the dance leader might refer to, for example:

- *Sensory qualities* – a trampoline / bouncing castle / parkour to help the dance participants to embody the resilient, acrobatic, high energy of the aerial movements.

- *Expressive qualities* – fast and furious, wild, fun, joyous, competitive, athletic, up tempo to help participants capture the dance style.

- *Formal qualities* – accumulating, increasing, amassing to help participants acquire a feeling for developments building to a climax (aspects of form / structure of the dance).

REFLECTION

1. Create a table similar to *Figure 6* above. Consider a dance performance that you have created. Complete your own examples of Smith-Autard's three qualities.

2. Review your teaching experiences to date. Reflect on the extent to which you address the feelingfulness of the movements that you teach, your dance participants create, you and your dance participants view.

3. Consider setting yourself a target in relation to your use of sensory, expressive and formal qualities.

Bibliography

Adshead J. (ed) 1988 *Dance Analysis: Theory and Practice*. London: Dance Books.

Bradley K. 2008 *Rudolf Laban*. London and New York: Routledge.

Laban, R. revised by Ullmann, L. 2011 [1950] *The Mastery of Movement*. [4th edition] Alton: Dance Books.

Newlove, J. 2004 *Laban for All*. London: Nick Hern Books.

Siddall, J. 2010 *Dance In and Beyond Schools*. London: Youth Dance England.

Smith-Autard, J. 2002 *The Art of Dance in Education*. [2nd edition] London: A and C Black.

Chapter 5

Session Planning (Part 1): Breaking Down Individual Tasks

Lorna Sanders

Introduction

All practitioners will share a belief in the importance of high quality dance experiences and, as highlighted in Youth Dance England's *Dance In and Beyond Schools* (2010), successful planning is considered essential to this. All planning, however, is underpinned by our notion of what *learning* is and historically this has changed considerably. In the nineteenth century, for example, it was more typical to see learning as a passive process, in which one simply acquired knowledge by being exposed to it. Learning has now come to be seen as more actively constructed by the individual and therefore the learner must be effectively engaged. Theories of learning are considered in Chapter 1, but it must be borne in mind that current perspectives on these and also what we personally value about dance education, will colour our planning choices and the tools we prefer to use.

It is necessary to break down material to assist learners. While it might seem obvious to split a long dance phrase in half, or teach a step pattern without arm gestures to those who struggle, it is productive to think beyond the immediate detail of the actions to the skills involved.

- Learners' needs can be effectively addressed by considering the layers within skills.
- Although skills are of many types (physical, cognitive, creative, social, for example), learning is assisted when they are broken down into a series of appropriate stages.

This has the benefit of offering clear differentiation opportunities and by underpinning individualised support for learning it furthers holistic approaches to dance education. As Buckroyd (2000) states: 'young people, by definition, do not have a fully developed sense of self. Because of their age and development stage, both children and adolescents have fragile self esteem [...] identity is strongly invested in the body and the developing sense of mastery of it' (pp. 2-3). Accomplishment of physical skills motivates interest in dance and encourages self esteem, but young people who find it difficult to learn skills that are inefficiently broken down by the teacher can assume it is their own ability which is lacking.

There are many planning tools offered by Education Theory and these tend to be based on development stages within cognitive skills. Two models are outlined in this chapter because they are adaptable to dance. Creative, technique, and appreciation skills are mapped against cognitive skills as examples of their application. Social skills, although important, are not dealt with here due to reasons of chapter length and perhaps are best approached by considering how a range of appropriate behaviours are encouraged through different dance / creative tasks, teaching strategies and styles. Links to differentiation strategies are discussed later.

1. Gagné's Model – Theories of Instruction

Gagné (1965) was influenced by his interest in information processing and computer systems. Proposing a hierarchical process, he suggests the need to focus on identifying lower level skills to be mastered first, before progressing to the next. His stages are based on distinctions within cognitive skills which progress from simple types of learning towards problem solving (a complex cognitive skill), but his model can be usefully adapted to dance. *Figure 1* illustrates Gagné's stages with an example of how it can be applied to a choreographic outcome: *understanding how to make a short rhythmic dance phrase using skipping and walking actions*. Read from the bottom of the table to the top.

Gagné's Stages	Dance example (Choreographic Outcome)
Problem Solving • Using the principles to solve complex issues or to test hypotheses.	For example, selecting and linking different ways of skipping and walking to make a rhythmical dance phrase. Applying principles of simple variation for choreographic interest.
Principles • Principles are made by combining ideas and concepts. • Value judgements are associated with this.	For example, understanding how to adapt actions of skipping and walking in an interesting way (as in travelling in different directions, or at different speeds).
Concepts • Using the characteristics of things to create groups or categories.	For example, recognising that particular ways of skipping and walking to music belong to a concept of travelling in dance. Actions are classified as dance.
Discriminations • Perceiving differences between items in collections of stimuli.	For example, learning to discern differences between fast lively music / skipping activity and music in slower tempo which requires a different action response (walking steps).
Basic Understanding / Simple Types of Learning • Stimulus and response.	Simple response develops by association of familiar ideas / feelings. For example, a child enjoys their first experience of skipping to music. Voluntary responses develop: when they hear music again they respond by skipping enthusiastically.

Figure 1: Adapted from Reece and Walker (2000) with added dance examples.

Prior Knowledge

- The seed of the completed nexus of skills in *Figure 1* lies in the initial experience of skipping because of the 'problem' to be solved.
- With this problem, as with more complex choreographic topics, while there is always a very basic underpinning level, older / more able learners may not need to engage in that simple level. It might already form their prior knowledge.
- We make progress by building on previously learned skills, so a basic level for older / more able learners can be more complex or higher up the scale.
- By considering the stages in skill learning, what is required as prior knowledge becomes more clear.

In Gagné's model, it is not always easy to identify the different *types* of learning involved (the first column). However by considering the different *levels*, even if you might determine somewhat differently between aspects of movement you might consider to be discriminations and concepts, it is easier to identify what a learner needs to know, or to be able to do, so that effective development can be facilitated. By attempting to identify all the stages, you are less likely to leave out important aspects or construct tasks that involve higher order responses before foundational understanding is in place. This puts the young people's learning at the centre of the decisions.

> **Case Study 1**
>
> By plotting the stages in the learning of skills, progressive tasks to accomplish mastery of these skills can now be clarified. For example, in response to *Figure 1*, what specific movement tasks would you construct to achieve the desired outcomes?

Skills of Technique

Figure 2 applies Gagné's model to a technical skill. Distinctions between mechanical and expressive skills are used to clarify types of learning. It is not suggested that expressive quality is discouraged until mechanical aspects are achieved. A cognitive model is adapted to physical skill and is thus not a perfect fit. We hope for expressive dancing at all levels and achieving a complex skill effectively may take many years of training.

Hierarchy	Technical Skill – a ballet pirouette (a turning action)
Problem Solving	Integrating all the information to perform a pirouette.
Principles (often to do with values – in this case the aesthetic values of the genre are to be considered): what will make this a good pirouette?	Using spotting to give a slick expressive quality; bringing the arms and gesturing leg quickly and strongly into clear accurate positions; holding the body shape efficiently throughout a continuous turn but without tension; using turn out; controlled closing in time with the musical pulse.
Concepts: (using characteristics of things) - what specific mechanical characteristics are significant in this pivot turn?	Upright torso; gesturing leg flexed to raise foot to supporting knee; arms brought inwards and held; balance on the ball of the foot; head uses whipping action.
Discriminations: (perceiving differences) there are many ways of turning - what kind of turning action is this?	Pivoting on one leg.
Simple level / Basics: what is the fundamental seed of the movement experience?	Simple turning and twirling around one's axis; feeling centrifugal force.

Figure 2: Deconstructing skills of technique

- This is not to suggest that one always begins to teach a pirouette by asking students to spin around on the spot (although this can be useful at times) but that, at a basic level, they require kinaesthetic understanding of this as foundational.
- Dance builds on human movement possibilities and the seeds of dance skills are found in our fundamental physical understandings drawn from our everyday movement experience.
- This is in line with Motor Learning Theory (see Chapter 2) which indicates we bring learned physical habits to our experience of learning new movement (this can be problematic as well as helpful).

The *types* of learning taking place are again not easy to identify, as *Figure 2* illustrates: it is problematic for example which characteristics of a pirouette are concepts and which are principles. It depends to some extent on your perspective of the difference between skill components (as mechanical requirements) and skills of stylistic expression (aesthetic principles). The illustrations in *Figure 2* suggest one way of using the model to assist your thinking and are not a set of rules. At which level in the hierarchy aspects such as spotting or turn out are placed is probably less important than attempting the analysis. For example, you might teach spotting as a concept or you might introduce it later as a principle, because a different emphasis is taken. By thinking through the process, you are better able to articulate the significance of that skill component.

Case Study 2

It can be very useful to consider Concepts as mechanical requirements because these would then require specific instances of strength, flexibility and coordination to be built. For example, *Figure 2* clarifies the importance of having the strength in the leg muscles to balance on one leg and having sufficient core strength to hold the torso upright.

- Identify a complex technical skill from your own style and analyse it into its stages.
- What specific skills of strength, flexibility and coordination are needed?

Skills of Appreciation

Gagné's model does not map easily across to appreciation skills because appreciation can be used in many different ways in dance: for example, to make judgements of others' choreography; to give performance feedback; to come to an interpretation of meaning in choreography; to support an expressive performance; to write a review of a dance. *Figure 3* below considers how Adshead's model for making interpretations (see Chapter 4) can be adapted. Children and young people need to understand how to develop their opinions and not be tied to stereotypes or prejudice. The topic considered is how to appreciate a specific dance phrase.

You need to imagine that the phrase in the example resulted from a workshop based on a theme of sibling rivalry drawn from Robert Cohan's *Hunter of Angels* (1959), during which the movement themes that were explored involved working with a partner and different ways of travelling. A simplified skill-set for interpretation is adapted from Adshead (1988) and illustrates how increasingly sophisticated observation leads to more in-depth understanding of what one sees.

Hierarchy	Appreciation Skill
Problem Solving: What does this phrase mean; what is my opinion of it?	**Appreciation and opinion draws on what has been previously noted about content and structuring of the phrase, taking account of how meaning is communicated within a contemporary dance style.** For example: "because of the way they travel and meet, it looks like the dancers are challenging each other. I thought this was interesting because I could hear the sounds of their hands making contact as they met in a strong balance. I liked the way that the symmetrical body designs during the balance suggested they were equals and had not resolved their rivalry. The tense music added to the mood."
Principles (often to do with values): what is drawn on to make an interpretation?	**Interpretation draws on relevant contextual information and understanding of how components such as costume, design and music aid expression of theme and create choreographic interest.** For example: the participant is aware that it is appropriate to notice certain aesthetic / artistic criteria and to draw on their understanding of the theme / the style / the starting points for the choreography.
Concepts: what characteristics are significant?	**Identifying structural components such as choreographic devices and over-all form.** For example: "the dancers are in unison, starting on opposite sides of the circle before they run around to meet half way; they balance facing each other using strong symmetrical arm lines; the second half of the phrase is a repeat of the first."
Discriminations: what kind of movements are there?	**Identification and description of individual movement components such as action, space, dynamics, flow.** For example: "two dancers run around in a circle, stopping briefly half way round in a strong shape."
Simple level / Basics: what is fundamental?	**Simple observations, discerning basic differences and similarities.** For example a participant might notice: "there are two dancers; they keep moving and there is very little stillness."

Figure 3: Deconstructing an appreciation skill

- By understanding how to observe detailed aspects of the movement in stages, a deeper understanding of the dance phrase is achieved.
- We need to give participants a language to use for feedback and interpretation.

> **Case Study 3**
>
> Identify a short dance phrase and make your own interpretation of it. It does not need to have a specific narrative meaning as in the example above.
> - Notice what language and terms you used to make your interpretation. What background knowledge assisted you and did you draw on the criteria of the style / genre in order to construct your interpretation?

2. Stenhouse's Model

This adapts Gagné's model and is particularly useful where creative skills are to be learned, so is helpful to adapt to dance. It is less linear than Gagné's as a process, initially, because it encourages a thought-shower method in which you try to formulate all the possible aspects / sub components that might be involved.

Stenhouse (1975) also widens the consideration by asking you to think about the three domains of learning that might be involved and this produces a holistic account of what might be covered. The three domains are:

- Cognitive (theoretical knowing, factual understanding).
- Affective (feeling / appreciating / valuing).
- Psychomotor (practical knowing / doing).

Once all the elements of the topic have been mapped, it becomes easier to see in what order they might be tackled. *Figure 4*, adapted from Reece and Walker (2000), illustrates a range of skills and understandings needed for learning how to play the violin and also the order in which one might introduce the basic subcomponents. It is still necessary to identify the skills in ascending order (as in Gagné's model) but having them all laid out as a mind map assists with the decisions. Again, you might have decided on the order differently but thinking through the process will mean that you have clear reasons for making choices and the subsequent effectiveness of these can be reflected on.

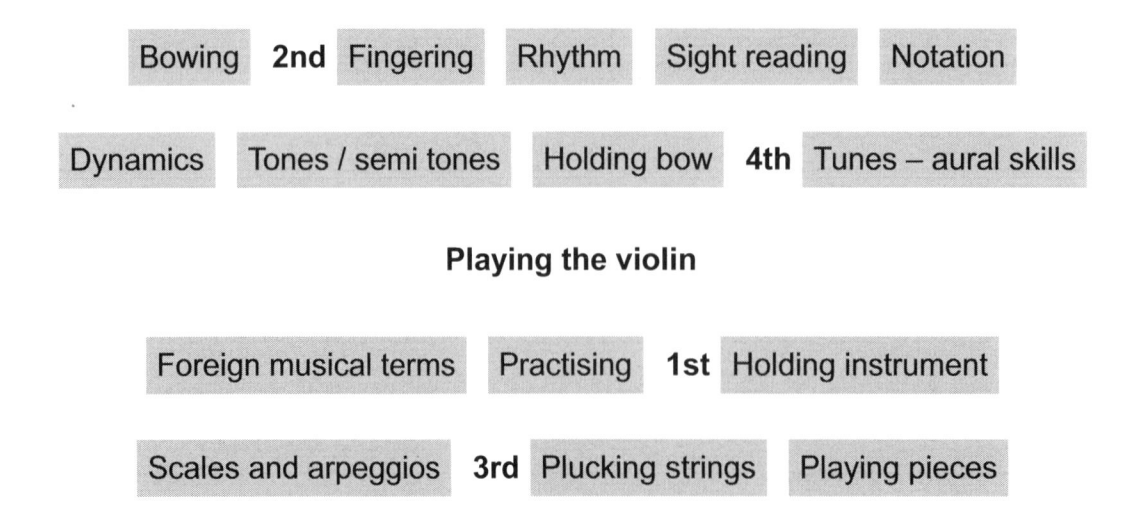

Bowing 2nd Fingering Rhythm Sight reading Notation

Dynamics Tones / semi tones Holding bow 4th Tunes – aural skills

Playing the violin

Foreign musical terms Practising 1st Holding instrument

Scales and arpeggios 3rd Plucking strings Playing pieces

Figure 4: Adapted from Reece and Walker (2000)

Note how the three domains of learning are included in the model without needing to categorise them as such: for example:

- Cognitive - students will learn 'Foreign Musical Terms'.
- Affective - students will appreciate tunes from an aural perspective, 'tunes – aural'
- Psychomotor – students will learn to pluck the strings.

Thinking in the round encourages consideration of the needs of the learner as they engage with the topic and this helps to clarify a wide range of areas where tasks can be planned.

Case Study 4

As with Gagné, Stenhouse's model can be applied to creative, technical and appreciation skills. Place any dance topic of your choosing in the centre of a large piece of paper and make a mind map of all the aspects of learning that you can associate with it.

Try to include something from each of the three domains, but making a free association of ideas sometimes results in this anyway.

It is important to note that applying either of these models focuses on identifying the sequencing of skills / understandings. Creating effective tasks and exercises depends upon your subject knowledge and the depth of understanding you have about your chosen dance style(s) / genre(s).

Differentiation

This provides individual and appropriate ways of achieving the learning for each student. There are several popular approaches (adapted from Stradling, 1991):

1. By **task** – various tasks are set for different ability levels.

2. By **outcome** – the same task is set for all; it is flexible and can be interpreted in different ways to allow students to work at their own level and produce a range of outcomes.

3. By **learning activity** – students tackle a similar objective at the same level, but in different ways (like the first bullet point but the activity itself will be very different, for example, performance, choreography, appreciation).

4. By **pace** – students cover the same content and at the same level, but take whatever time they need to complete it.

5. By **dialogue** – the teacher discusses the work with the individual and they negotiate how to tailor this to the individual's needs.

Research shows that differentiation by **outcome** is the one most often used by teachers in formal education (Harland, J. 2000) and developing a wider palette of choices would be useful. Application of either the Gagné or Stenhouse model assists you to identify the stages in learning and also alerts you to the essential ingredients that must be mastered and the prior learning that needs to be in place. Differentiation can thereby be clarified.

For example in *Figure 2*, taking the bullet points on differentiation in order from the top of the list:

1. while some learn a pivot on one leg, some students could practise turning on two feet and some could be given strength developing exercises;

2. all could attempt the same pivot turn but are allowed to use whatever leg and arm gestures they are comfortable with;

3. some could be in the centre learning by practising while others could be learning by observation (watching to give feedback);

4. some students could be given a longer time to practise a half turn while others attempt a full turn;

5. the teacher could discuss with the more able how they might apply the information to practise double pirouettes.

> **Case Study 5**
>
> Identify a technical step or creative task of your own choosing. Break it down using one of the Models above. How would you use differentiation to promote personalised learning?

REFLECTION

1. How have you planned the break down of material in the past? Did you experience any occasions where participants did not achieve what you intended? Why do you think this was?

2. How might you take into account the need to provide participants with a language to use for appreciation / feedback skills. How can you develop their observation and language skills?

3. What kind of differentiation strategies do you typically use? Reflect on why this might be.

4. Do you have sufficient subject knowledge to identify appropriate tasks to achieve the stages in learning? Could you find a workshop / class to observe in order to see how another practitioner constructs their tasks?

Bibliography

Adshead, J. (ed) 1988 *Dance Analysis*. London: Dance Books.

Buckroyd, J. 2000 *The Student Dancer*. London: Dance Books.

Gagné, R. 1965 *The Conditions of Learning*. New York: Holt, Rinehart and Winston.

Gagné, R. Briggs, I. and Wager, W. 1992 *Principles of Instructional Design*. Orlando: Harcourt Brace Jovanovich.

Harland, J. Kinder, K. *et al.* 2000 *Arts Education and Effectiveness in Secondary Schools*. Berkshire: National Foundation for Educational Research.

Kimmerle, M. and Côté Laurence, P. 2003 *Teaching Dance Skills: A Motor Learning and Development Approach*. Boston: J. Michael Ryan.

Reece I. and Walker, S. 2000 *Teaching, Training and Learning.* [4th edition] Sunderland: Business Education.

Stenhouse, L. 1975 *An Introduction to Curriculum Research and Development.* London: Heinemann.

Stradling, R. Saunders, L. and Weston, P. 1991 *Differentiation in Action: a whole school approach for Raising Standards.* London: HMSO.

Chapter 6

Session Planning (Part 2 – macro level issues): A Planning Framework

Alysoun Tomkins

Introduction

For DDTAL purposes the terms *Work Plan* or *Teaching Work Plan* are used. Others may prefer the term *Scheme of Work or Programme of Study* for example. All are acceptable. Similarly, *Learning Outcomes*, *Learning Objectives*, and *Objectives* are all acceptable terms.

The overall purpose of a work plan is to dissect its main aims into step by step areas of study which guide learners to predetermined learning outcomes. This chapter considers the content of a work plan and individual lessons, what to include and how to structure information in clear and workable formats. See also Purposes and Planning in Chapter 12.

Work plans and lesson plans are working documents created to act as guides. They should be presented clearly and effectively, so that another teacher picking them up would be able to deliver the sessions and provide successful learning experiences for the students.

> The use of schemes of work [work plans] allows individual learning sessions to be placed in a wider context and related to the overall aims and content of a unit of learning. Knowledge, understanding and skills can be shown building up systematically over a period of time.
>
> (Avis, Fisher and Thompson, 2010, p. 136)

Work Plan Framework

A work plan demonstrates progression and development of the skills, knowledge and understanding required by the aims of the work plan and measured in the learning outcomes. McCutcheon states that a work plan is made up of related lessons that address common aims and outcomes: 'they focus learning experiences on an important focal point (or topic) in dance [...] such as a dance style, theme, choreographic work, or a combination' (2006, p. 419).

In dance teaching the work plan might concentrate on skill acquisition of a particular style of dance where fundamental principles of anatomy and body management need to be mastered before more complex technical skills are attempted. Or it may be concerned with developing creative responses to given stimuli which require the learner to increase their knowledge of movement language and / or choreography in order to find more sophisticated responses to tasks. Progression and development of the material and learning through the individual lessons must be shown whatever the focus.

Gathering information for the Work Plan

I would propose that, particularly when working in the informal sector where you may not know the context or the group you will be teaching, it is important to begin your planning with researching both these areas in order to inform the aims, content and learning outcomes of your work plan and sessions.

Suggested order of planning a Work Plan:

Step 1	Context and Group.
Step 2	Aims – Movement and / or Personal and / or Social.
Step 3	Evaluation of aims.
Step 4	Learning Outcomes.
Step 5	Assessment of learning outcomes.
Step 6	Content – Lesson planning.
Step 7	Progression and development.
Step 8	Delivery – teaching styles and strategies; differentiation.

Steps 1-8 can be adapted according to the circumstances in which you are working. If you read McCutcheon (2006, p. 420) you will see that she is looking at a one year, long range plan containing 5 units of study, divided into individual lessons given within a statutory educational establishment.

The principle of planning which McCutcheon proposes is relevant to shorter time spans, for example 10 weeks. Due to the context within which her learning and teaching is occurring she will know her students. It is because she has pre-knowledge of both the context and the student group that McCutcheon suggests you consider the learning outcomes first – what do you want your participants to have achieved by the end of the scheme? (Step 4 below).

Next, she suggests, you consider how you will assess that learning to give evidence that the Learning Outcomes have been met (Step 5 below). Thirdly, she proposes you plan the learning experiences which you will give your students along the way (Step 6 below).

Step 1 – Context and Group

Establish the following information about the group:
- Age and Gender.
- Ethnic background and language ability.
- Amount of previous dance knowledge, experience and ability.
- Any physical, sensory or learning disabilities within the group.
- Whether they are an established group who know each other or newly formed.

And the context within which the teaching occurs:
- Within school curriculum; or within school building but not within curriculum time.
- Pupil referral unit.
- Pre-school nursery.

- Youth centre / sports hall / private dance school / dance agency.
- CAT scheme.
- Outreach group linked to a professional company.

This list is not exhaustive but gives an idea of the range of contexts within which one might be working with children and young people. Taking cognisance of the types of young people with whom you are working, and where, and in what context you are teaching them, should inform the work that you will devise for them. Armed with this knowledge you can start creating your work plan. It can be useful to start this planning process in a more visual format.

Mind Mapping a Work Plan

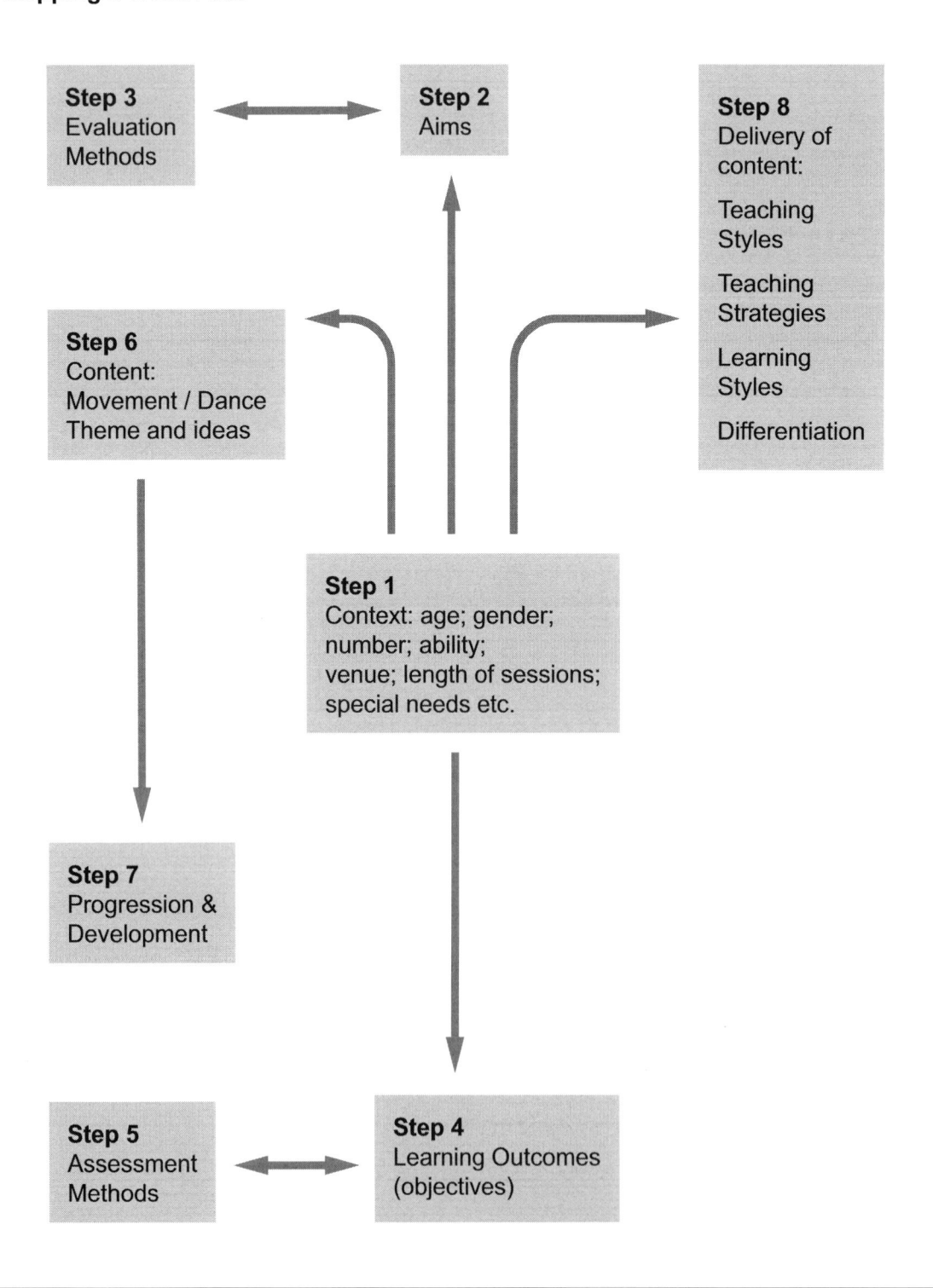

Step 1
Context: age; gender; number; ability; venue; length of sessions; special needs etc.

Step 2
Aims

Step 3
Evaluation Methods

Step 4
Learning Outcomes (objectives)

Step 5
Assessment Methods

Step 6
Content: Movement / Dance Theme and ideas

Step 7
Progression & Development

Step 8
Delivery of content:

Teaching Styles

Teaching Strategies

Learning Styles

Differentiation

Step 2 – Aims

One can adopt a *depth-first* or *breadth-first* approach:

> [...] a purely logical development may not always be the best pedagogic approach [...] a *depth-first* [approach is where] a particular topic is explored in detail before moving on to the next one, and a *breadth-first* [approach is one] in which a topic is taken only as far as is needed to be used in other topics
>
> (Avis, Fisher and Thompson, 2010, p. 136)

In dance, an example of the above might be seen in the teaching of a sequence: one can either demonstrate the whole sequence with the learners observing and 'having a go' (breadth – approach) or break the sequence down and explore all aspects of each section in terms of space, weight, time, (depth approach) before performing the whole sequence. If teaching a particular dance style, a depth approach might teach a routine in the chosen style whereas a breadth approach may begin by considering the social, historical and stylistic aspects before attempting the routine.

It is important to recognise the difference between aims and learning outcomes / objectives and the relationship between them. **The aim is the driving force behind the work.** Consider what your Aims are – an aim identifies what you want the learners to know, demonstrate or understand by the end of the work plan. Learning outcomes / objectives, how you achieve these Aims, are the driving force behind what you teach, how you teach it and what you assess to demonstrate the learner's skill, knowledge and understanding. (See Step 4 below). Gough (1993, pp. 7-9) gives a clear framework from which movement material can be selected for the focus of an aim.

According to Kassing & Jay (2003, p. 202), aims and their associated learning outcomes can be divided into:

Cognitive – what theories and facts students will learn:

- To recognise creative dance vocabulary (artistic).
- To listen and follow teacher's instructions (personal).
- To conduct a self or peer evaluation of a beginning creative movement or dance performance (artistic / social).

Affective – feeling, appreciating, valuing:

- To know and demonstrate etiquette for the creative dance class (personal).
- To demonstrate movement confidence (personal).
- To interact successfully with other persons in the class (social).

Psychomotor – practical knowing / doing:

- To execute basic creative dance elements and vocabulary (artistic).
- To demonstrate the dance forms' relationships to music (tempo, rhythm, counts) (artistic).
- To perform concepts as they relate to creative dance (personal and general space) (artistic).
- To create dances with a beginning, middle and end to meet the learning outcomes of the activity (artistic).

Case study 1

Which of these aims and learning outcomes do you typically address?

As seen on the previous page, there will be aims concerned with movement / artistic development undoubtedly, but you may also include personal and social aims. Further examples are:

- To improve confidence and self-esteem.
- To negotiate with others when working in pairs or a group.
- To observe and give feedback to peers.
- To develop leadership skills.
- To develop critical skills.

Further information on Aims can be found in Chapter 10.

Step 3 – Evaluation Methods

Evaluation Methods can be found in detail in Chapter 10. After considering your aims, it is necessary to indicate in your work plan how you will evaluate those aims to ensure that they have been met. Inevitably, when doing this, you will need to reflect on your practice (the content you devised and the methods of delivery) as these aspects of your teaching will have an effect on how well the aims are met.

Step 4 – Learning Outcomes / Objectives

If Aims are the driving force behind the work, then **Learning Outcomes (objectives) are the driving force behind what you teach, how you teach it and what you assess to demonstrate the learner's skill, knowledge and understanding.** A helpful model for deciding learning outcomes is Bloom's taxonomy. This is discussed in McCutcheon (2006, pp. 80-82; 265), summarised in the table below and helps to give both areas of learning and levels at which these may be achieved. The levels are identified as moving from a recalling of basic facts, through to creative and critical thinking.

The six types of thinking are written along the top of the chart below. Each type of thinking will apply to any age group but 'there are […] degrees of sophistication, difficulty or complexity within each thinking level…from simple to complex depending on the age and cognitive maturation of the child' (*ibid* p. 81).

It is important to make a distinction between the learning activities that you will undertake and Learning Outcomes. Learning Outcomes are what students will achieve.

Learning Outcomes need to be written in such a way that they can be measured (assessed) so the language used in the 'Verbs to use' row in the chart below will be helpful.

For example: The student will… + verb… + criteria:
            The student will… identify… the 5 ways of jumping.

	Knowledge Level 1	Comprehension Level 2	Application Level 3	Analysis Level 4	Synthesis Level 5	Evaluation Level 6
Synopsis	Recalling specific information.	Understanding information without relating it to other information.	Using information in a new situation.	Breaking down information into its constituent parts.	Putting parts together to make a whole.	Making and defending judgements.

	Knowledge Level 1	Comprehension Level 2	Application Level 3	Analysis Level 4	Synthesis Level 5	Evaluation Level 6
Key Words	Know Describe	Understand Explain Describe	Demonstrate Use	Examine Analyse	Compose Create	Critique Judge
Descriptors	Fact based: who, what, when, where. Basic information. Acquiring details.	Recognise Identify Describe material	Explaining Showing Demonstrating	Categorise Identify Describe	Combining Composing Creating	Judge Merit Assess quality
Process	Recalling and remembering	Grasping the meaning of material i.e. different levels.	Applying what one knows to what one does e.g. applying choreographic form to dance making.	Breaking down material e.g. observing a work and describing its use of space.	Putting material together to form a new creation.	Judging artistic merit. Critiquing a dance composition or performance quality.
Verbs to use	List Name Observe Memorise Remember Recall	Identify Summarise Describe	Explain Apply Show Use Sequence Organise Imagine	Characterise Categorise Examine Distinguish between Describe Analyse	Create Choreograph Relate Invent Plan Compose Construct Design Improve Edit, Refine	Evaluate Critique Judge Value Conclude Rate Solve

> **Case study 2**
>
> Use this chart to craft 3 Learning Outcomes for a group you are teaching / leading.

Step 5 – Assessment Methods

Assessment methods can be found in detail in Chapter 9. By assessing the learning outcomes against predetermined criteria one is providing evidence to show how much the students have progressed, what the students have learnt and at what level. In the Work Plan you need to identify what you will assess, the types of methods you will use and the criteria against which you are determining the level of achievement.

Step 6 – Content - Selection of content and lesson models

Having completed Steps 1-5 you will know the context and group with whom you will be working, you will have decided upon the purpose of the work plan (the aims) and how you will evaluate these and you will have identified what skills, knowledge and understanding (the learning outcomes) the learners will gain and how you will assess them. Within that broad structure you now need to fill in the content – the material and teaching methods you will use to explore the aims in order to achieve the outcomes. This involves dividing the learning experience into manageable pieces: the lessons.

Historically, there have been different models for teaching dance based on the purpose and educational thinking of the time. The 'Professional Model' is used to train highly skilled technical dancers for performance within a vocational context, for example the technique class. The 'Educational Model' was developed as a more child centred approach to learning and teaching and focuses on the process of exploring dance rather than the product, for example in creative or modern educational dance. Smith-Autard (1994) developed a model which she called the 'Midway Model'. This model, based on the concept of the art of dance in education, amalgamates the above two models. Here process and product are given equal value. Similarly, Gough (1999, pp. 26-34) states that she uses a 'Dance as Art' model and outlines the structure as:

- Compose.
- Perform.
- Appreciate.

A lesson structure is then proposed with the following headings:

- Dance Style [or Dance Idea, or Theme or Stimulus].
- Movement Aims.
- Warm up.
- Movement Exploration .
- Development.
- Dance [perform].
- Appreciation and evaluation.

McCutcheon (2006, p. 411) advises starting each lesson with an introduction which includes information on the theme or aim, and the learning outcomes to be achieved by the end. She also states that one concludes the lesson with a review and reflection on the lesson and what has been learnt (sometimes referred to as a Plenary). Between the introduction and conclusion she proposes either a five or eight step lesson plan, both of which can be adapted for the ability and needs of the group. As can be seen in the table below, it is clear that the structure of these three lesson models is similar, the differences being in the number of stages that the teacher takes the learners through. **It is also imperative that warm up and cool down are included to ensure safe practice. A Plenary to close the lesson is also useful.**

These models can be used for both technique and creative classes:

Gough's model	McCutcheon 5-step plan	McCutcheon 8-step plan
Dance style / theme / stimulus	Introduction to topic	Introduction to topic
Aims	Introduction to topic	Introduction to topic
Warm up		
Exploration	Explore	Explore
	View	View
Development	Compose	Compose

Gough's model	McCutcheon 5-step plan	McCutcheon 8-step plan
Dance (perform)	Show	Show
		Analyse
		Refine
		Perform
Appreciation / evaluation	Evaluate	Critique
	Reflection	Reflect

> **Case study 3**
>
> Examine a lesson plan you have written in the past. Which of these models is it similar to?

Kassing & Jay (2003, p. 130-133) propose several areas to be considered when beginning to plan the lessons:

1. Who and what the teacher will teach; the population and content

2. What supporting materials and equipment are necessary to teach the class?

3. What are the exercises, combinations, dances [tasks] and when are they presented in the class?

4. What teaching and management strategies are identified for the class?

5. Why are you teaching this content or the objectives of the class?

6. How will the student learning be assessed?

What is omitted above is the question on how you will evaluate the aims of the class.

Step 7 – Progression and development within each lesson and in the work plan

A work plan must show how progression and development enable learners to increase their skills, knowledge and understanding. Progression and development may also refer to the development of material, which may be technical, stylistic or creative, or all three. If one refers again to Bloom's taxonomy above, one can see that the levels of learning indicate progression from recalling basic information through to making and defending decisions made. For example, one might teach a sequence; can they recall and reproduce that sequence accurately? After setting tasks such as: *re-structure the sequence in any order and change the direction and speed of the movements*, one might ask the learners to explain their choices, thus requiring them to make and defend those choices.

See Chapter 5 for further information on layering and developing movement.

Step 8 – Delivery of Content

Finally, once Steps 1-7 have been completed, the methods of delivery to be employed can be determined. The teaching styles and strategies chosen will depend on the material, the learning styles of the students (see Chapter 1) and how one might need to differentiate tasks and outcomes. (See Chapter 3 for information on Teaching Styles and Chapter 5 for Differentiation).

REFLECTION

1. Consider how you articulate your Learning Outcomes or Objectives. Do you make a distinction between the learning activity (what you will do) and what you will assess? Learning Outcomes address what participants will know, understand or be competent in doing by the end of the lesson.

2. Using (and adapting if required) either Gough or one of McCutcheon's Lesson Model plans above, devise in broad outline:

    a) a technique class

    b) a creative class.

3. Using Bloom's taxonomy of learning to show progression and development of learning and material, write down:

    a) a technical exercise and how you would develop it

    b) a creative task and how you would develop it.

Bibliography

Avis, J. Fisher, R. Thompson, R. (Eds.) 2010 *Teaching in Lifelong Learning – A Guide to Theory and Practice.* Berkshire: McGraw- Hill.

Gough, M. 1993 *in touch with dance.* Lancaster: Whitehorn Books.

Gough, M. 1999 *Knowing Dance. A guide for creative teaching.* London: Dance Books.

Kassing, G. & Jay, D. 2003 *Dance Teaching Methods and Curriculum Design.* USA: Human Kinetics.

McCutcheon, B. 2006 *Teaching Dance as Art in Education.* USA: Human Kinetics.

Siddall, J. 2010 *Dance In and Beyond Schools.* London: Youth Dance England.

Smith-Autard, J. 1994 *The Art of Dance in Education.* London: A & C Black.

Chapter 7

Inclusive Dance Practice: Barriers to Learning

Christina Kostoula

Introduction

> Through fear and lack of awareness we don't get the development we need.
> Other people think that they should know, and then lack the confidence to admit they don't know –
> few of them ask the simple question 'what works for you?'
>
> (Caroline Bowditch, in Jones, 2010, p. 36)

The definition of inclusion is constantly debated and its implementation always negotiated between those who "include" others in their practice (in our case dancers / teachers) and those who are "excluded" and wish to "integrate" (disabled dancers / participants). This chapter gives an overview of the agenda of inclusion and its impact on how we think about specific groups of students, especially those defined as "different" from "us". The way we think about "difference" and the ways we deal with individual physical, mental or cultural differences are results of historical change and shifts in social theory and policy.

Most importantly, as dance teachers and artists we can shift existing attitudes and through our practice propose new models of inclusive behaviour. We can, for example, stop perceiving disability as a problem and a barrier to learning dance.

- To be inclusive is to consider how our own training, practice and outlook may be a barrier to the learning of others.
- To be inclusive is to ask questions about what we value as ability, talent and body image in dance.
- To be inclusive is to confront the challenges posed by the people in our classes and studios who may not fit into a mainstream view of what a dance artist / student is or looks like.

What is Inclusion?

Inclusion is a term designating curricula and policies that deal with social disadvantage. Inclusion can be valued as an action compensating for the exclusion of people who are seen as different from the norm. Inclusion also addresses disability, ethnic and social background. When we consider difference and discrimination we also need to consider the ways social divisions overlap. Gender, class, race, sexuality, age and disability combine in important and varying ways to exacerbate or modify the experience of exclusion in our society. We can all reflect on examples of disablism, sexism, racism from real life that intersect in marginalising some people. We may then start unravelling these intersections to combat discrimination.

Perceiving "Disability": The Social Model versus The Medical Model

There are two distinct models of thinking about "disability" and they affect the ways we may include a disabled person in our practices or not. These models also affect the language we use to refer to disability and its experience. Since the 2002 *Disability Discrimination Act* (DDA), the terms 'disabled people' and 'non-disabled' people are favoured over the term 'people with impairment or disability'. The term 'disabled people' is preferred because it supports the social model of disability, in which a person is disabled by the way society is organised, not by his / her own body or impairment. The point therefore is not to cure disability, as in the medical model, but to address attitudes and barriers that contribute to discrimination against someone with a different body or mind.

The social model of disability has assisted people in their political fight for their rights. It opposes the conventional way of perceiving disability as the patient's problem. According to the medical model, only if patients recover can they be integrated into society, thus society does not need to change to accommodate them. According to the social model, disability is a social category and can be experienced as a positive cultural identity, not dissimilar to gender and ethnic identity. Thus, an inclusive social outlook on disability does not locate it in an individual's body or mind as personal stigma, but rather in the cultural attitudes that often dis-able or exclude people, with the aim combatting these.

Case Study 1

It is not the lack of legs that disables a person but the existence of stairs linking two floors. According to the social model, disabled students are not disabled by their wheelchairs but by the fact that a teacher delivers a lesson based mainly on footwork without reference to their needs. A blind student is equally disabled by a teacher who only demonstrates visually without reference to alternative learning styles.
Consider the facilities where you teach. Do they dis-able anyone?

Legislation: Equality Act and the Challenge of Accommodating Disability

From October 2010 the DDA was replaced by the *Equality Act* which also outlaws discrimination of disabled people in education. Discrimination is defined as,

> treating a disabled person less favourably than you would treat a non-disabled person for a reason relating to that person's disability. Failing to provide a reasonable adjustment.
>
> (www.direct.gov.uk/Disabledpeople/RightsandObligations)

According to the *Equality Act*, making reasonable adjustments could include:
- Changes to practices or procedures.
- Changes to physical features.
- Changes to how learners are assessed.
- Providing extra support and aids.

(www.direct.gov.uk/Disabledpeople/RightsandObligations)

Inclusion in Dance

There are many historical and cultural factors that served to promote inclusive dance practices in Britain. In his seminal book on dance and disability *Making an Entrance* (2002), Adam Benjamin (founder of CandoCo, one of the first contemporary dance companies to employ disabled dancers) offers an account of the influences that heralded the emergence of disabled artists. There have been trends and innovations within dance experimentation and choreographic developments that helped to expand traditional movement vocabulary and challenged dominant notions of ability and technique. British companies such as CandoCo, Amici, Green Candle, Jabadao, Salamanda Tandem, Anjali, Common Ground, and StopGAP have established accessible community projects to address difference and diversity. The influential community arts movement of the 1970s and 1980s helped to promote a more inclusive dance and theatre culture.

Dance that aims at inclusion is nowadays a distinct area of training and performing and it can be defined as,

> a field of transformational practice with the potential to affect personal and social change. Its facilitation relies upon the dance practitioner's skill, commitment, awareness (of self and others) and enthusiasm for engaging with this particular form of dance work
>
> (Victoria Hunter quoted in *Animated*, Autumn, 2009, p. 36)

It is important to recognise that there are no agreed guidelines or standards of training in inclusive dance education. The dance sector currently develops a home-grown approach to delivering inclusion. There are courses such as East London Dance's *People Moving* on adapting movement material to meet different needs. Because of the different approaches and methodologies of inclusive dance delivery, there is a lack of precision in how we define inclusion as a sector. In the field of dance practice, inclusion is an open-ended creative process, rather than a ready-made product and policy. Together with their students, teachers are the agents of inclusion.

Different Models of Inclusivity

There are many and disparate interpretations of inclusivity, materialised within a range of dance organisations. Despite commonalities in outlook, every dance organisation is different and has developed its own inclusive methodologies, using different terminology and descriptions of difference. For instance, some curricula refer explicitly to impairments (see Hills (2003) who includes descriptions such as quadriplegic and muscular dystrophy), whereas others like ChickenShed Theatre Company avoid them. Hills promotes the need for more knowledge of the effects that particular conditions can have on individuals, whilst ChickenShed's inclusive methodology avoids language that re-creates social distinctions within its "inclusive space".

Individual Needs versus the Need for Group Cohesion

Hills (2003) argues that inclusive leaders and support assistants need to be able to deliver activities that match the members' diverse preferred learning styles. For example, she spells out a list of possible needs often relevant to dancers with short attention span:

> need for clear boundaries, consistency, relevant stimuli, relevant pace, change of activity, physical movement that often wears them out, attention from others, appropriate support.
>
> (Hills, 2003, p. 30)

CandoCo's *Accessing Dance and Performance Training Model* (ADAPT) also pays attention to the specificities of individual embodiment and encourages dance teachers to think about adapting movement tasks to suit individual profiles and needs.

In contrast, ChickenShed's terminology does not refer to physical / mental disability or issues of socio-cultural exclusion, but invests in a symbolic use of words such as "all", "together" and "everybody". This makes it easy for a wide range of individuals to recognise themselves in the company's imagery. For ChickenShed, it is the leader's job to monitor and evaluate participants' needs as part of general classroom practicality ensuring the flow of group activities, rather than as an opportunity for the participants' reflective practice. Hills promotes the idea of 'physical listening' (2003, p22) a holistic and kinaesthetic awareness of other people's needs.

People Moving (Parkes and Connor, 2003) and Candoco's ADAPT and *Foundation Course for Disabled Dancers* promote a different type of pedagogic assessment / evaluation; one that combines tutor assessment with self-assessment and peer assessment, as well as reflective practice at all levels. *People Moving* suggests that individual needs and Individual Goal Monitoring should be explained to the students to empower them towards self-monitoring and self-evaluation (2003, p. 14).

ChickenShed's methodology establishes the notion that creativity, in the context of inclusive instruction, equals not so much the desire to act towards individualised expression but 'the desire to act upon ideas and direction of others and for others' (NITTDP, 2003, p. 19). According to this model of inclusivity, group cohesion is the goal. *Focus, attention, respect* become instrumental for structuring cohesion and conformity to the inclusive rules.

Case Study 2

Thinking critically: Identify strengths and limitations in the above inclusive approaches. Think of it as a problem: Those who look around passing focus, giving cues for people to talk, orchestrate responses and identify the needs, are those who hold the authority to control the inclusive framework. A look can serve easily as a discreet and silent device of inclusive authority. For the sake of the group and of continuity, the leader has to take spontaneous decisions to intervene and regulate individual expression to the benefit of collective communication.

How can this be a barrier to learning? What divisions operate between those *facilitated to look* at others and those positioned as *to be looked at / after by others*? How can we challenge this division?

Beyond Inclusion and Towards Empowerment

The nexus between non-disabled leader and disabled participant should always be acknowledged in inclusive practice. Hills warns against the repeated positioning of participants in the same roles and activities that deny them the chance to vary their experience of inclusion. Dancers should take turns as appraiser, dance critic, rehearsal director and choreographer (2003, p. 17).
She stresses the need of inclusive dance to:

      a) Foster the ability to create dance as opposed to someone who purely follows instructions,

      b) the ability to shape dance pieces through an aesthetic awareness and

      c) the understanding that there are different ways of doing things and making decisions.

                                                                                       (Hills, 2003, p. 65)

Dancers should be encouraged to make choices that are not simply responses to a framework given by the leader – to build a choreographic knowledge through a range of activities.

Candoco's ADAPT is also part of a trend of inclusive pedagogy that goes beyond inclusive morality and instead promotes the methodological and systematic challenging of existing habits and hierarchies of teaching dance. Norwood, who designed the accredited professional course for Anjali Dance Company (whose members are all learning-disabled), outlines a pedagogy geared towards the professional development of learning-disabled dancers. She argues for the concept of equality in all learning platforms:

> [give access to] an equal opportunity to contribute within any given creative process, a structure that actively supports different learning styles, and the use of common language.
>
> (Norwood, 2007, p. 22)

Case Study 3

Thinking critically: Are some more "equal" than others in our practice?

To ensure equality we need to ask each time "WHO" possesses the tools of dance knowledge - all or a few - and what is the selective criterion (ability, background, gender?) To be truly inclusive we need to ask "who speaks and on behalf of whom" and why? We always need to challenge the effectiveness of the activity format in terms of equality.

Inclusive Choreographic Tools – Working Towards Creative Equality

Somatic approaches can help to introduce dancers to concepts such as breathing and relaxation, so that they may feel less inclined to take the short-cut of mirroring without reflecting on the movement for themselves. Accessible dance forms such as release and contact improvisation also encourage ownership of the movement. However, it is difficult for inexperienced participants to understand that not being told exactly what to do is part of the creative process of teaching and learning dance. Offering critical explanations, while encouraging physical involvement using evocative description, could give students the option of learning to understand the process of individual creativity in dance (Parkes, 2003, pp. 22-23). Benjamin also warns those newly converted to improvisation that, if taught and practised uncritically, it can result in ignoring the real issues of difference, buying instead into a ready-made theory of creativity that allows 'dancing around the problems rather than valuing them' (2002, p. 46).

In general, less rigidly-structured and non-pressurised workshops facilitate intimate acts of moving from within. Even ordinary movement, when given space and time to breathe, can have its own particular kind of beauty. Hills identifies not just flow and de-contraction but also 'stiffening, tensing, withdrawing body parts, fidgeting, giggling and giving more weight to partner as physical responses that need to be valued, and as individual creativity to stimulus that should be further developed within work in pairs' (2003, pp. 116-117).

In addition to the empowering imagery of improvisation and somatics, existing inclusive dance curricula offer inclusive tools:

- Use of enabling words (examples: "walk" can become "move", "travel". "Stand" can become "stand or sit", "See" can become "sense, hear, become aware of").

- Person-centred techniques (examples: use of touch, emphasising the role of senses, use of alternative styles of training - "floor barre", the Simpson board, "sign song", "eye contact", "movement through touch" (Jones, 2010).

A Common Dance Language – The Need of Translation / Adaptation

Candoco's *Foundation Course for Disabled Dancers* argues for the creation of a new role within inclusive dance settings, that of Dance Support Specialist (DSS), working as an interface between tutors and students. Technique is a core component of the course and allows students to have a language that they can use in other dance environments. DSS are trained dancers who apply their knowledge of dance technique to translate and work towards the implementation of technical requirements in and by the body of individual dancers.

Here is a definition of inclusive translation and adaptation:

> to provide the same or equally positive sensation rather than reproduce the same visual form and aesthetic outcome. Encouraging students to identify what an exercise is for, recognising that the information is the same even if the felt sensation and physical outcome is different for each individual dancer, based as it is on each individual dancer's body.
>
> (Whatley, 2007, p. 13)

In inclusive practice we need to consider:

- The deeper syntax of movement, breaking it down for the student, through an internal understanding of the intention behind the movement.
- How students can be facilitated to identify ways to adapt movement to their needs whilst retaining the core aims of the exercise.
- How to know / question what we are trying to achieve (making meaning through dance) rather than imposing a certain *know-how* on people.
- How to identify the core principles of our chosen technique (elements which identify or define a codified style / technique) and be prepared to translate them.

Example of adaptation led by a disabled dancer:

> I have been working out how to adapt various techniques to fit my body – the dancers give me insight into what needs to be going on in the body behind the movements – for example, I realised that a low box to sit on could provide me with a way in which I could feel a sense of gravitational pull, this enables me to work harder and feel how to work correctly.
>
> (Caroline Bowditch, in Jones, 2010, p. 35)

Case Study 4

Example of adapting ballet technique: the key movement idea behind a tendu in ballet is extending the line of the leg by pointing the foot, or strengthening the feet for landing from jumps. How could the idea of tendu be translated for someone who is a wheelchair user? Translating the key movement idea to the arms or even the torso might be a way.

Select a movement of your own and consider how it can be adapted.

Inclusive Performance: Process-led versus Product-led Approaches

There are undisputed benefits in performing in front of an audience. However, when prioritising inclusion we need to ensure we do not *impose* synchronisation and symmetry. Rhythm and repetition are of course adding the power of collective to individual movements and they can be seen as staples of inclusive performance of groups such as ChickenShed Theatre Company, Anjali and StopGAP. However, other groups find that public performances and emphasis on product versus process can prove to be problematic in terms of inclusivity.

Companies such as Salamanda Tandem, for example, prefer to share work-in-progress or offer open workshops that incorporate some performance rituals. These are often structured with an orchestrated opening and ending and take place in front of an audience that functions more like a witness than a spectator. The event is more like an exchange of ideas between equals rather than a conventional show.

Many inclusive arts organisations choose to emphasise the value of the dance process over a final dance product. They share improvisations, exhibit film and photographic documentation from workshops, or sound recordings. Inclusive performance in this sense is more like an extension of a good creative process, or the process being made transparent. Arguably, the participants feel less pressurised (than in traditional public performance set ups), whilst enjoying the creative and empowering benefits of a heightened awareness of sensation and an awareness of environment, in the presence of others.

Inclusive performance aims to draw spectators into the creative action, helps them to feel the heavy breathing and sweating of the performers and to gain a kinaesthetic knowledge through perceiving their bodies in a way that antagonises visual detachment. Inclusive performance can thus be seen as anti-spectacle, a kind of active witnessing, a radical aesthetic shift. Most of all, it is about seeing people collaborate.

Conclusion

Even if not actively engaged in teaching disabled people, dance teachers need to understand that there is no one-size-fits-all approach to learning, simply because there are always varying degrees of learning ability within even the more mainstream and homogenous of dance classes. All teachers have to use problem-solving skills to adapt material and understand their students' needs; each and every one of them has different needs and abilities to consider.

The presence of a disabled student in the studio inevitably highlights the shortcomings of a teacher who does not acknowledge individuality and difference in general. Delivering dance in an inclusive manner means that we prepare and organise a class so that the presence (or not) of a different body will not pose problems to the ethos and the purpose of the lesson. Teaching inclusively means that we plan for and include the possibility of different needs within our teaching from the very start.

REFLECTION

1. Return to the three bullet points on page one of this chapter. Consider your beliefs and attitudes towards inclusivity. How might you define it?

2. Consider your own attitudes in relation to the social and the medical models. Which do you find the most persuasive and why?

3. Try to record yourself teaching. Listen to the terms you use. How might you adapt these for inclusive practice?

Bibliography

Anonymous, 2009. *Animated Making Dance Matter*, Foundation for Community Dance, Suffolk: BC Publications, Autumn.

Benjamin, A. 2002 *Making An Entrance, Theory and Practice for Disabled and Non-Disabled Dancers*. London: Routledge.

CandoCo Dance Company, ADAPT, *Accessing Dance and Performance Training*, unpublished document, Inset for Urdang Academy, January, 2008 and Training Day, June 2008, by Susie Cox (Course Director for CandoCo's Foundation Course for Disabled Dancers)

ChickenShed Theatre Company, 2003, National Inclusive Theatre Training and Development Programme (NITTDP) Booklet One: *Inclusive Performing Arts – Group Inclusion – Principle into Practice*. Unpublished company literature.

Cooper Albright, A. 1997 *Choreographing Difference, the Body and Identity in Contemporary Dance*. Hanover: Wesleyan University Press.

Hills, P. 2003 *It's Your Move! An Inclusive Approach to Dance*. Birmingham: The Questions Publishing Company.

Jones, I. 2010 *Dance and Disabled People, Pathway to practice for Dance Leaders working with Disabled People*. London: Foundation for Community Dance.

Kuppers, P. 2000 Accessible Education: Aesthetics, Bodies and Disability. *Research in Dance Education,* 1, 2, pp. 119-131.

Norwood, S. 2007 Routes to Integration for Learning Disabled Dancers. *Animated*, Autumn, pp. 22-23.

Parkes, M and Connor, C. 2003 *People Moving, Towards an Integrated Learning Culture for Dance*, curriculum commissioned by East London Dance in partnership with the Dance Department of the Arts Council of England.

Whatley, S. 2007 Dance and Disability: The Dancer, the Viewer and the Presumption of Difference. *Research in Dance Education*, 8, 1, April, pp. 5-25.

www.chickenshed.org.uk

www.direct.gov.uk/Disabledpeople/RightsandObligations

Chapter 8
Fostering Creativity in Dance Education
Linda Rolfe

Introduction

This chapter introduces the discussion surrounding creativity and offers ways of framing creativity in dance education. It draws on current educational practice, relevant literature and suggests how ideas might work in practice.

Why explain creativity?

Explaining creativity can help educators teach more effectively and contributes to the identification and realisation of every person's unique creative talents. Creativity is not a mysterious force that some people are just endowed with, but it is complicated. Through the centuries there have been different conceptions of creativity, and there is no single historically continuous definition of the term. It may be useful to acknowledge that our conception of creativity is not universal and society may change its conception of creativity in the future. Explaining creativity also requires us to know a lot about the culture, society, and historical period in which it occurs.

It is recognised that creativity is mostly conscious, often hard work and uses everyday mental processes involving improvisation, collaboration and communication (Sawyer, 2006). Skills, knowledge, training and conscious deliberation are all essential for creativity wherever it occurs.

Creativity frequently includes a balance between imitation and innovation, whilst recognising the key role played by convention and tradition. Making reference to the professional dance repertoire of choreographers, dancers and companies of past and present is thus of great value. It is this canon of work which is a resource for the creativity of dance in the future, where transformation and invention, variation and change are the building blocks of new dance work.

Creativity in Education

Education in many parts of the world has been promoting creativity for several years. The multiple current discourses on creativity which are evident in English creativity in education are now well documented, (for example, Banaji, Burn and Buckingham, 2010). In England this can be traced back to *All Our Futures: Creativity, Culture and Education*, a report produced by the National Advisory Committee on Creative and Cultural Education (NACCCE, 1999) which ultimately led to Creative Partnerships, a flagship government initiative in 2002.

NACCCE defines creativity as: imaginative activity fashioned so as to produce outcomes that are both original and of value (1999, p. 29). There are many definitions in the literature, however, this one serves as a useful starting point in helping to explain and understand creativity.

In Craft's work (2005, 2008, 2010, 2011) and that of others who have investigated creativity in dance (Chappell, 2008; Rolfe *et al*, 2009), it is argued that:

> creativity is about imagination and multiple possibilities, about shared generation of ideas, about immersion in the flow and about capturing unexpected and exciting new ideas.
>
> (Chappell, 2011, p. 4)

Despite the attention and importance given to creativity there are concerns that British education within the formal sector is driven by a narrow focus on literacy and numeracy. These issues were raised in the NACCCE report (1999) and the government of the day responded by introducing educational policies and initiatives designed to encourage creative and cultural learning in schools. The most significant were: Artsmark (2000, www.artsmark.org.uk), Creative Partnerships (2002, www.creativepartnerships.com), a new Secondary Curriculum (2008, www.qcda.co.uk), and Find Your Talent (2008, www.findyourtalent.org). The Roberts report, *Nurturing Creativity in Young People* (2006) proposed a framework for how creativity could be developed for children and young people. The new secondary curriculum (2008) reflected this concern to develop creativity and it included a creativity strand in the programme of study for all of the ten subjects in the curriculum. Despite these developments and also subsequent to the change of government in 2010 there remains anxiety amongst educators that creativity is stifled by increasing pressures to assess attainment and measure success across all phases of formal education. In particular within dance examinations there is concern that this can result in choreography which lacks originality or authentic original dance ideas. Creativity can be assumed as a product of dance education but national inspection reports from the Office For Standards in Education express concern this is not always the case (Ofsted 2006).

Perspectives on creativity in dance education

Creativity in dance education has been studied and framed in a number of different ways. Although rarely defined for analysis, creativity in dance education embraces abilities such as innovation, being able to put aside the familiar and the safe, questioning what is already made, and using imagination, knowledge and skills. Of particular relevance is Smith-Autard's (2002) Midway Model which advocates an equal emphasis on creativity, imagination, individuality and acquisition of knowledge of theatre dance. Gough (1999) emphasises that creative dance teachers should make classes relevant, respect students as individuals, generate enthusiasm, be flexible and build good relationships. The Dance Partners for Creativity (DPC) research found that the creative relationship developed between a dance artist and a teacher working in partnership is one that could be replicated between a teacher and a group of learners by:

- building trust
- allowing another person to contribute ideas
- valuing others' ideas
- negotiating leadership, with power and control going back and forth.

(Malcomson, Watkins, Rolfe and Jobbins, in Chappell, 2011, p. 44)

These factors can provide a teaching environment in which creativity can be sparked and flourish. This co-construction of creativity, with both teacher and learners actively engaging in the creative process, (suggesting ideas, using imagination, taking risks) is at the heart of an education within dance.

In order to provide a framework for some of these views we can draw on Chappell's research which showed that dance teachers were using 'three dimensions of pedagogy which were intricately intertwined when teaching for creativity' (2009, p. 181). These are outlined in the *Figure* below which has been adapted and extended for this chapter to include a fourth dimension:

Chappell's views about individual, collaborative and communal creativity (this is developed from Craft's (2000) notion of *creativity-in-relationship* using John-Steiner's (2000) notion of *creative collaboration*). Learners and the teacher are required to shift between all four interrelated and intertwined dimensions.

Dimension of pedagogy	Description	Dance example
Prioritisation of creative source – '*inside out*' or '*outside in*'	Whether the task source was mainly the children's or the teachers' ideas / dance knowledge. This means shifting between inside or outside for the sources of dance idea, movement and opinion, ensuring that learners experience the creative impulse as their own in order to authentically give voice to ideas which are meaningful to them in dance.	**Inside out** Learners contribute ideas on what the dance should be about and the kinds of movement it might include. For example: using poetry written by the learners as a stimulus and they suggest how the words / ideas in the poem might be represented in movement. **Outside in** The teacher initiates the dance idea and sets the creating tasks. For example: the teacher selects a professional work and uses the dance idea and some of the movement vocabulary.
Degrees of proximity and intervention	Supporting and challenging creative ideas, providing reactions from a distance or close-up interaction. Proximity is indicative of the amount of freedom teachers allow the learners *per se* for creativity.	**Distance** Teacher gives learners greater freedom to respond to a task and then reacts to their work with praise. For example: 'All try to explore counterbalance with your partner, I think the ideas from this duet are really working well as they are clearly communicating their closeness'. **Close proximity** Teacher intervenes more proactively whilst the learners are creating, also guides and suggests answers to the task. Responds with critical praise. For example: 'This duet have used both hands in their counter balance now can they try to extend their arms and stay closer to the floor.

Spectrum of task structures - *purposeful play to tight apprenticeship*	Moving between play-based task structures (characterised by '*risk-taking*', '*acceptance of failure*', '*fun, silliness and mess*'); and apprenticeship structures (characterised by '*tight parameters*', '*safety*' and '*structured stages*', where progression is contingent on '*step-by-step success*' and '*hard work*'). Appropriate to the situation, this means: • Sharing responsibility for the creative idea. • Allowing differing amounts of control and freedom which allow for differing amounts of space within tasks for 'bursts of creativity' or more sustained creative explorations.	**More open tasks** 'Explore different ways of taking weight onto different parts of your body'. **More structured tasks** 'Start by taking weight onto your hands, now try shifting the weight so that you have your back in contact with your partner'.
Interrelating layers of individual, collaborative and communal embodied creative activity	What the learners communicate, and how they want to communicate it, individually or collaboratively. Communal creativity encourages a strong focus on empathy, shared ownership and group identity.	**Individual** 'In your own space improvise different ways to rise and fall to the floor'. **Collaborative** 'With a partner use your rising and falling ideas to create a phrase in unison. **Communal** 'Share your duet with another pair. Watch each other's work and give comments about the content and meaning in order to develop it further'.

Figure 1: Adapted from Chappell (2009, p. 182) with added dance examples.

Case Study 1

Consider how the open and structured tasks referred to above might be related to Mosston's spectrum of teaching styles. See Chapter 3 for information on these.

In the following section the four dimensions of pedagogy are applied to creating dances. In most examples the four dimensions are interrelated and not discrete, they are overlapping, although some may be more prevalent than others.

The 'what' of creativity in dance

In this section the focus is on creativity in making or creating dance, rather than on viewing or performing dance. Siddall (2010, p. 22) identifies the constituent features of creating dance thus:

Aural setting   *Movement*

DANCE IDEA

Dancers   *Physical setting*

Structure

Dance Idea

Dance ideas originate from many different sources and whether they are visual, auditory, kinaesthetic or ideational they should have the potential to be transformed into movement. Consider whether this is '*outside in*' or '*inside out*', and quite possibly the generation of ideas will shift between the two as learners and teacher contribute and share thoughts and feelings. Try to select something that learners can connect to their prior experience and which excites and stimulates their imagination.

Case Study 2

- Select a dance idea (for example a painting, a poem, a story). Does it have the potential to engage and inspire?
- Write down the possibilities for movement, i.e. action, space, dynamics, relationships. Are physical challenges and risk-taking involved?
- Choose compositional devices that could be used to structure the dance. Are there individual and collaborative opportunities?

Movement

To generate a movement vocabulary the process of developing the dance idea involves setting movement tasks. A variety of tasks will allow learners to experience a spectrum across purposeful play to tight apprenticeship. Depending upon the learning aims the teacher should select which approaches are most appropriate for the dance context. Answer the questions in the case study.

a) Asking questions

Case Study 3

More **open questions** encourage *play* and *risk-taking*. Dance idea: Flight
- How does it feel to have the wind pushing you in different directions?
- What parts of your body are taking your weight?
- When is there rhythm in your movements?

The use of **open questions** hopefully provoked you to a variety of different responses which could help to generate a rich mixture of movement outcomes. These may then be explored further and refined to create a bank of movement vocabulary.

The use of **closed questions** will encourage a narrower range of outcomes and require *safe structured* stages for example:

>Dance Idea: Flight
>
>Can you move in different directions? Try up and down, side to side.
>
>How can you take weight on your hands? Use both hands and then just one.
>
>Have you tried changing the speed? Travel slowly and gradually speed up.

Asking learners to generate more questions is a way to develop movement ideas, encouraging them to take greater ownership of the creative process. This can be encouraged when they are watching the work of their peers and giving feedback by getting them to ask why, what, where, how and when questions.

It is also helpful to offer strategies for thinking about connections and different ways of solving problems in order to foster creativity. This might result in recalling previous experiences in dance or referring to the work of other learners or professional dance for exemplification. As the learners and teacher become more experienced at challenging assumptions and initial responses the movement should become more innovative, demonstrating informed understanding of the problems being solved. Leaving more space physically and mentally for learners to develop ideas can allow them to create their own answers to movement problems. The teacher shifts between *close proximity* and *greater distance* when giving feedback and intervening in the creative process.

b) The use of images

Images can help learners to imagine a range of possible movement responses to a dance idea. The use of language or other stimuli can evoke images which elicit an imaginative response. This approach is centred on the learner initiating a movement response which connects to them personally, from '*inside out*'. Images may allow learners to connect the idea to the physical generation of movement. The example below is taken from the Dance Partners for Creativity research project which collected data in English secondary schools over two years. The project explored the kinds of creative partnerships manifested between dance-artists and teachers in co-developing the creativity of 11-14 year olds, and how these partnerships develop. Full details can be found on the DPC website: http://education.exeter.ac.uk/dpc

Lîla Dance are a professional company who work with young people in different educational contexts. They make extensive use of imagery to generate movement material with the dancers when co-constructing the choreography. In the following extract Abi Mortimer, a founder member of the company, explains their ideas and how they work in practice:

>'What do we mean by an image? In our practice an image is an idea that is planted into the body and mind to trigger a human response, be it emotional, physical or intellectual. The emphasis is always on the intrinsic relevance of the image so that the young person understands the movement they generate from a kinaesthetic point of view. An image could be evoked from a number of sources, such as visual stimuli, music / sound, or the use of language [...]
>
>For example:
>
>A: Sit down, cross legged. Go to place your hand on the floor, but do so with a slow and steady pace and with a steady hand. Reach with your fingertips. The moment your fingers touch the floor, pull your hand away in a direct line and with speed.

B: Sit down, cross legged. Imagine the floor is covered in hot coals, go to touch it. What would your reaction be?

A causes a cognitive response through following instructions that explain what and how to do a specific movement. B provides the possibility for a more personal response, as an image is evoked through the choice of language that recalls movement memories.

The response from B is also evoked through using less words, it is immediate and powerful because it speaks to knowledge already held in the body. By using an image, emphasis is placed on the 'why' and 'how' of the movement and this in turn informs how the movement itself is perceived and understood. The movement response therefore feels like it comes from the self as it is personal.'

(Mortimer in Chappell *et al*, 2011, p. 48)

Case Study 4

- Think of images that you could use when teaching a technical movement. For example visualising the spine as a string of pearls when rolling down towards the floor from standing.
- What language can you use to evoke a physical and feeling response in the learners? For example smooth, successive, flowing, rippling. How does this assist a creative response to learning technique?

c) Demonstration and modelling

Creativity in dance can be developed through demonstration and modelling of movement. Frequently led by the teacher, who selects the stimulus and initiates the tasks, (*outside in*), the learners make progress in *safe and structured stages* (this can also include skilful learners demonstrating to their peers). Physical demonstration of movement by the teacher inspires interest and enthusiasm in learners. They enjoy learning through watching the teacher perform. This might include the teacher demonstrating the skills needed to complete a task such as travel, spin and fall, to give an idea of movement vocabulary. This can clarify the movement and add new physical challenges. The dancers can then copy and select movements to create a movement sentence. This could then be followed by a choreographic task, for example asking learners to use question and answer to build a duet, which is part of the dance structure.

Providing models of the completed task, such as a movement motif or a concept such as suspension, gives learners an opportunity to observe and develop a conceptual model of the task or process before attempting to perform it. This provides an example of what might be possible. The professional dance repertoire provides a rich resource to show many possibilities of what movement is realisable in dance. Showing learners extracts from dance on DVD can extend their imagination and inspire them to create beyond their previous experience.

Case Study 5

Dance Idea: A day at the beach

Dance section based on swimming. Consider the table below. Select your own idea and a professional work and suggest how you would use modelling and demonstration.

Teacher	Dancers
Demonstrate arm gestures of breast stroke using variation of directions and levels. Use language to explain what they are doing as they perform	Watch the teacher, and then copy the gestures as a whole class, mirroring the movements. This could lead to them using the movements to create a phrase.
Perform an example of a movement motif based on breast stroke, providing a model of a completed task	Watch the teacher, and then learn the motif. This could lead to them creating their own motif.
Show an extract from *Waterless Method of Swimming Instruction* (Cohan 1974)	Identify the dynamics used by the dancers and include them in their own movement phrase / motif

Structure

The structure of the movement into phrases and eventually dances is a part of the creative process, involving both knowledge about choreographic tools and open ended creative dance experiences. A balance between the two is desirable, rather than one being taught at the expense of the other. You need to consider how to provide a safe environment by clear teaching about dance structures, before participants can be confident to try something new and unknown. Excessive emphasis on structure can restrict students' imaginative and creative responses. It is essential to allow them to be spontaneous, experiment and take risks beyond their experience and knowledge. This involves shifting between the four dimensions outlined above, overlapping the pedagogic approaches as appropriate.

Case Study 6

- In a duet about relationships, which choreographic tools or devices are appropriate to communicate the dance idea? For example: question and answer, contact between dancers, repetition, changing the direction of movement.
- How might each section of the duet relate to the whole dance? For example: use of contrast, variety, transitions, balance.

Dancers

The partner and group relationships, formations and sensitivity to others within a dance highlight the value of the creative space between individuals. New ideas are shared and grow out of questioning and challenging, as well as collaborating with others. Both learners and teacher can work together, co-constructing the dance. The dynamics of interacting with others can ignite ideas and imaginative responses with learners creating from *inside themselves to the outside and outside themselves to the inside*. Being able 'to bring themselves and their ideas into conversation with other people, other people's ideas, and the developing artistic idea' (Chappell, 2011, p. 94) is a vital aspect of creativity in dance. A shared creative group identity can also provide a safe place to create within and requires considerable empathy. Learners may develop their own sense of support for one another with social relationships thoughtfully enacted, which supports the group identity and creative work.

Summary

To quote Warburton (2009): 'creativity is a skill that can be practised, a process to be pursued, and a performance to be enjoyed' (p. 157). Successful outcomes take time to achieve and success can be viewed as progression towards a goal, involving breaking the work down into achievable sections within a realistic time scale. Learners can then build their creative practice confidently and the level of challenge can gradually be increased. This requires familiarity with known boundaries, awareness of what may be the next step and the courage and ability to go into new areas of dance experience.

REFLECTION

1. Explore your own views and attitudes towards creativity. Why do you consider creativity to be important? How would you explain creativity? What do you think your participants would understand by creativity? What value is placed on it?

2. What kind of creative processes do you usually engage in with your participants? *Outside in* or *Inside out*? Why do you select these methods? Remember that creativity is involved in all strands of dance education.

3. It was suggested that teaching strategies include close *proximity* and *distance*. Consider how you use these in your own practice.

4. In the early part of this chapter the co-construction of work between teacher and learners was identified as a useful approach. Read the quotation by Malcomson again and consider how you can apply this to your own practice – whether this is creative or technique-based.

5. Creative tasks need to be built progressively. Consider what frameworks have been provided in this chapter to assist you with planning. Return to Case Study 5 and construct a series of creative tasks to develop the dance idea.

Bibliography

Banaji, S. Burn, A. and Buckingham, D. 2010 *The rhetorics of creativity: a literature review*. [2nd edition] London: Creativity, Culture and Education.

Chappell, K. 2008 Towards Humanising Creativity. UNESCO Observatory E-Journal *Special Issue on Creativity, policy and practice discourses: productive tensions in the new millennium*. 1, 3, December. http://www.abp.unimelb.edu.au/unesco/ejournal/vol-one-issue-three.html

Chappell, K. Craft, A. Rolfe, L. and Jobbins. V. 2009 Dance Partners for Creativity: choreographing space for co-participative research into creativity and partnership in dance education. *Research in Dance Education: Special Issue Creativity* 10, 3, pp. 177-197.

Chappell, K. Rolfe, L. Craft, A. and Jobbins, V. 2011 Introducing the research project. In Chappell, K. Rolfe, L. Craft, A. and Jobbins, V. *Close Encounters: Dance Partners for Creativity*, Stoke on Trent: Trentham Books, pp. 88 - 100.

Craft, A. 2000 *Creativity across the primary curriculum. Framing and developing practice*. London: Routledge.

Craft, A. 2005 *Creativity in schools: tensions and dilemmas*. Abingdon: Routledge.

Craft, A. 2008 Trusteeship, wisdom and the creative future of education? UNESCO *Observatory E-Journal Special Issue: Creativity, policy and practice discourses: productive tensions in the new millennium.* 1, 3, December.

Craft, A. 2010 *Creativity and Education Futures.* Stoke on Trent: Trentham Books

Craft, A. 2011 Becoming meddlers in the middle: stretch, challenge and leap? In Chappell, K. Rolfe, L. Craft, A. and Jobbins, V. *Close Encounters: Dance Partners for Creativity.* Stoke on Trent: Trentham Books, pp. 113-127.

Gough, M. 1999 *Knowing dance: A guide for creative teaching.* London: Dance Books.

John-Steiner, V. 2000 *Creative collaboration.* Oxford: Oxford University Press.

National Advisory Committee on Creative and Cultural Education. 1999 *All our futures: Creativity, culture and education.* London: DFEE.

OFSTED 2006 *Creative Partnerships: Initiative and impact.* London: Ofsted.

Roberts, P. 2006 *Nurturing Creativity in Young People.* London: DCMS.

Rolfe, L. Platt, M. Jobbins, V. Craft, A, Chappell, K. and Wright, H. 2009 Co-participative Research in Dance-Education Partnership: Nurturing Critical Pedagogy and Social Constructivism. *Conference on Research in Dance, Conference Proceedings* (pp.98-109). Illinois: University of Illinois Press.

Sawyer, K. 2006 *Explaining Creativity: The Science of Human Innovation.* Oxford University Press.

Siddall, J. 2010 *Dance In and Beyond Schools.* London: Youth Dance England.

Smith-Autard, J. 2002 *The art of dance in education.* [2nd edition] London: A and C Black.

Warburton, E. 2009 Editorial. *Research in Dance Education: Special Issue Creativity.* 10, 3, pp. 157-159.

Chapter 9
Assessment in Dance
Lorna Sanders

Introduction

For teachers within school-based education, assessment is an accepted feature of the role, but for some dance practitioners this aspect can be less familiar. During assessment, the level, value and worth of your participants' achievements are judged. It is necessary for the processes to be *valid* (measure what they are supposed to measure); *consistent* (be applied to all participants fairly); and *reliable* (give similar results when applied to similar participants over time). In this chapter, the tools that can help you design valid and reliable assessments are considered, however consistency comes with experience; applying judgements fairly; and having a thorough understanding of your subject.

In some education literature, evaluation and assessment are occasionally used as interchangeable terms. For the purposes of DDTAL, the following distinction applies: **evaluation** is something you do to yourself (for example, you might evaluate your delivery or planning to consider its effectiveness); **assessment** is something which you do to others (for example, you might examine or judge the progress of your participants).

Assessment supports learning, assists participants in the development of their skills and understandings, and also celebrates their achievements. It can be positive and enabling. Whenever assessment is being applied however (different types and methods are outlined in this chapter), it is essential to consider the self-image, self-esteem and motivation of participants because a negative experience can be damaging, not just demotivating.

- I am not what I think I am.
- I am not what you think I am.
- I am what I think you think I am.

(in Coopersmith, 1967, n.p.)

Invalid, unpredictable, unreliable judgments contribute to negative feelings, but even justified assessment, which aims to be helpful, can be misunderstood. Assessment is of limited value 'if it presents children with low marks and adverse teacher comments but without illuminating the child's mind as to why these results were produced, and what can be done to remedy the situation in the future' (Fontana, 1995, p. 164).

It is important therefore that positive reinforcement informs assessment feedback so that participants understand quite specifically what it is they have achieved and how they can improve. Your sense of self worth is shaped by the feedback you receive from others.

Case Study 1

Is the feedback that you give to participants GOSPEL?

- **G**enuine (tone of voice and body language matter too)
- **O**ften
- **S**traightforward, accurate and realistic (or it will not be believed)
- **P**ositive
- **E**ngaging (indicates the processes / activity for improvement)
- **L**inked specifically to the task, skill or understanding

Assessment: Products and Process

In dance examinations such as GCSE and A Level, a three-strand dance curriculum has been established (performance, choreography, appreciation). Outcomes (dances, performances, written papers) are the products of the learning that are assessed. However, the processes in which participants are engaged can be valued in and of themselves. A significant research study in secondary schools found that the effects of dance most often mentioned by school pupils were:

> developments in technical skills and capabilities associated with their dance lessons – specific types of movement, as well as more general comments on increased movement and motor skills [...] there was little mention however of any increases in knowledge about the art form and very little pertaining to the social and cultural domains. Neither did pupils perceive any effects of dance relating to communication skills or, surprisingly, in developing a sense of one's emotions.
>
> (Harland, 2000, p. 267)

In addition to physical and creative aspects therefore, wider areas of understanding might be assessed depending on the context, the participants, and your aims and objectives: for example, health and fitness, cultural awareness, artistic and aesthetic understanding, appreciation skills, personal skills, social understanding, learning skills and literacy more broadly (see Bramley, 2002, p.13). A series of employability skills can be added to this, such as 'communication and negotiation […] problem-solving, leadership skills, flexibility and experience of working in different ways' (Siddall, 2010, p. 9).

Case Study 2

- In the dance sessions you lead, what types of understandings and skills do you tend to assess? This might be through formal methods where you apply the strict criteria of an external organisation for example; or where you come to an informal judgement of your participants' progress.
- Do you assess physical skills (technique / performance or choreographic) in the main?
- What other aspects of dance understanding and experience do you/might you address in your assessment of participants' success?

Whatever the skill or understanding involved, valid assessment relies on having clear objectives (see Chapter 6). There are three general purposes for assessment: diagnostic; formative and summative. Before exploring these, it is useful to consider some of the widely known types of assessment processes developed in Education Theory. These offer ways of identifying valid and reliable benchmarks against which judgements of success can be made for any of the three general purposes.

Norm-Referenced Assessment Processes
• An individual's achievement is set against what their peers within the age group are normally expected to achieve. • This produces an average, achievable by many of those to be assessed. • The less able and more able are distributed around this average benchmark - termed in statistics as a normal distribution curve (fewer participants achieve results at the bottom and top and the greater bulk will be ranged in the middle). **Benefits:** participants are assessed based on what is normally achievable by most others in their age group. **Challenges:** where there is no prior notion of what might be normal this needs to be realistically decided upon. Setting the average at too high / too low will be problematic.
Criterion-Referenced Assessment Processes
• An individual's achievement is judged against predetermined criteria which are related to the task / skill itself. • Participants meet the expected competence against this benchmark or they do not. **Benefits:** a simple pass / fail judgement is made solely on personal progress in respect of the skill to be achieved. **Challenges:** the skill, its purpose and pre-determined standard must be closely related.
Grade-Related Assessment Processes
• This is a version of criterion-referenced assessment – but here a range of different levels in achievement of the skills / understandings is decided in advance. • A description of what is to be achieved is allocated to different grades. **Benefits:** achievement is matched to a set of statements that describe positively what participants must know or be able to do at the different levels. One can distinguish between participants with different abilities who achieve different levels of mastery. **Challenges:** mastery and understanding must be clearly described and levelled.

Figure 1: Assessment Design. Based on Child (1995).

The General Purposes of Assessment

1. Diagnostic Assessment

Whether meeting new or known groups, you need to gain a clear picture of what they do not know yet, and *why* they do not know it. This allows you to address participants' specific needs. In diagnostic assessment you will need to:

• Identify what gaps there might be in their current knowledge and skills.

- Identify what misunderstandings, general approaches or habits of thought they bring to their working / learning processes.

> Diagnosis depends upon prompting children to articulate their processes and strategies ('What did you do to arrive at that answer?'), and plays a vital role in determining which learning tasks are appropriate for each child.
>
> (Fontana, 1995, p. 164)

Before reading further, consider what opportunities and methods you typically undertake for diagnostic assessment. Do you address both of the bullet points above?

Case Study 3

- Think of a new group you taught recently (or which you might in future). What objectives did you plan? Now identify an early opportunity / task you used to diagnose the group's needs in respect of one of these objectives.

  For example, a Centre for Advanced Training (CAT) course for 12-13 year olds – after the warm up, a practitioner might teach a set phrase with some complex actions to assess participants' abilities to pick up new material because this is an objective for the course.

- What method did you undertake in order to achieve a diagnosis for your group?

  For example, in respect of the CAT above, after dancing the set phrase with the group the practitioner might ask participants to work alone to remember it. This provides an opportunity for the practitioner to observe and make an informal assessment of who achieves it and what tactics they bring to bear. After a second run through, the practitioner might ask what they did to recall the phrase and map their responses against their performance of the material to see who has effective learning strategies.

- What benchmarking process did you select for diagnostic assessment of your group?

  Look at *Figure 1*: do any of the processes there match how you set up an expectation that you can make your judgement against?

  For example, the practitioner teaching the CAT group might tap into a notion of what might be expected normally of this age group (norm-referencing their assessment). They understand from experience that this age group might *normally* get the order of the actions and some accurate use of space and dynamic range. Judgements are based on this.

Based on the considerations in Case Study 3, create a simple check list for aspects that you might judge in diagnostic assessment. For example, during the warm up activity when meeting a new group, one might estimate: if they have ability to follow instructions; can respond physically with confidence; have basic spatial understanding; use the space safely; can observe and copy movement; have some self-discipline or understanding of dance; and have any special needs. The judgement will be based on what you normally expect or have experienced in similar circumstances (norm referenced).

Diagnostic assessment is often informal because the focus is on assisting you to decide if adaptations to the work plan and adjustments to your delivery are needed. Informal methods can be less stressful for participants because they may not know that it is occurring. This does not mean that formalising your expectation in some way if needed, such as constructing a description of what you are looking for in advance, might not also be useful. Strategies for creating descriptions are considered later. Whether diagnostic assessment is formal or informal depends on what you want to achieve by doing it in that particular way and the choice can often be yours to make.

2. Formative Assessment

The purpose of formative assessment is to support learning so in some respects it is like a continuation of the diagnostic process. It does not usually count towards the final assessment. The practitioner helps the participant to identify their progress (reciprocal feedback between class members can also be used for this). The assessment method and feedback (GOSPEL) should be supportive and motivating; it can also help the participants to take responsibility for their own learning.

Formative assessment takes place informally throughout a session (this is assessment for learning) but opportunities for more formal methods could be planned for during a course / workshop if appropriate. For example, look at *Figure 1* and consider how grade-referenced processes might be used to focus specific feedback for different abilities. Descriptions created in advance, sometimes referred to as a rubric, set the criteria against which achievement is judged. The task and description must be closely linked. The clearer this is, the easier it is to match work against it and ensure your assessment will be valid.

Case Study 4

In the *AQA GCSE Dance Specification*, a composition task requires candidates to select three motifs from a set professional dance. They are required to develop these into a short solo which must have a clear structure and they must apply analysis and evaluation to bring about improvement of the dance.

The criteria for assessment are:
- Imaginative development of selected or given material through actions, space and dynamics.
- Successful integration and linking of the motifs into the composition.
- Structuring and use of choreographic devices and principles.
- Analysis and evaluation to bring about improvement during the progress of the piece.

The work of a candidate in a low band will match the following rubric / description (*AQA GCSE Dance Specification* p.16):

> 'The material is not developed but some of the original motifs are apparent. Evidence of structure and the use of choreographic devices is limited. The candidate demonstrates limited analytical and evaluative skills to bring about improvement'
>
> (AQA, 2011, p. 16)

The teacher can match work against this description to identify lower achieving candidates and then construct formative assessment methods to support learning.

Notice how the statements in the rubric relate strongly to the task, assessment criteria and expected outcome (a clearly structured solo using three motifs). What is meant by structure? The dance needs a variety of choreographic devices which develop the selected motifs. This clarifies what aspects to improve on. For example, the teacher could now assist candidates to improve the structure of their solo by giving lower achieving students a chart for reciprocal feedback to each other which focuses on ensuring development:

Watch your partner's solo twice.	Did they change the level?	Did they change direction?	Did they change the order of the actions?	Did they change the dynamics / or speed?
How did they develop their actions from last week?				

3. Summative Assessment

This provides a summing up of achievement and is a final judgement of success. It usually takes place at the end of a course / workshop, although a series of ongoing points might also be selected where it is important to monitor progress which counts more specifically towards the final grade.

It might assess the process the participants have been involved in (for example, their ability to collaborate effectively in creative tasks) and / or the products they produced (for example, the effectiveness of the choreography at expressing their intentions).

Whether formal or informal methods are used, clear benchmarks must be set and it is good practice to share this information with participants. As Case Study 4 above indicates, it is useful to create assessment criteria and then the rubrics which build on these, to express the detail of what successful outcomes will be. The rubrics should articulate the full range of skills / understandings that are needed and be tightly related to the task and the original objectives set for the course / session.

Rubrics and Likert Scales

Levels in achievement can be indicated by using a rating scale. In Education Theory these are called Likert Scales and when associated with rubrics these can produce valid, reliable judgements. This approach is useful for developing grade-referenced assessment processes in particular (and also criterion-referenced processes with only pass / fail levels).

Creating a Likert Scale

- A Likert Scale must be based on the objectives set for the course / workshop (see Chapter 6). First, the objectives need to be clearly articulated and achievable.
- You must pre-determine the attributes of success suggested by the objectives.
- Create a rubric which describes what success will be, and identify levels within this.
- A rating scale of 1 to 3, 4 or 5 provides broader, more general bands for identification of success; 1-10 provides for more fine discriminations in achievement. 5 or 3 point scales for example provide a middle point where the average would lie.
- Set a benchmark for the pass / fail border – identify what would achieve zero and what this might look like (norm-referenced expectations can be useful for this).
- Decide what terms you will use to describe your levels. For example:

5 = very good   or distinguished, exemplary, excellent
4 = above average   or good, accomplished
3 = average   or confident, proficient
2 = below average   or apprentice, developing
1 = barely passing   or beginner, basic, satisfactory
0 = fail   or below pass rate, ungraded.

The terms in the list are commonly used to articulate the levels. Notice how different choices of terms might affect a participant's perception of their achievement.

Two examples of different layouts for rubrics and Likert scales follow. They are adapted and reproduced from Kassing and Jay, 2003, pages 148 (Example 1) and 152 (example 2). Both have as their task *rolling down through the spine* as set within an exercise.

Example 1:

Assessment Rubric

Knowledge: sequence of specific movement and transition (knowledge of the exercise?)

Timing: correct counts and phrasing (moving on the correct beat?)

Execution: correct performance with appropriate technique (executes individual movements accurately?)

Placement: body alignment throughout (safe and correct posture and placement throughout?)

Energy: correct energy during the sequence (accurate dynamics and movement quality?)

Musicality: ability to transcend counts and give expressive performance (use of breath and phrasing?)

Rating 0-4 (4 = the highest score)

Name of Student	Knowledge	Timing	Execution	Placement	Energy	Musicality

Example 2:

Assessment Rubric

Beginning (1): student executes the body rolls rarely applying performance criteria – a basic level of performance.

Developing (2): student executes body rolls sometimes applying performance criteria – reflecting development and movement towards mastery.

Accomplished (3): student executes body rolls most of the time applying performance criteria – reflecting mastery.

Exemplary (4): student always executes body rolls always applying the performance criteria – highest level of performance possible.

Rating 0-4 (4 = the highest score)

Selected Criteria	Beginning (1)	Developing (2)	Accomplished (3)	Exemplary (4)
Rolls down through the vertebra				
Returns through the vertebra				
Connects counts to exercise				
Applies technique				
Applies principles of element				
Uses breathing				

REFLECTION

1. Consider why it might be important to understand what unconscious or un-clarified benchmarks might be in operation and affecting your judgement when you assess achievement.

2. Consider how you might make further use of the different assessment processes outlined in *Figure 1* in your own practice. For example, since grade-related referencing is useful for determining a range of levels in achievement, you could demonstrate to a sponsor of a project that all the participants have achieved some improvement in learning. Take each of the three processes in turn and identify how you might make use of these in your practice.

3. Based on Case Study 3, you will have created a simple check list for aspects that you might judge in diagnostic assessment. Explore whether this is best achieved through formal or informal methods. Why might you choose one or the other of these methods? When you teach your next new group, or new material to existing groups, try this out and log the results in your Reflective Journal. Note how judgement will be based on what you normally expect or have experienced in similar circumstances (norm referenced). Try to articulate what you normally expect and identify this clearly for yourself.

4. Look at Examples 1 and 2 of rubrics and scales which closed the chapter. Although they are assessing the same physical activity, what is the difference between them? How might their different approach and presentation make them useful in different circumstances? Identify a task in your own practice that could be assessed by adapting either Example 1 or 2. Design and write the rubrics and the Likert scale fully for your use. Consider how this might help you achieve more consistent assessment.

5. Look at the tasks, assessment criteria, grades and descriptors in the DDTAL syllabus. For Unit 1 in particular, consider how the aims of the Diploma and the content link to the tasks that address assessment. Look at how these are in turn linked to the assessment criteria and the 3-point Likert scale (Pass, Merit, Distinction). Or look at how assessment can play a part in raising the standard of dance projects and adding to the evidence base (see Lord et al, 2012).

Bibliography

AQA. 2011 *GCSE Dance Specification*. www.aqa.org.uk

Bramley, I. 2002 *Dance Teaching Essentials*. London: Dance UK.

Child, D. 1995 *Psychology and the Teacher*. [5th Edition] London: Casell.

Coopersmith, S. 1967 *Antecedents of Self Esteem*. San Francisco: Freeman.

Fontana, D. 1995 *Psychology for Teachers*. [3rd edition] Basingstoke: Palgrave Macmillan.

Harland, J. Kinder, K. *et al* 2000 *Arts Education and Effectiveness in Secondary Schools* Berkshire: National Foundation for Educational Research.

Kassing, G. and Jay, D. 2003 *Dance Teaching Methods and Curriculum Design*. Illinois: Human Kinetics.

Lord, P. Sharp, C. Lee, B. Cooper, L. and Grayson, H. 2012 *Raising the Standard of Work By, With and For Children and Young People: Research and Consultation to Understand Principles of Quality*. Slough: National Foundation for Educational Research.

Siddall, J. 2010 *Dance In and Beyond Schools*. London: Youth Dance England.

Chapter 10
Evaluation of Dance Teaching Practice
Alysoun Tomkins

Introduction

How do you know how good a teacher you are? Have your students, or someone who has watched you, told you? Do you ask anyone? Do you evaluate your own practice? How do you, or the people you ask, know how good you are? What are they basing their critiques on? What is being measured? This chapter will examine those questions and look at educational theory on evaluation to determine how best to evaluate our teaching in order to develop practice.

Evaluation processes provide us with the opportunity to assess our own teaching practice and through so doing, improve upon it.

> Evaluation is part of our professional practice – the process of evaluation helps artists [practitioners / teachers] engage in the debate about what constitutes good practice.
>
> (Amans, 2008, p. 174)

As dance teachers we are often required to evaluate projects with which we are involved, by stakeholders, funders or various authorities. These partner organisations will want to evaluate their own desired aims and outcomes:

> **Programme and Project evaluation:** This form of evaluation is typically concerned with making judgements about the effectiveness, efficiency and sustainability of pieces of work.
>
> (Smith, 2006, n.p)

These aims may differ slightly from the teacher's and may not contain all the information teachers require in order to understand if their role in the project has been successful.

> **Practice Evaluation:** This form of evaluation is directed at the enhancement of work undertaken with particular individuals and groups, and to the development of participants (including the informal educator). It tends to be an integral part of the working process [...] Such evaluation is sometimes described as educative or pedagogical as it seeks to foster learning. But this is only part of the process. **The learning involved is oriented to future or further action**. It is also informed by certain values and commitments.
>
> (Smith, 2006, n.p)

In this chapter the focus is on the evaluative processes which help the teacher to reflect on their practice, provide evidence to support judgments made about the work and inform future teaching. As a teacher, you need to show through evidence that your approach to teaching a particular group in a specific context demonstrates best practice, or highlight areas for development which, when implemented, will progress your teaching practice.

As stated in Chapter 9, assessment and evaluation are sometimes used interchangeably.

> Assessment relates to the measurement and testing of performance; evaluation considers the 'value' or worth of what has taken place. The results of assessment generally inform evaluation.
>
> (Avis, Fisher and Thompson, 2010, p. 240)

Hence, evaluation is about making judgments to do with value (the worth of what you intend the students to learn and why) and quality (standard of content and delivery) of the teacher's work within a lesson or project. This chapter further examines why we evaluate our practice, what we are evaluating, when we evaluate, and looks at methods of collecting and interpreting evidence in order that the value judgments we make are objective rather than subjective.

For the DDTAL qualification, evaluation is concerned with something that you do to yourself (assessment is something you do to others).

WHY evaluate

Evaluation of the teacher's performance in a project should provide the teacher with an opportunity to learn from the experience and thus develop their practice. Gough (1999) describes evaluation as 'being the process of making a value judgement on, for example, the effectiveness of the project' (p. 109) and Woolf (1999) states that evaluation is 'making judgments, based on evidence, about the value and quality of a project [lesson]' (p. 7).

In the same way that assessment supports the learning of the participants, evaluation supports the learning and development of the practitioner. Avis, Fisher, and Thompson (2010) state that it is important for teachers to consider their own values and beliefs in order to achieve useful information through evaluation to aid development of understanding and skills in teaching (p. 240).

To summarise – by evaluating their teaching practice teachers will:

- Identify their values and beliefs as a teacher.
- Contribute to their Continuing Professional Development.
- Develop skills as a reflective practitioner.
- Improve their teaching by learning from mistakes and building on success.
- Aid flexibility in their work plan / delivery / content.
- Gather evidence of their abilities / strengths / experience.
- Inform future teaching work.

WHEN do we evaluate

Like assessment, evaluation can be both *formative* and *summative*. (For explanations of the terms formative and summative see Chapter 9) Therefore it is both continuous (formative) throughout the lesson / work plan, as well as final (summative). It needs to be *practical*, that is to say you have both the time and resources to evaluate, *appropriate* to all involved as you may wish input from your students and others and *relevant* within the context of the project. Evaluation is part of reflective enquiry and as such could be termed action research undertaken by the practitioner.

> Evaluation is the systematic exploration and judgement of working processes, experiences and outcomes. It pays special attention to aims, values, perceptions, needs and resources.
>
> (Smith, 2006, n.p)

Evaluation needs to be integral to the whole process and not seen as something that is just achieved through questionnaires at the end of the work plan. In order to react to the needs of the group, teachers must be able to change, adjust, and be flexible in both their delivery and content. If I am driving along the wrong road there is no point continuing as I will not reach my destination: I may need to turn around, take a detour or choose, or be persuaded, to go to somewhere completely different!

In a one hour lesson it may not be possible to include many methods of evaluation but we can observe and ask questions of our students. We can take time after the session to jot down notes which will help inform the following session. In a longer project, evaluation should be built into the structure of the project from the start. Methods of evaluation are discussed later. Time must be allocated to the evaluation as should any costs, such as those incurred when employing an external evaluator.

WHAT are we evaluating

It is crucial when you are planning a lesson or series of lessons that the **aims** of those lesson(s) are absolutely clear. If the teacher does not identify exactly what it is that s/he wants the learners to know, demonstrate or understand by the end of the session(s) then the content delivered and the learning outcomes will also be vague. Clarity of the aims will give purpose to the learning.

> If we are clear about the aims [...] and our objectives or outcomes [...] it will be easier to measure whether or not we have been successful. Measures of success are sometimes called performance indicators.
>
> (Jayne Stevens, in Amans, 2010, p. 51)

To achieve clarity with the Aims and enable you to make effective evaluations it is helpful to use the **SMART** test:

Specific	Measurable	Achievable	Realistic & Relevant	Time achievable
Start with the word 'to'. Use action verbs. Clearly define the **aim**. Be precise about what you are going to achieve.	How will you evaluate this **aim**? How will you know that change has occurred? How will you measure how well the **aim** has been met?	Are you attempting too much? Is it feasible and easy to put into action?	Do you have the resources to make the aim happen? Are the **aims** relevant to the group? Are the **aims** relevant to the context?	State when you will achieve the **aim**. Use a time frame to set boundaries around the **aim**. Ask yourself if this **aim** can be achieved in the lesson / work plan time.

Example 1

Specific	Measurable	Achievable	Realistic & Relevant	Time Achievable
Aim: To understand the use of weight and how this affects the dynamic of the movement.	Observation of the physical responses to given tasks. Dialogue with participants. Self-reflective questions.	The exploration will occur in lessons 1-3 in preparation for contact work.	The floor, walls and resistance bands will be used to aid kinaesthetic awareness. The group are 10 - 11yrs.	Each lesson is 1 hour. The exploration phase will be complete in week 3.

As seen in the above example, the (movement) aim is to give the children an experience, over 3 lessons, of how weight might be used in the body. By using the SMART test, the evaluation methods and props required have been identified and a time limit given to achieving this aim.

Case Study 1

In the table below identify an aim from a recent lesson / work plan and test it using SMART.

Specific	Measurable	Achievable	Realistic & Relevant	Time Achievable
Aim:				

In order to evaluate whether the aims of our work plan have been met, it is necessary to consider the relevance of the content, the effectiveness of the methods of delivery, including teaching styles and strategies, and the level of achievement of the learning outcomes.

In Example 2 below, consideration is given to both the content of the three lessons referred to in Example 1 and the delivery method of that content.

Example 2

Aim:	Content: Lesson 1-3	Teaching Styles and strategies:
To understand the use of weight and how this affects the dynamic of the movement.	Rising and falling. Pulling and pushing. Rolling. Sinking. Balancing. Resisting. Lifting and letting go.	Command for warm up and cool down – demonstration and imagery (verbal and visual) to support changes in weight. Guided (divergent) discovery - to set tasks which require exploration of the use of weight in the body. Choice of accompaniment to reflect 'strong and light'.

Case Study 2		
In the table below, insert the aim used in Task 1 and outline both the content and teaching styles and strategies used in its delivery:		
Aim: What is it you want the learners to know / understand and demonstrate?	Content:	Teaching Styles and strategies:

HOW do we evaluate?

Methods of collecting evidence for evaluation purposes are varied. Some are indicated in the charts above and further examples given below. Input from all involved can help ensure the objectivity of the final analysis.

Gough (1999) gives examples of evaluation pro forma for: planning; external evaluator; participant and teacher (pp. 109-115).

Once the evidence has been collected, one then needs to find a method of measuring how successfully the aim has been met and how the content and delivery have supported (or hindered) the achievement of that aim. The measuring strategies proposed for assessment, the use of a rubric or Likert Scale (Kassing and Jay, 2003, p. 146) can be adapted for use in measuring evaluation data. For further information on these see Chapter 9.

Methods of Evaluation

Avis, Fisher and Thompson (2010) advise that, in order for evaluation to be effective, there needs to be a 'range of perspectives' (p. 241). Therefore, the inclusion of information from a variety of sources ensures that different experiences and viewpoints are voiced. Data can be both quantitative and qualitative: numerical information is useful and easily obtainable; data on 'value' is not so concrete and therefore collecting and interpreting qualitative data needs to be done within clear parameters such as the Aims and Learning Outcomes.

Quantitative Data

- Attendance register / number of participants enrolled and retained.
- Number of boys versus girls.
- Number of young people with disabilities or learning challenges.
- Different ethnic groups represented.
- Number of hours / weeks / days the project lasted.

- Number of practitioners, musicians, or others involved such as support workers.
- Availability of resources.
- Standard of facilities.
- Level at which learning outcomes were met.

Qualitative Data may be gathered through:

- Self-reflective questions: Possible questions on content for teacher, for example:
    - Were the aims appropriate for the needs of the group?
    - Were the movement aims clearly established?
    - Was the warm up effective?
    - Did the exploration and development section stimulate creative responses / imaginative material?
    - Was there natural [and logical] progression from one section to the next?
    - Was the accompaniment suitable?
    - Were the aims and Learning Outcomes achieved? If not why not?

- Possible questions on delivery for teacher:
    - How effective was: use of voice, demonstration?
    - How effective was my observing and critiquing?
    - Was I well organized?
    - Did I manage time effectively?

(Gough, 1993, p. 54)

- Ethnographic method: observe, listen and note down comments by participants or others involved.

- Dialogical approach: talking to or interviewing participants / others:
    - How did this session help you develop as a dancer / choreographer?
    - What did you enjoy most / least?
    - What have you learnt?
    - Did anything surprise you about the session?
    - What are you proud of?

- Questionnaires: 'happy faces'; yes / no tick box answers; graded answers; space given for further comments.

- Other sources of evidence:
    - Recalling previous week's material (see if students remember and how well).
    - Asking students to demonstrate.
    - Asking students to give feedback to each other.
    - Filming at intervals through the project.
    - Teacher's reflective journal.
    - Student's diary.
    - Sketch book / notebook throughout lesson.

- 'Post-its' on wall / graffiti walls – these can be grouped under different headings.
- External evaluator / critical friend.
- 'Hot chair' – teacher sits in the chair and is questioned by students.
- Comments box – this allows for anonymity.

Example 3

Aim:	Content:	Teaching Styles and strategies:	Evaluation Methods:
To understand the use of weight and how this affects the dynamic of the movement	Rising and falling. Pulling and pushing. Rolling; sinking. Balancing. Resisting. Lifting and letting go.	Command for warm up & cool down – demonstration and imagery (verbal and visual) to support changes in weight. Guided (divergent) discovery – to set tasks which require exploration of the use of weight in the body. Choice of accompaniment to reflect 'strong and light'.	Observation of individuals and group. Dialogical approach: - how did that feel? - did the images / music help? How was the feeling different from…? Demonstration by learner. Peer feedback: - how were they using weight? Teacher's Reflective log: - Did the tasks help the exploration of weight? - Were my demonstrations / images clear enough? - Were the aims met?

Case Study 3

Insert the aim, content and teaching styles and strategies used in Task 2 and add how you would evaluate:

Aim:	Content:	Teaching Styles and strategies:	Evaluation Methods:

Making sense of the data collected

> It is only when an analysis of results leads to action to improve that evaluation becomes worthwhile.
>
> (Avis, Fisher and Thompson, 2010, p. 24)

One can respond to questions using a simple YES / NO response
　　OR
Give a graded response – using a rubric or Likert scale (as proposed for assessment in Chapter 9) and changing the terms to be relevant to evaluation. For example, when adopting a rating scale of 1-5 to measure how well the aims have been met, the relevance of the content and effectiveness of the delivery, the terms might be:

　1. Not at all

　2. Minimally

　3. Reasonably

　4. Mostly

　5. Totally

Or for a more simple scale of 1-3: 1 Not at all; 2 Reasonably; 3 Totally.

Example 4: the above scale is used to measure how well the Aim has been met.

Aim:	Content: Lesson 1-3	Teaching Styles and strategies:	Evaluation methods	Grading method: Scale 1-3
To understand the use of weight and how this affects the dynamic of the movement.	Rising and falling. Pulling and pushing. Rolling. Sinking. Balancing. Resisting. Lifting and letting go	Command for warm up and cool down – demonstration and imagery (verbal and visual) to support changes in weight. Guided (divergent) discovery – to set tasks which require exploration of the use of weight in the body. Choice of accompaniment to reflect 'strong and light'.	Observation of individuals and group. Dialogical approach: - how did that feel? - did the images, music help? How was the feeling different from…? Demonstration by learner Peer feedback: - how were they using weight? Teacher's Reflective Log: - Did the tasks help the exploration of weight? - Were my demonstrations, imagery clear enough? - Were the aims met?	2 2 3 3 2 3 2 3 2
The above results demonstrate that the students' cognitive understanding of weight was better than their physical demonstration of the use of weight in the body. Therefore the aim has been met totally in terms of cognitive exploration and reasonably through physical experiencing.				

Unit 2 - Professional Knowledge of Dance Teaching

Case Study 4
How would the above evaluation inform the planning of: • The same sessions for a new group of learners? • The next session for this group?

Case Study 5
Insert the aim, content, teaching styles and strategies and evaluation methods used in Case Study 3; add the grading method used to evaluate how well the Aim has been met.

Aim:	Content:	Teaching Styles and strategies:	Evaluation methods:	Grading method:

REFLECTION

REFLECTION 1	
Do I work towards Aims developed by consideration of the needs of the group?	
Am I clear about the Aim of each session I teach and how the teaching styles and content support the learning?	
What are my strengths as a teacher?	
How has the work that I have done so far on DDTAL helped me to improve practice?	(If you are not studying DDTAL, consider how this chapter might help you improve your practice.)
How do I know the answers to the above?	

REFLECTION 2	
Use the table below to answer the two questions. Reflection on our values and beliefs helps to underpin why we teach dance and what we consider important and through evaluation of our practice, identifies areas for development.	
As a dance teacher, what are my values?	
As a dance teacher, what are my beliefs?	
REFLECTION 3	
Through evaluating my practice, what areas have I identified for development?	
How and where might I find the mentoring / training that I need?	

Bibliography

Amans, D. 2008 *An Introduction to Community Dance Practice*. Basingstoke: Palgrave Macmillan.

Amans, D. 2010 *Passport to Practice – An Induction to Professional Practice in Community Dance* Leicester: Foundation for Community Dance.

Avis, J. Fisher, R. Thompson, R. (Eds.) 2010 *Teaching in Lifelong Learning – A Guide to Theory and Practice*. Berkshire: McGraw-Hill.

Gough, M. 1993 *in touch with dance*. Lancaster: Whitethorn Books.

Gough, M. 1999 *Knowing dance. A guide for creative teaching*. London: Dance Books.

Kassing, G. and Jay, D. 2003 *Dance Teaching Methods and Curriculum Design*. Illinois: Human Kinetics.

Smith, M.K. 2001 / 2006 'Evaluation', in the *encyclopaedia of informal education*, www.infed.org/biblio/b-eval.htm

Woolf, F. 1999 *Partnerships in Learning*. London: Arts Council England.

UNIT 2

PROFESSIONAL KNOWLEDGE OF DANCE TEACHING

Chapter 11
Youth Dance Contexts (part 1): Arts, Culture and Sports Contexts

Jeanette Siddall

Introduction

This chapter offers an overview of key themes pertinent to youth dance purposes and practices. There are separate chapters on the specific contexts of health and youth justice (Chapter 12), and of formal education (Chapter 13). This chapter offers a general introduction that explores what we mean by 'youth dance', a brief history and examples of practice.

By way of a wider context:

- dance has a particular appeal for young people as physical activity, second only to football, and as a means of expressing their identity, the way they see themselves and the world around them;
- youth dance is integral to the professional practice of the art form, for example companies such as the Royal Ballet are closely associated with a training school, while others facilitate youth dance groups and projects;
- professional dancers, like musicians, have to start their training at a young age and many professional dancers would be classified as 'young people' by the European Commission definition (up to the age of 26);
- dance is the 'new kid on the block' in terms of public recognition and funding compared to its sister art forms of music and drama; many of today's policy-makers grew up with limited experience or understanding of dance, and dance receives less attention and funding than music or drama;
- today's young people will become the artists, audiences, promoters and policy-makers of tomorrow – their understanding of dance will directly affect its future.

This particular set of circumstances gives dance a unique cultural context. It is important to the lives of young people; by the European Commission definition young people are a significant proportion of the professional dance workforce; and the artistic, cultural and political future of dance will be shaped by young people's experience of dance today.

What is youth dance?

Youth dance is an umbrella term that embraces a wide range of activities. It includes youth dance companies that may be facilitated by a dance company, dance agency or a theatre; by another kind of organisation such as a school or local authority; by an individual dance artist / practitioner; or by young people themselves. It also includes time-limited projects that may lead to a live performance in a theatre, shopping centre, park, or museum, or to a film, or to a different kind of outcome. Centres for Advanced Training (CATs) and regular classes and workshops for young people provided by private dance teachers, dance agencies and others are all part of young people's dance experience.

Youth dance is not a particular dance style or genre but can embrace any and all dance styles. It could be argued that it enables young people to develop their creative, personal and social skills and to realise their potential in and through dance. It could also be argued that good practice in youth dance is inclusive, purposeful and relevant to young people, and enables them to progress and to experience the roles of creator, performer, audience, critic and leader.

A key defining factor in the practice of youth dance is purpose – why is the activity, project or initiative being provided, and what are its objectives? One way of thinking about purpose is to consider the spectrum between intrinsic and instrumental objectives:

Intrinsic – dance as arts practice, promoting artistic development such as in execution, concepts, creation, production;

Instrumental – dance as a means of promoting personal and social development such as confidence, working with others, and well-being.

Both purposes have value, and most youth dance practice delivers both intrinsic and instrumental values. Good practice in artistic purposes such as technical, choreographic, and performance development involves, for example, building confidence, team-work, taking responsibility for themselves and others, decision-making and reflection. Instrumental purposes are more effectively realised when the dance content is purposeful and of high quality. The prime purpose will determine *how* the activity is taught or facilitated, rather than the *what*, or content of the session.

A brief history

There is no definitive starting date for youth dance. Peter Brinson (1991) referred to the first National Youth Dance Festival organised by the Leicestershire Education Authority in 1975 as demonstrating that youth dance must have existed before that date.

The growth of youth dance is, however, closely connected with the development of contemporary dance, particularly the residencies undertaken by London Contemporary Dance Theatre from the later 1970s that broke down barriers between dance performance and participation through lecture-demonstrations, classes, workshops and discussions. Around the same time, the community arts movement was emerging, and promoting the idea that everyone could engage in the process of making and presenting art, and dance animateur posts were being established across the country.

In 1979 there were three dance animateurs funded by the Calouste Gulbenkian Foundation: in Cardiff, Cheshire and Swindon. The Arts Council of Great Britain (now Arts Council England) built on these pilot programmes by providing funding in partnership with local and regional partners. Numbers grew, national conferences were held, and a national association was established in 1984 (now Foundation for Community Dance). Animateurs worked across different communities in their areas, but the establishment of youth dance groups was a major strand of the work of most animateurs. The Arts Council funded professional choreographers to create work with youth dance groups and, in 1992, published a directory of 175 youth dance groups, *On the Move*. Animateurs arranged youth dance exchanges which involved workshops and performances shared between two or more groups from different areas. Annual festivals were held that brought together groups from across the country. In the 1980s the National Youth Dance Company was established to provide high-level training, creative and performing opportunities for young people with exceptional talent.

So, by the early 1990s youth dance was established, visible and growing. There was a developing infrastructure of local delivery, national festivals organised on a voluntary basis by individual animateurs and a national company. Dance was embraced by Physical Education within the National Curriculum in schools with an artistically focused programme of study, although being optional for secondary schools to offer.

Eventually the youth dance movement grew too large for national festivals to be managed as an 'add-on' to the responsibilities of a single animateur or organisation, and it became increasingly difficult to raise the funds needed for national festivals and the National Youth Dance Company. There was a sense that youth dance was established, that flag-ship initiatives were no longer necessary and no longer fully represented the diversity of youth dance practice. By the mid-1990s there were no more National Festivals and the National Youth Dance Company was able to accommodate fewer young people, drawn mainly from the professional training schools. Youth dance activity continued at local level, but it was less visible in public policy and among decision-makers. Opportunities for young people to progress, or to work with professional choreographers and their peers from other parts of the country became fragmented and reduced in scope and scale.

The next stage of development was driven by the Department of Education's *Music and Dance Scheme*. This had been established in the 1970s to support young people attending one of the specialist boarding schools. From the late 1990s, this remit expanded, following research that identified inequality of opportunity in different parts of the country and lack of provision in, for example, contemporary, urban and South Asian dance forms. The Scheme aimed to support young people with exceptional talent and potential in music and dance, it now recognised the need to increase access and develop new models of provision. Youth Dance England (YDE) was established in partnership with the Arts Council in 2004, to champion dance for all young people, and Centres for Advanced Training were established in partnership with professional dance organisations, to identify and nurture young people with exceptional dance potential.

Brinson (1991), the House of Commons Select Committee for Culture, Media and Sport's *Inquiry into Dance Development* (May 2004), and Tony Hall's *Dance Review* and the *Government Response* (March 2008) all recognised the need for a national organisation to support and promote dance opportunities for young people. Youth Dance England was established as that organisation. Following extensive consultation, it developed a programme that included:

- A national network of youth dance co-ordinators, then strategy managers and sub-regional youth dance hubs.
- The development of a framework and resources for local, regional and national youth dance performances, *U.Dance*.
- Programmes for young people with exceptional potential in choreography, *Young Creatives*, and leadership, *Stride!*
- A new qualification, the Diploma in Dance Teaching and Learning (Children and Young People) (DDTAL) in partnership with Trinity College London.
- A pilot School Dance Coordinator programme.
- National conferences, commissions and publications.
- A website containing information, guidance and resources.

As a result, YDE has been able to demonstrate significant growth in youth dance. For example, the number of youth dance groups grew from 463 in 2006 to 850 by 2008, and in February 2011 there were celebrations to mark 100,000 young people having danced as part of *U.Dance*. The numbers are impressive, but perhaps less important than the qualitative difference YDE is making by providing opportunities for progression and for exceptionally talented young people from across the country to work with their peers; by supporting artists and practitioners through conferences, publications and the new DDTAL qualification; and by raising visibility, profile and providing a voice for youth dance with national partners and policy-makers.

Among the issues identified in Tony Hall's *Dance Review* were: significantly less funding and a more limited infrastructure for dance compared to music; dance being 'lost' in the National Curriculum by being positioned within Physical Education; lack of diversity; and lack of information. The government's response to the *Dance Review* highlighted:

"Youth Dance England has been building a solid foundation for youth dance since its establishment in 2004. DCMS, DCSF and ACE are committed to strengthening YDE's position by enabling it to develop fully as a strategic organisation to lead on youth dance and dance in schools. Strategic funding will be invested in YDE over three years from 2008-11." (*Dance Review* and *Government Response*: free to download at www.yde.org.uk/publications).

Three years later and a change of government in 2010, policy had changed. Dance had been given as an example of a 'soft' subject by Michael Gove MP (the new Secretary of State for Education), public expenditure has been cut, and the Arts Council did not include Youth Dance England among the organisations to be funded as part of its national portfolio programme, although Youth Music and the National Youth Theatre both continued to be funded by the Arts Council. None of these decisions took apparent account of the significance of young people to dance as its future artists, audiences and promoters, nor of the previously identified need for a national youth dance organisation, or of the impact of Youth Dance England.

In practice

Youth dance embraces a wealth of practice and providers. Attempting to offer a comprehensive overview is not possible and the examples of practice given below offer a flavour of the range of possibilities and show something of the extent to which youth dance matters to all kinds of people, for all kinds of reasons.

Individuals working with young people and dance have an important role in sign-posting opportunities and they need to understand where their work sits in a wider local and national context. This needs a breadth of understanding about the possibilities, and being open to other ways of working that puts the interests of the young person centre-stage. For details of the Henley *Review of Cultural Education* (2012) and how this might impact on dance, see Chapter 13.

Dance Companies and organisations

Most dance companies provide a range of education and participation opportunities. This often includes activity that is connected to the company's repertoire although the nature of this connection can be wide ranging. Further information about these projects can be found on the companies' websites.

> **Birmingham Royal Ballet** created a production of *Romeo and Juliet* with young people as the culmination of its *Bally Hoo!* in 2006, a project that included young people learning the work. For its *Ballet, Birmingham and Me* project in 2010, it began with the idea of Cinderella but facilitated young people in developing the concept, storyboard and production from scratch.
>
> **New Adventures**, in partnership with the Theatre Royal Glasgow, created a new production of *Lord of the Flies* in 2011 over a year-long collaboration. With a cast of local young men, it involved dance and film, and the same creative team as any other New Adventures production.

All these projects engaged young people with the company and its work, happened over an extended period of time, developed personal and social skills and created a high profile for young people's achievement in and through dance.

> **Rambert Dance Company** runs a youth dance company, *Quicksilver*, for talented young dancers aged 15-24 who perform new contemporary works at various locations such as the opening of Eurostar from St Pancras Station in 2007.
>
> **The Place** has a resident youth dance group, *Shift*, and selected six youth dance groups to perform at *ReFresh 2011* who were challenged to create new work to music selected by professional choreographers.

Dance is a good medium for integrating young people of different abilities, cultural abilities and with different generations.

> **Candoco Dance Company** runs two Youth Dance groups for disabled and non-disabled young people aged 14-25 years old, one at **The Place** and one at the **Siobhan Davies Dance Studios**. New dancers can join at the start of each term and no previous dance experience is needed. Sessions include a range of techniques and creative tasks, and the groups perform across the country at youth dance platforms, conferences and festivals.
>
> **Balbir Singh Dance Company** and **Srishti** worked with 9 schools across Lancashire to introduce Kathak and Bharatanatyam to pupils and teachers, supported by a resource pack and CPD sessions. In 2010 young people were able to access the Dance India summer school at **The Lowry**, create a piece for a *U.Dance* performance and a dance film with **Srishti** that would be part of their performance at **The Lowry**.
>
> **Greenwich Dance** commissioned Rosemary Lee to create *Common Dance* as part of *Dance Umbrella 2009*. It was designed for the Borough Hall, with commissioned music by Terry Mann, and involved the Finchley Children's Music Group and 52 dancers aged from 8 to 82.

These examples also demonstrate the importance of partnerships in creating large-scale, impactful projects with young people.

> **Wayne McGregor | Random Dance** created *SENSE* for Endeavour House in Ipswich with 80 participants from four local schools in 2008. It was an artistic collaboration between Wayne McGregor, Random Dance, Stevie Wishart and Britten Sinfonia in partnership with **DanceEast** and funded by the Department for Education.

Boys Dancing

There are many social and cultural reasons that mean boys have been traditionally disadvantaged in terms of opportunities to engage with dance. One response to this has been the development of groups and projects specifically for boys and young men.

> **Being Frank Physical Theatre**'s artistic director Dave McKenna in partnership with **Warwick Arts Centre** built on previous boys' dance work through being commissioned by *Dancing for the Games*, part of the West Midland's Culture Programme for *London 2012*. It is working with schools, youth centres, Pupil Referral Units and other agencies across the West Midlands, to create work for performances in theatres, site specific work and dance films. A network of professional male dance artists is being developed through the project.
>
> **Wayne Sables Projects** in partnership with Doncaster's *Hot House Festival* and **South Yorkshire Dance Hub** has run boys' projects in 2010 leading to performances. There are plans to develop the projects into a longer-term programme that includes an Academy, residences and film projects.

Progression

For many young people, dance is an important part of their life. For some it is a passion and / or a career aspiration. Enabling young people to realise their potential in and through dance is a responsibility for all those involved in youth dance.

> **Youth Dance England** offers national opportunities for young people with exceptional potential in a range of aspects of dance:
>
> *Stride!* is the national leadership and development programme for young people aged 14-19, helping them to discover the different career opportunities available within the dance sector. They take part in a residential where they devise projects, in a placement with a professional organisation, and receive support from a mentor.
>
> *Young Creatives* is for choreographers aged 14-19. In 2011 they were mentored by professional choreographers, took part in a residential at the **Royal Ballet School** and created new work that was performed in the Linbury Theatre at the **Royal Opera House**.
>
> *National Youth Dance Performances* highlight the breadth of youth dance by involving groups from across the country. The *U.Dance* performance framework supports groups to perform locally, regionally and nationally. In 2013 there was an overall increase of 20% in applications to perform, demonstrating both the success of the event in 2012 and illustrating the enthusiasm within the youth dance sector.
>
> *National Young Dance Ambassadors* selects motivated and inspiring young dancers as advocates for dance. In *U.Dance* 2012 they also programmed performances in the **Clore ballroom**, taking on the roles of compere, programmer, stage manager and steward.

> **Centres for Advanced Training (CATs)** provide advanced training and development for young people with exceptional potential, funded by the Department for Education's *Music and Dance Scheme*. Most programmes focus on contemporary dance, but there are programmes in urban dance (Swindon), ballet (Yorkshire) and South Asian Dance (Birmingham). Places are awarded by audition. **CATs** also work in partnership with schools/other organisations to offer workshops and other activities.

Sports and Arts

Agencies and organisations promoting sport with young people are often interested in embracing dance for its particular appeal for girls and its capacity to engage them in physical activity. Dance can also enhance certain skills that are useful in sports. This provides opportunities for partnerships between arts and sports organisations.

> **Sadler's Wells** runs *Jam Free*, a performance project for **School Sports Partnerships** based in outer London boroughs, designed to inspire girls aged 11-16 to take part in physical activity. A performance takes place at a school, inviting other schools to attend, and including guest youth dance groups and work by a professional choreographer, with a celebratory performance at the Lilian Baylis Studio at **Sadler's Wells** (as occurred in 2009). Each Partnership is also visited by the professional choreographer within curriculum time, providing a repertoire based practical workshop and opportunity for discussion about their creative process. A Teacher's Pack is available to all schools within the Partnership.

Dance unites art and sport. This has given it a key role in the *Legacy Trust UK* regional projects intended to create excitement in the run up to the *Olympic and Paralympic Games 2012* and ensure its legacy.

> **Big Dance** began in 2006 and became the *Legacy Trust* project for London, providing almost £3 million for **Big Dance** between 2010 and 2012. Five Big Dance Hubs have been established to connect with every London Borough, and partnerships with heritage, other art forms, health and sport are enabling a wide range of participatory and performance projects, many of which involve young people. For example, 2013 offers a 3 minute Pledge Performance for everyone to join choreographed by artists from English National Ballet using London 2012 and the 7 Olympic Values as inspiration.
>
> **Dancing for the Games** is a key strand of the West Midlands *Legacy Trust* programme. Organisations have been invited to apply for funding for projects that encourage participation and promote the core values of the Games. Again many of the projects involve young people.

Conclusion

These examples indicate the breadth of youth dance in arts, culture and sports contexts. There are many more that could have been included. While all the examples have a local impact, the focus here has been on projects that also have a wider impact and involve a range of partners. In addition, thousands of local initiatives and youth dance groups are where most young people engage with dance, and the Youth Dance England website includes 'Insights' into projects from every region that include the voice of young people.

To an extent, youth dance groups that create and perform their own dance work are the core of youth dance. Such groups may be led by young people, dance artists or teachers and be part of the work of dance companies, organisations, theatres, local authorities or schools, or they may be independent of any other organisation. They exist in a context where there is a myriad of other opportunities for young people to develop performance, creative, leadership and critical skills.

REFLECTION

1. In your own work with children and young people, what purposes are you trying to achieve and why are these important to you? If you are not teaching yet, consider what purposes you would hope to address.

2. Consider how your own work fits in with the local and national picture outlined above. What local or regional activity might you signpost children and young people to as progression from your group? If you are not teaching yet, research the dance activity in your area.

3. Select two case studies from the article for further research that reflect different purposes or ways of working with children and young people. Consider how these projects reflect their different purposes and what you might learn from them.

4. Find out why the young dancers that you teach / lead attend dance activity. For example, devise an anonymous questionnaire that prompts a general response rather than specific comments on your sessions. Compare their thoughts with your purposes (as considered in point 1 above).

5. Research a national scheme such as the CATS. See www.education.gov.uk for links to the Music and Dance Scheme and contacts for CATS.

Bibliography

Brinson, P. 1991 *Dance as Education: Towards a National Dance Culture*. London: Falmer Press

Hall, T. *The Dance Review*. 2007 Department for Children, Schools and Families. Available from www.yde.org.uk/otherpublications

Government Response to Tony Hall's Dance Review. 2008 Department for Children, Schools and Families. Available from www.yde.org.uk/otherpublications

House of Commons Culture, Media and Sport Committee. 2004 *Arts Development: Dance* (HC 587). Sixth Report of Session 2003 - 04. Norwich: The Stationery Office. Available from www.parliament.uk

Chapter 12
Youth Dance Contexts (part 2): Health and Youth Justice
Jeanette Siddall

Introduction

Dance integrates physical activity with creative and expressive purpose in a social, collaborative context. It can, therefore, contribute to a range of wider social agendas. A range of projects have demonstrated some of the instrumental values of dance in health and youth justice contexts and shown that dance can provide a means of promoting healthier and more positive and responsible attitudes and behaviour. Dance can promote:

Physical health – coordination, control, posture, agility, flexibility, strength, balance, energy, physical confidence.

Emotional and psychological well-being – confidence, self-esteem, focus, concentration, aspiration, positive attitudes.

Social skills – team working, communication, trust, leadership, collaboration.

Learning – memory, patterning, observation, analysis, exploring, motivation.

(Siddall, 2010, p. 9)

This is not an exhaustive list, and it is possible to see how improvements in one area might impact on others. For example, improved posture and energy is likely to promote higher self-esteem and confidence, which in turn might facilitate communication and motivation.

In addition, dance can provide an introduction or alternative to physical activity for those less interested in competitive sport and is often seen as a valuable means of engaging girls and women in physical activity. It can also raise awareness of health issues such as obesity, and can enable the development of coping strategies such as for the management of nerves and anger. Dance can also be simply enjoyable.

> Dancing is affirmative, optimistic and democratic. It embodies the idea that the world can be a better and happier place.
> Editorial in *The Guardian* (20 December, 2008, n.p. accessed www.guardian.co.uk)

Health

In 2006, the then Minister for Public Health and the Minister for Culture provided a joint foreword to the Arts Council England document *Dance and Health* produced with the National Health Service. They said:

> Dance can have a powerful effect on people's lives and we want to see the physical, emotional, mental and social benefits extended to as many people as possible.
>
> Efforts to improve health and well-being need to reach everyone in our society. Anyone can dance and enjoy dancing – young or old, disabled or non-disabled. The vibrant range of styles drawn from different cultures gives dance an impressive reach in our multicultural society. Dance has a long history of successfully working with hard to reach groups and building a sense of social cohesion within communities.
>
> (Arts Council England, 2006, n.p.)

Governments, and government attitudes change, but it is clear from this quotation that dance has established a role in the promoting of health for all ages and abilities, for different cultures and in creating a more cohesive society.

A great number of dance artists, companies and organisations have engaged in health-related dance initiatives. Youth Dance England's website has a Dance and Health section that includes a wide range of examples of projects, some of which are highlighted here as case studies.

The first of these is particularly rigorous in terms of its objectives and research methodologies, and includes useful findings from previous research.

Case Study 1: NRG2

A research collaboration between **Hampshire Dance** and **Trinity Laban** with the support of the **National Health Service, West Sussex Council Council, Big Lottery Fund** and **Youth Dance England**.

The evaluation report includes the rationale for the research that outlines relevant previous research including:

- Decreases in physical activity during adolescence, especially the transition from primary to secondary school; girls participating less in physical activity than boys; relationship between physical activity in adolescence and in later life (Biddle *et al*, 2004, in Amstel *et al*, 2010).
- Less active adolescents being more likely to engage in risky health behaviours such as smoking (Pate *et al*, 2006, in Amstel *et al*, 2010).
- Sedentary behaviour linked to orthopaedic conditions and reduced life expectancy (Kreimler *et al*, in Amstell *et al* 2010).
- Physical activity linked to increased mean academic achievement (Grissom 2005, in Amstell *et al*, 2010) and improved mental health and self-esteem (Ortega *et al*, in Amstell *et al*, 2010).

The research found significant improvements in aerobic capacity, hamstring flexibility, competency and a positive impact for physical and psychological well-being for girls taking part in a 10 week programme of creative dance activity. PE teachers found that children who had never previously relished physical activity were inspired by the dedicated dance classes. Participants who did not enjoy PE felt the dance classes were fun and enjoyable.

Have you noticed a similar impact in your participants?

There are various examples of partnerships with General Practitioners, Primary Care Trusts and between dance organisations, local councils and the NHS. See Case Study 2.

> **Case Study 2: Salsa on Prescription**
>
> A partnership between **NHS Gloucestershire, Stroud District Council** and local leisure centres builds on an existing exercise referral scheme for people over the age of 14. Those referred receive 12 weeks of dancing at a heavily subsidised rate followed by a review.
>
> The majority identified improvements in their general health with specific examples including improvements in asthma, with reduced use of an inhaler, weight loss, improved mood and focus, and increased confidence.

The case studies are useful in offering ideas and examples of the range of health-related dance possibilities. With changes in government health policies, reduced public funding for the arts and shifts in Arts Council priorities it may be that most of the case studies are no longer directly replicable. They may still inspire new ways of delivering high quality health outcomes through dance. The following case study outlines a course that brought together dance artists and health professionals to enhance mutual understanding and promote the quality of dance and health practice.

> **Case Study 3: Dance Active**
>
> A training course for dance artists and commissioning health professionals delivered on behalf of the **Department of Health** and **DanceXchange** in partnership with **Youth Dance England**.
>
> The course ran in March 2010 and covered national and regional strategic health priorities, best practice through case studies, practical dance work focused on delivering specific health outcomes, networking, and the commissioning process.

Specific health outcomes might involve particular settings, particular groups and health issues, for example:

> **Case Study 4: Settings, groups and issues**
>
> **Hospitals – Protein Dance**
> **Protein Dance** works in a range of settings including schools, Pupil Referral Units and Hospitals. Their work in children's hospitals places an emphasis on fun, inclusion and confidence building and invites children, parents, staff and friends to join in.

Young Women – Dare2Dance

A project to encourage young women to become involved in physical activity through Hip Hop and Street Dance. Launched as part of *Big Dance 2008* and developed in partnership with **Pro-Active**, the sports development agency for London, with **London Youth Dance**, **Nike** and **Southbank Centre**.

Obesity - darts (Doncaster Community Arts)

Darts ran a project designed to address teenage obesity among girls. Participants were referred by their General Practitioner and sessions included moderate dance activity followed by aspects related to fashion and appearance, such as make-up, that provided both a motivation for attendance and promoted self-esteem.

Dance is amenable to mass participation events that can raise awareness, motivate participation and promote a wide range of causes. Such events may not be directly focused on specific health outcomes, but can build the visibility of dance and help create an environment that is conducive to the use of dance in meeting wider social agendas.

Case Study 5: Promotion and mass participation

Big Dance and Dancing for the Games

Big Dance 2012 is the *Legacy Trust UK* programme for London and *Dancing for the Games* is the programme for the West Midlands. Both embrace a wide range of projects, for example *Big Dance Schools Pledge* has collaborated with **The British Council**'s *Connecting Schools* programme and *5-a-day Fitness* that involves a five minute on-screen dance routine. Schools from Germany, Sri Lanka, India and Lebanon joined schools across the UK in performing the routine in their school grounds.

www.dancingforthegames.co.uk
www.bigdance2012.com

Dance for Life (known as *Dance: Make Your Move* since September 2011)

An initiative by the **Red Cross** to celebrate youth dance and to raise funds for the work of the **Red Cross**. It brings together schools, colleges and youth groups to create a routine that reflects an aspect of the **Red Cross**' work and perform at events across the country. The website contains blogs and videos of participants, and information on volunteering opportunities and funding.

www.redcross.org.uk

continued on next page

> **Dansathletic**
>
> A collaboration between **Protein Dance** and **East London Dance** exploring the sporting ideals of the *Olympic and Paralympic Games*. It involved 100 young people from the five Olympic Boroughs and performed at Canary Wharf as part of *Big Dance* and at Stratford Station to launch the *Newham Arts Festival*. A resource pack for teachers was written by Luca Silvestrini and Kathryn Sexton and is available from **East London Dance**.
>
> www.eastlondondance.org

Youth Justice

The Arts Council's *Dance Included* programme focused on promoting good practice in dance and social inclusion. Several projects involved aspects of youth justice.

> **Case Study 6: Dance Included**
>
> **Dancing Inside** – a residency and performance project led by **Motionhouse Dance Theatre** in HMP Dovegate that aimed to address issues of violence and reinforce positive attitudes among the men. Outcomes included improved health and well-being, pride, confidence, self-esteem and trust.
>
> **Physical Justice** – a dance-led programme for young offenders and young people at risk of offending by **East London Dance** that aimed to prevent young people from becoming engaged in criminal activity, and to contribute to educational learning.
>
> **Men at War** – **Dance United** worked with young men and staff at **Her Majesty's Young Offender Institution Wetherby** to raise self- and peer-esteem, and confidence, and develop key skills such as literacy. Outcomes included trainees achieving educational qualifications, feelings of pride, promoting trust and teamwork and changes in behaviour and outlook.
>
> **The Water Project** – led by **The Place** and **Cardboard Citizens** it worked with homeless people to address issues related to health, such as drink and drug use that often leads to criminal behaviour. Outcomes included participants feeling better physically and psychologically, new friendships and increased confidence.

Dance United has gone on to develop its work with the Youth Justice Board to establish Academies for young offenders in Bradford, London and Wessex and to work in women's prisons and young offender institutions. A range of youth offending teams have used dance to promote positive activity for young offenders and those at risk of offending, many involving Dance United working in partnership with dance agencies.

Purposes and Planning

Dance in health and youth justice contexts usually has instrumental purposes. Clarity about the purposes, the specific aims and outcomes required from the work is critical to planning the structure, content and methodologies employed in the work. The following questions are intended to prompt further questions that might be helpful to ask, depending on the particular context:

What do you need to know about the participants?

This could include who they are, the challenges they face, the choice they have about participating, their motivation, their age, previous experience, expectations.

What do participants need to know about you, the project / activity, expectations of them?

This might include consideration of the kind of relationship you want to create with participants, how you can contribute to their motivation, commitment and aspiration through their understanding of the activity, establishing ground-rules around attendance and behaviour.

What change is desired?

This relates to the overall aims and purpose of the activity and to ensuring clarity and precision about the two or three priorities for change. The more precise a shared understanding of the desired change, the more likely it is that the project will succeed.

What role will the commissioner play?

The commissioner may be a physical activity coordinator, General Practitioner, or Youth Offending Team member. Understanding their role and expectations of the project and ensuring they are able to advocate for the project with participants and others might require more discussion than expected.

What will success look like?

How will you and others know that the project has been successful? What change will be visible and evident and how else might change be demonstrated? This might include feedback from participants and evaluation measures which may need to be built into the project.

How can the activity best deliver the change and success?

This includes thinking about ways of engaging participants at the start of the project, ensuring the activity is achievable, rewarding, and owned by participants, thinking about progression in terms of the complexity of tasks, participants' sense of autonomy, building confidence and collaboration, approaches as well as content, reflecting and reviewing progress and change – all related to achieving the specific outcomes that have been identified.

What has happened before?

This includes researching examples of effective practice in previous projects and building on established practice. It might also be relevant to consider participants' and / or the organisation's previous experience of dance / arts projects.

What might happen next?

Is it a one-off project, or a pilot that might be sustained in the future? How does this affect what can be achieved in the time scale and how the success of the project is understood and / or evaluated?

Practicalities?

How much time will you have, what is the space like, how might the wider environment impact on what is possible, the motivation of participants, and your role? This might also include contractual issues, the logistics of arrival and departure, responsibility for participants' behaviour.

Performance

Performance can have both intrinsic and instrumental values in health and youth justice contexts. The intrinsic values include performance being the logical conclusion of dance activity. The instrumental values include: performance as a motivating goal; the experience of performing which promotes coping strategies, non-verbal communication, responsibility for own and each other's performance, team building, focus, memory and concentration, being totally present in the moment; and the confidence that comes from overcoming a challenge. Being a focus of attention and applause also provides extrinsic recognition of achievement.

Performance can be through an informal sharing and / or a fully produced performance with costumes and lighting. It might also be on film and / or made for the screen. The setting of the performance might involve different degrees of instrumental value, as will ensuring that participants are well prepared, have a sense of ownership of the material they perform and look as good as possible.

In some contexts, it may be that regular participation cannot be relied on. Participants may be taken out, or opt out of projects for a range of reasons. This might mean that flexible choreographic strategies are more useful, for example everyone being spread out or close together rather than being more specifically positioned in the space.

Performance can also have an instrumental value in changing the attitudes of audience(s) who might include commissioners and policy-makers. It might challenge their assumptions about participants and enable them to be seen in a new light, and it might enhance the understanding of the value of dance in the context.

Case Study 7: Performance

Think about a project you have led or can imagine.
- What is the significance of performance in the project?
- What is your role in developing the performance, for example is it as creator, facilitator, editor, artistic director, and how does this impact on the intrinsic and instrumental quality of the performance?
- What was / might be the audience response?
- What could you do to make the audience response as positive as possible?

Evaluation and Impact

Performance is one means of demonstrating the impact of the project. It can be complemented by evaluation which might be more easily and widely disseminated.

Evaluation can be internal or external. Its purpose needs to be clear and considered before the project starts; just as with assessment, valid evaluation relies on having clear objectives.

Evaluation aims to identify what has worked well, what has worked less well and what might be done more effectively in the future, it is about revealing learning from the project. Evaluating the extent to which aims and purpose have been met might involve methodologies such as a baseline questionnaire at the start compared to a final questionnaire to identify change. It might include quantitative data such as attendance rates, and qualitative data gathered through interviews. It is useful to understand the potential audience for the findings of the evaluation, and whose views need to be incorporated. Views can be captured through questionnaires, interviews, quotations, on film and through photographs. Further information on assessment and evaluation can be found in Chapters 9 and 10 respectively.

The *NRG2* report also describes the rationale for the research methodologies and references relevant literature. For example, it describes the three basic psychological needs of autonomy, competence, and relatedness as being related to the motivation an individual must feel in order to perform a given activity and which are essential to psychological growth and health. Using established scales, and referencing academic or scientific authorities, can help shape the evaluation strategy and add credibility to its findings.

Useful websites

www.artscouncil.org.uk

www.yde.org.uk

www.dance-united.com

www.dancingforthegames.co.uk

www.bigdance2012.com

www.dh.gov.uk

www.justice.gov.uk

REFLECTION

1. Select one of the case studies noted above to research further. Use some of the questions provided under Purposes and Planning and see if you can obtain enough evidence about the case study to answer these.

2. Research one of the organisations such as Dance United. What kind of projects do they support? What are the aims of the organisation?

3. Research the projects which have taken place in your local area.

Bibliography

Amstell, S. Blazey, L. Quin, E. and. Redding, E. 2010 *NRG2: Youth Dance and Health*. Report. Hampshire Dance and Trinity Laban.

Arts Council England 2006 *Dance and Health*. www.artscouncil.org.uk.

Bramley, I. and Jermyn, H. 2006 *Dance Included*. London: Arts Council England.

Siddall, J. 2010 *Dance In and Beyond Schools*. London: Youth Dance England.

Chapter 13
Dance in the Formal Education System
Veronica Jobbins

Introduction

Dance has been part of the formal education system in England for well over 100 years, whether it be folk dance in the 1900s, Laban-based Modern Educational Dance in the 1960s or Contemporary Dance and Hip Hop in the 2000s. It has always had to justify its place within the education of children and young people but equally managed to thrive and develop, in part because of the determination of dance teachers but also because it has been recognised as having a valuable place within both physical education and arts education. It is significant that dance among young people is the second most popular activity in the country following football, with ever increasing participation rates.

The term formal education is used in this chapter, to refer to the statutory education system of schools, further education and higher education. It will focus mostly on dance within primary and secondary schools as being the main employment area for dance practitioners working with children and young people within the formal sector.

Dance in the School Curriculum

The school curriculum is influenced by many factors; primarily the national curriculum prescribed by government and enshrined in law as compulsory. However, the values and ideals of the school community, be it individual teachers, Head teacher, parents and governors, as well as the interests of the pupils and wider community, will influence what is taught and what educational opportunities are provided beyond the parameters of the national curriculum.

The introduction of the national curriculum in 1992, and all subsequent revisions to date, have located dance within the statutory physical education (PE) curriculum, making dance a compulsory activity within Key Stages 1 and 2 (primary schools) and optional at Key Stages 3 and 4 (secondary schools). This has ensured that dance is taught to some extent within most primary schools and the majority of girls' and mixed secondary schools, but rarely in boys' secondary schools. However, the time available for the subject, the content of the curriculum, and the specialist skills, knowledge and understanding of the teacher vary considerably from school to school and across the country. The commitment and enthusiasm of individual teachers or head teachers may well be the deciding factor as to whether dance is taught widely in a school or perceived as a very minor part of the curriculum.

In early years settings (children aged 3-5) and primary schools (pupils aged 5-11) dance is largely taught by the classroom teacher who will probably have quite limited dance skills. Dance lessons, frequently creative in focus, may be linked to other aspects of the curriculum such as History, Maths, English or Science topics, be influenced by prevailing popular dances such as Hip-Hop, or reflect cultural education by including folk or other dance styles.

In secondary schools the picture is equally varied. While for the purposes of the national curriculum dance is currently placed within PE, it may be located within different areas; within PE, performing or creative arts departments, or as a subject in its own right. Some large secondary schools devote considerable resources to dance, ensuring that there are high quality dance facilities, specialist teachers and sufficient budgets to invite professional dance artists and practitioners to contribute to the curriculum. Other schools provide very little. However, the increasing number of dance examination courses, such as GCE A and A/S level, BTEC and GCSE qualifications on offer to pupils at Key Stage 4 and in the sixth-form of schools or within Further Education (FE), has established dance more securely within the formal education system and provided progression for young people interested in improving their skills.

Dance: Physical Education or Arts Education?

It is not possible to discuss dance in schools without considering the issue of whether dance should be placed within PE for the purposes of the national curriculum or more closely allied with the other arts. The debate is a complex one. While many within the dance sector are determined that the subject, as one of our major art forms, should be taught alongside the other arts, historically it has generally been taught as part of physical education. The significance of this debate comes to the fore each time the national curriculum is reviewed (as it is at the time of writing).

The National Advisory Committee on Creativity, Culture and Education (NACCCE) recognised that whilst placing dance within PE had ensured dance was taught in schools, the PE national curriculum had failed to sufficiently acknowledge the artistic, cultural and creative dimensions of dance as an art form:

> The position of dance within physical education has provided short-term security for the discipline, but long term lack of teachers and too little emphasis on the artistic nature of dance.
>
> (NACCCE 1999, p. 181)

The report *Arts Education in Secondary Schools: Effects and Effectiveness* agreed with this view:

> in recognition of their contribution beyond that of PE and English, dance and drama should be given comparable status in the National Curriculum to that of art and music.
>
> (Harland, Kinder *et al*, 2000, summary, p. 10)

It is likely that dance in the foreseeable future will continue to be taught across the school curriculum in physical education or the arts depending on the school. However, the central rationale for the subject being taught in schools embraces both artistic and physical.

Case Study 1

Dance Examinations: look online for the GCE A Level and GCSE Dance specifications (www.aqa.org.uk)

- What kind of dance content and assessment tasks do they contain?
- Look on You Tube for examples of work. What kind of material and dance styles are in evidence? What standards of performance and choreography are in evidence?
- What kind of opportunities might be on offer to dance practitioners given that many of the teachers are not subject specialists?

The National Dance Teachers Association (NDTA) stated in their document *Maximising Opportunity* that the distinct and unique value of dance for children and young people is:

> As one of the major art forms, its intrinsic value lies in the possibilities it offers for the development of pupils' creative, imaginative, physical, emotional and intellectual capacities. Because of its physical nature, dance provides a means of expression and communication distinct from other art forms and because of its expressive and creative nature it stands apart from other physical activities.
>
> (NDTA Policy Paper, 2004, n.p)

Thus dance contributes to young people's artistic, creative and cultural development but also their health, fitness and well-being. Additional benefits include personal and social education, giving pupils the opportunity to develop self-confidence and pride in individual and group work, encouraging their independence and initiative, and giving opportunities to explore the relationship between feelings, values and expression.

Conceptual Framework for teaching dance in schools

Since the early 1980s and the work of Jacqueline Smith-Autard, dance teaching in schools has been underpinned by the three inter-related strands of performing, composing and appreciating dance which underpin lesson planning and are evident in the content of all the public examinations in dance. (See also Chapters 4 and 22).

Creating or Composing in Dance is concerned with making up dances: i.e. shaping movement material into clear, repeatable form or structure.

The skills developed include:
- Selecting and responding to stimuli.
- Improvising, experimenting and exploring ideas in movement.
- Selecting movements and dance ideas to express an idea or feeling.
- Repeating, varying, developing and refining movement.
- Forming and structuring movement into dances using compositional devices.

Performing in Dance is concerned with being able to perform phrases of movement, sequences or complete dances in any dance styles.

The skills developed include:
- Physical and technical skills, such as co-ordination, posture, alignment, strength, flexibility, control, balance and movement memory.
- Expressive skills, such as focus, projection, musicality, sense of style and communication of choreographic intention.

Appreciating Dance is concerned with looking at dances and understanding more about them. It involves describing, interpreting, analysing, appraising and evaluating dance that children may see in the theatre, on film or those created by their peers.

Case Study 2

Look online and find the current national curriculum:
- How easy is it to access?
- What does the national curriculum include?
- What activities are compulsory? What are optional?
- Can you see evidence of the 3 strand model in the programmes of study?
- Does it include different dance styles?
- Do you think it matters that dance is included under the PE Curriculum, or do you think it would be best if it was allied with the other arts such as drama and music?

Government Policy and Initiatives

Dance in schools has benefitted considerably from various government policies over the last ten years or so that have supported a number of initiatives, providing increased funding and opportunities for the subject. These have been directed at raising achievement in poorly performing schools through using the arts instrumentally, as well as focusing on creativity and cultural education. The NACCCE Report in 1999 advocated increasing arts activities in schools and prompted the then Labour government to introduce a national programme, *Creative Partnerships*, facilitating creativity in school through a range of artist led projects. In February 2008 another initiative *Find Your Talent* was introduced. This scheme, to ensure that every child had a minimum of five hours per week of high quality arts and cultural activity, was discontinued by the incoming Coalition Government in 2010.

Just as the rationale for dance in schools can be seen as identifying its creative and artistic value as well as physical benefits, government initiatives promoting health and fitness for children and young people have been as significant for dance in schools as creative and cultural policies. In 2003, the *PE, School Sport and Club Links (PESSCL) Strategy* was launched. This was a major investment aimed to ensure that all 5-16 years olds have access to two hours PE and three hours beyond the curriculum; and 16-19 year olds have three hours of sport outside of the curriculum.

Over time, *PESSCL* ensured dance was included among the roll out of activities alongside football, gymnastics and other sports and developed continuing professional development for teachers, after school activities and gifted and talented work. A document, *Dance Links: a guide to delivering high quality dance to children and young people* (2005) was written by Youth Dance England with the National Dance Teachers Association (and endorsed by the then Ministers for Sport and Culture) to highlight how high quality dance in and beyond the curriculum could be developed, especially how children and young people could link with out of school dance agencies and clubs. The notion of good practice entailed in *Dance Links* is outlined in Chapter 23.

It is interesting to note that *Artsmark*, a national award scheme managed by Arts Council England, that recognises schools with a high level of provision in the arts has been retained over many years. The award scheme open to all schools in England (primary, secondary, special schools and pupil referral units), both maintained and independent, shows its commitment to the wider development of young people and teachers and to raising the profile of the arts in the school and local community.

> **Case Study 3**
>
> Access information about the *Artsmark* (www.artscouncil.org.uk/artsmark)
> - What are its underpinning values?
> - What job opportunities do you think it opens up for dance practitioners?

Role of Dance Artists in Schools

Finally, it is important to consider the role of dance artists and practitioners who go into schools either independently or as part of a larger dance company or agency. They can provide the expert specialist dance knowledge that many primary and secondary school teachers lack by complementing the existing dance curriculum, inspiring children and young people and developing their dance skills. Most dance companies offer a range of projects to schools, frequently linked to their current repertory, making a strong link between the professional dance world and pupils in schools. Many freelance dance practitioners deliver regular after-school clubs as well as dance projects in curriculum time, often in the case of secondary schools supporting GCSE Dance or other examinations courses. Such projects and activities have enriched dance in schools and supported the growth of the subject.

The Future of Dance in Schools

This chapter has been written at a turning point for the education system in England as the Coalition Government, as all previous governments, plan to change the national curriculum and education structures to make them more effective, relevant to the current world, and reflect the values and ambitions of the government of the day. A new *Education Act* was passed by Parliament in November 2011 and a national curriculum review is currently taking place (February – April 2013).

Additionally, Darren Henley's *Review of Cultural Education*, which began in 2011, aims "to create a definition of what a solid cultural education should comprise of and how to make sure that all young people benefit from it" (Henley, 2012a, n.p.). On publication of the Review in February 2012, Henley offered proposals that cover all areas of cultural education. They are:

> intended to ensure that all children leave school as "well-rounded individuals with a knowledge of the world, past and present, around them".
>
> (2012b, n.p.)

Whatever the changes that occur I am confident that dance will survive in some way or other, as the dance and education sector over the last 20 years have achieved much to embed dance education within schools, further and higher education enabling many children and young people to enjoy and progress in dance.

REFLECTION

1. Non-British Models of Education. Research non-British curriculum models on the internet. In particular, look at the Arts Curriculums in New Zealand and New South Wales in Australia. How do they differ from the English national curriculum for dance and the arts? Reflect on whether they give any ideas for your own practice.

2. Government Initiatives: research one of the initiatives or government policy papers relating to dance or arts in schools. For example, see the *Henley Review*. Welcoming the announcement that a review was to be undertaken Michael Gove (Secretary of State for Education) said: "Every child should be exposed to rich cultural opportunities. Too often, this is a privilege reserved for the wealthy few. This must change. This important review will play a key role in ensuring that children from all backgrounds can reap the benefits of our culture and heritage." (2012a, n.p)

When it was published in February 2012, what did this Review recommend? How might it impact on the teaching of dance in schools? For information, see document listed in Bibliography: DfE, DCMS (2012).

3. How do you think dance in formal education has changed since you were at school? Do you have any current experience within the formal sector? Reflect on the changes and what part you might play in the future. If you are not familiar with this sector it would be useful to arrange a visit to a school which offers dance as part of their curriculum.

4. Research current government proposals and consultations: www.education.gov.uk.

Bibliography

Abbs, P. [Ed] 1987 *Living Powers: The Arts in Education*. London: Falmer.

Dance Links 2005 *Dance Links: A guide to delivering high quality dance for children and young people*, DCMS/DfES. Document Ref: PE/DL. November.

DfE, DCMS. 2012 *Cultural Education in England: The Government Response to Darren Henley's Review of Cultural Education*, February, http://media.education.gov.uk/assets/files/pdf/g/government response to the henley review.pdf

Hall, T. 2008 *The Dance Review: A Report to Government on Dance Education and Youth Dance in England*. London: DCSF. www.teachernet.gov.uk/publications.

Harland, J. Kinder, K. et al 2000 *Arts Education in Secondary Schools: Effects and Effectiveness*. Berkshire: National Foundation for Educational Research.

Henley, D. 2012a Announcement of Review of Cultural Education. http://www.culture.gov.uk/news/news_stories/8041.aspx

Henley, D. 2012b *Review of Cultural Education*. Press Notice. February. www.education.gov.uk/inthenews/inthenews/a00204075/vision-for-cultural-education-will-inspire-all-children-and-enrich-lives

NACCCE 1999 *All Our Futures: Creativity, Culture and Education*. National Advisory Committee on Creative and Cultural Education, Suffolk: DfEE Publications.

National Dance Teachers Association, 2004. *Maximising Opportunity: Policy Paper*. www.ndta.org.uk

Siddall, J. 2010 *Dance in and Beyond Schools: an essential guide to dance teaching and learning*. London: Youth Dance England. www.yde.org.uk.

Smith-Autard, J. 1994 *The Art of Dance in Education*. London: A and C Black.

Chapter 14

Dance Training (part 1): Anatomy and Child Development

Janet Briggs

Introduction

This chapter is divided into 2 sections. First, the anatomical systems of the body are outlined. It is recommended that you make use of the reading list at the end of this section to further your understanding. Second, information on child development is provided. The sections can be approached separately for study purposes.

The Anatomical Systems

The circulatory system

This is made up of the heart, arteries, veins and capillaries which are only one cell thick. The blood is a transport system for bringing oxygen and nutrients to the cells and for removing carbon dioxide and waste products which are then transported either to the lungs or kidneys for excretion.

The heart is made of cardiac muscle – a specialised muscle which continues to work throughout life. The heart rate is rapid in the new born – over 100bpm and gradually reduces until it reaches the adult rate.

Circulation is generally good in children because the heart does not have to pump the blood as far as in an adult.

The respiratory system

This consists of the lungs, bronchioles, trachea, nose and mouth. The function of the respiratory system is to extract oxygen from the air to supply the cells, and to remove carbon dioxide.

Respiration is fast in children and gradually slows as the lungs grow and the system becomes larger and more efficient.

The digestive system

The digestive system allows nutrients and elements to be extracted from the diet to provide energy for cell production and function such as muscle contraction.

The nervous system

This is divided into the central nervous system and the peripheral nervous system. The central nervous system is made up of the brain and spinal cord and consists of thousands of inter-neurones or nerve cells. The peripheral nervous system is made up of sensory and motor neurones which are bundled together to form nerves. Neurones communicate with each other at synapses. Some neurones can be very long e.g. from the spine to the big toe.

At birth the nervous system is immature and development is rapid. The new born goes from being reflex driven, to one capable of complex, intricate movements. The plasticity of the nervous system allows new connections to be made between neurones, which results in learning. This process is continuous throughout life but is most rapid in the early years when much is being learnt and neuromuscular pathways are being established. If a movement is repeated enough times it becomes an automatic response or movement pattern which is difficult to change.

The brain does not consider individual muscles when carrying out movement but thinks in terms of *the goal to be achieved*, and thus there will be *many ways to execute a dance step*. If the dance technique requires a certain type or quality of movement, this will involve conscious thought, preparation and practice in order to execute the step correctly.

The sensory system feeds information into the central nervous system about where the limbs and joints are in space – this is known as proprioception or kinaesthetic awareness. During growth spurts and particularly in boys, this sense can become disrupted and awkwardness or clumsiness appears, sometimes for several months.

The sympathetic nervous system helps control the temperature of the body. There is some evidence that children sweat less and that thermoregulation is less effective. For example, children can become more easily overheated in hot conditions and while undertaking vigorous dance activity.

The skeletal system

The axial skeleton is made up of the bones in the skull, spine, thorax and pelvis. The appendicular skeleton is made up of the bones in the arms and legs. At birth much of the skeleton is a framework or blue print of hyaline cartilage with only the shafts of the long bones ossified (primary centres of ossification). The ossification process, where bone replaces cartilage, progresses towards each end of the bone. The terminal regions of the long bones are ossified by separate centres of ossification, known as secondary centres of ossification, some of which do not appear until the teens. The growth plates or epiphyseal plates are where the two centres of ossification meet. Thus in a long bone such as the tibia there are three centres – the shaft and the two ends. A further centre of ossification (or a lip from the upper end of the tibia) appears from about the age of 12 years, which is aligned with the patella tendon. This secondary growth plate can become irritated if the adolescent is very active or working on inappropriate floors. The pain and swelling that occurs is known as 'growth apophysitis' and is given the eponymous name Osgood Schlatters Disease. Both Severs Disease, in the heel where the Achilles tendon attaches onto the calcanium, and Jumpers Knee, at the distal end of the patella, are examples of growth apophysitis.

If bone growth is very rapid 'growing pains' may occur. These tend to occur at night and may disturb sleep. They may start at about 7 years of age and go on whilst the long bones are growing. Because the bones of children are not as hard as those of adults, they may bend rather than break – these are known as green stick fractures. Fractures which occur through an epiphyseal plate can interfere with bone growth. Where training and / or dietary constraints are taken to extremes, such as with anorexia, bone density can become impaired.

Irregular bones, most of which are found in the axial skeleton, have several centres of ossification e.g. the scapula has eight centres of ossification which may take until the 20th year to fuse completely.

Connective tissue system

There is an extensive network of connective tissue throughout the body which includes fascia, ligaments, tendons and the tissues surrounding structures such as bones (periosteum) and muscles (epimysium).

Ligaments are made of tough connective tissue which joins bones to each other. Tendons are made of similar connective tissue which joins muscle to bone.

Joints

Joints are where two bones meet. There are many different types of joints which are adapted for the function required of them. Most joints in the appendicular skeleton are synovial – the joint surface of each bone is lined with hyaline cartilage. Their joint surface is surrounded by a joint capsule which is lined with synovial membrane, and produces synovial fluid which lubricates the joint space. In addition the joint is strengthened by ligaments which support and restrict the movement available.

Muscular system

The muscular system is made up of the contractile elements of the muscle which is surrounded by connective tissue (epimysium). This in turn is attached to the bone via a tendon. When a muscle contracts, it causes a joint to move. Muscle can contract and shorten (isotonic contraction), or tense and cause stability (isometric) or it can relax and lengthen. When a muscle contracts and shortens (the prime mover), the muscle on the other side of the joint has to relax to allow the movement to take place (the antagonist). The 'relax and lengthening' of a muscle is used for certain stretches for example 'hold relax' stretches.

Slow twitch muscles are those which have a good blood supply and are capable of long term low grade contractions; fast twitch muscles are those which are capable of large contractions but which fatigue quickly. Each muscle will be made up of a mix of these muscle fibres so the muscle is capable of carrying out the work expected of it. Genetics, training and nutrition will influence the balance of fast and slow twitch fibres within a certain muscle.

The 'deep muscle system' tends to contain muscles which are predominantly slow twitch and work over a single joint. Their main function is to control the stability of the joint and to maintain equilibrium. This system will include the postural muscles, such as the deep abdominals. The superficial muscle system tends to have predominantly fast twitch muscle fibres and is made for locomotion and movement, rather than stability e.g. the gastrocnemius muscle in the calf which is involved in running and jumping.

With training, the balance and number of muscle fibres can change, depending on the workload. This will have an effect on power and stamina. The length of a muscle will change with growth and with appropriate stretches. In adolescence, muscle mass and shoulder width increases in boys.

Unless fitness is maintained or improved there is a tendency for muscles to become weaker and stiffer. A common view is that muscles and soft tissue grow in response to long bone growth. During periods of growth, unless gentle stretches are undertaken, there is a tendency for the joints to become stiffer and less mobile.

For more detailed information it is strongly recommended that you read the following:

Cash, M. 1999 *Pocket Atlas of the Moving Body*. London: Ebury Press.

Blakey, P. 2000 *The Muscle Book*. Stafford: Bibliotek Books.

Bramley, I. 2002 *Dance Teaching Essentials*. London: Dance UK.

Jarmey, C, contributor Thomas Myers. 2006 *The Concise Book of the Moving Body*. Lotus Publishing.

Howse, J. and McCormack, M. 2009 *Anatomy, Dance Technique and Injury Prevention*. [4th edition] London: Methuen Drama.

Grieg, V. 1994 *Inside Ballet Technique - Separating anatomical fact from fiction in the ballet class*. London: Dance Books.

IADMS Education Committee 2000 *The Challenge of the Adolescent Dancer*. free resource, www.iadms.org

Koutedakis, Y. and Sharp, C. 1999 *The Fit and Healthy Dancer*. Chichester: John Wiley.

REFLECTION

1. Research the impact of the growth spurt further (see Bramley, IADMS or Koutedakis and Sharp listed above). What kind of injuries might be associated with this? What might you need to adapt or avoid in your teaching?

2. Design a safe stretching program for adolescent dancers.

3. Analyse the muscle action for one exercise. Identify the prime movers and the antagonists. Why do you think antagonists are the most easily injured? What can you do to avoid this?

Child Development

This section gives a brief introduction to child development which is all that can be covered here; further reading on the subject is strongly recommended. Children develop and mature at different rates due to factors such as culture, diet, genes and social factors. However there are general developmental stages that most children go through. Treating children as if they were 'little adults' can result in confusion, misunderstanding and possibly injury for the child.

Birth - 2½ years: The Sensory Motor Stage

Physical

At birth a baby is flexed with no extension of the cervical or lumbar spinal curves which will give the mature shape of the spine. The skeleton is mainly cartilaginous and far from complete. Development and growth is rapid in all areas, the ability to maintain an upright posture, movement control, saving reactions, developing over the months, so that by the age of 2 years the baby has become a toddler who has learned to run, squat, and can go upstairs whilst holding onto something for support.

Cognitive

The infant is learning about itself and the world through the developing sensory and motor activity. Infants grow from being only able to respond through reflexes and random behaviour to goal oriented toddlers. The child learns that it exists apart from other things, so that by 2 years old they can name everyday objects and show association between objects, for example, a spoon and dish go together, or shoes go on feet.

Psycho-social

A baby is soon open to stimulation and begins to show interest and curiosity – it will smile readily at 3 months old. It learns to communicate by crying and can be soothed by being spoken to in a soothing manner. By 2 years old a toddler can attend to communications directed to them and has learned about fifty words, and is also able to put two words together. The infant can carry out simple commands. At some point between 2 and 3 years the toddler becomes toilet trained and will be dry, at least through the day.

Attachments

Attachment is a reciprocal enduring emotional tie between a baby and the care giver (Ainsworth, in Papalia, 2009, p.202). There are different types of attachment and no agreed way of assessing it. The baby will form attachments with both parents and different types of attachment will develop between the baby and each parent. The more secure a growing child's attachment to a nurturing adult, the easier it is for the child to eventually become an independent adult capable of developing good relationships with others.

Case Study 1

Some toddlers start dance classes at 2 ½ years old.

- Think about what could be expected of a child at this age and stage both physically and cognitively (see Chapter 1 for further information).
- What language would it be helpful to use and what might limit progress at this stage?

---

3 - 6 years old: The Pre-Operational Stage

Physical

At 3 years old the child is able to run, turn corners and negotiate around objects but has difficulty stopping suddenly. They can jump with two feet together and perform a running jump of between 40 - 60cm. They will be learning to skip and some may be able to start hopping. They can rise onto the toes and stand on the preferred leg momentarily. Movement to music comes naturally.

At 3 years the toddler is beginning to 'slim down and shoot up', the babyish roundness becomes more slender, and the abdominal muscles develop so the baby tummy starts to tighten. The limbs grow longer. However, the heart and abdominal contents still take up a proportionally large amount of space so abdominal control is limited and a balletic posture is impossible for example.

The brain and nervous systems are developing fast, along with skeletal development. By 6 years old the child can jump higher, hop easily and perform simple sequences of movements.

Cognitive

The child is not ready to engage in mental operations that require logical thinking. They tend to focus on one aspect of a situation and neglect others. By 3 years the toddler has grown out of the 'terrible twos' and behaviour has become more amenable, and is more able to understand how others may feel (empathy). By 4 years old the child will describe themselves in concrete observable behaviours and external characteristics.

Their thinking tends to be all or nothing and may be unrealistically optimistic, "I can balance on one leg and one day I am going to be a ballet dancer". They realise that events have causes but may jump from one thought to another and see causes where none exist, e.g. "I didn't point my foot well, therefore I am bad".

They can show some appreciation of the difference between the present and past, and of the need to defer satisfaction of wishes into the future. They can count and deal with quantities and follow simple commands – '8 skips and stop'. However, between the ages of 3 and 6 years they do not understand that two feelings can coexist.

Psycho-social

The child uses implicit memory in the dance class thus remembering movements without conscious awareness. They may be a little anxious at separation from the carer when starting dance classes. They will have acquired self-awareness, and may show self-evaluative emotions such as pride, shame and guilt, also a knowledge about society's accepted standards. They can evaluate their own thoughts, plans and desires. The child is probably ready to start more formal dance classes, and will learn by copying and trying movements out for themselves.

The securely attached child will have larger, more varied vocabulary and more positive interactions with peers. From 3-5 years securely attached children are more curious, competent, empathetic, resilient and self-confident than those who are insecurely attached.

Case Study 2

Children at this stage are not ready to learn movements that require detailed muscular co-ordination. I worked with a 6-year old gymnast who needed to learn intrinsic foot exercises. To start with she tried hard but soon became distressed when she was not able to do what I asked her.

- How could I have achieved what I wanted without upsetting her?
- What images or imagery could I have used to help her?

Middle childhood - 6 years to 11 years: The Concrete Operational Stage

Physical

At this stage girls are superior in movement accuracy to boys. The boys are superior to girls in forceful, less complex activities. One footed balancing without looking becomes possible and they can hop and jump accurately. Children are able to learn more steps and complex movement patterns. It seems that at this stage movement patterns become more established – thus it is important that the teacher of younger students establishes good movement patterns in every area of dance. The children at this age become taller and are able to engage abdominal muscles more accurately and so dance posture improves. Rough and tumble play is enjoyed, more than the social or symbolic play of earlier years. Improvements in strength and endurance help to build healthy bones and control weight.

Cognitive

At this stage children use mental operation to solve actual problems. They are able to think more logically because they are able to take multiple aspects of a situation into account. However, they do tend to think in the here and now, and may not be able to readily transfer what is learned to other situations. For example, in a ballet class a correction at the barre may need to be repeated in the centre.

The child begins to integrate specific features of the self and to articulate a sense of self-worth, eg "I'm good at dancing but I can't add up". A child with high self-esteem will work at something difficult and will try different ways to achieve the goal.

Psycho-social

A clearer idea of guilt and shame develop and the child acquires a more sophisticated understanding of simultaneous emotions. Children begin to understand the motivation for actions. Friends at a class will enhance the enjoyment of the dance class and they may start to look to the teacher as a role model. Pressure to engage in long hours of practice and emphasis on winning or passing exams may discourage participation in exercise. It may be better to encourage skill building rather than passing exams with good marks.

Giftedness and intelligence

Early talent may not lead to excellence in later life. A love of the pursuit, drive to excel, and hard work along with encouragement and guidance are more likely to nurture excellence.

Intelligence is intellectual skill or knowledge, mental brightness and information communication. Eight different types of intelligence have been suggested by Howard Gardner: linguistic, logical or mathematical, musical, bodily or kinaesthetic (dance), interpersonal and naturalist (see Chapter 1). High intelligence in one area is not necessarily accompanied by high intelligence in any other abilities.

Case Study 3

At this stage children become more able to engage in detailed motor action. Core stability exercises can be learnt and practised.

- What things could you use / suggest that would help to motivate a child to practise physical homework exercises?

The 11-year old: Preparation for Adulthood

Physical

The increasing physical strength and endurance, and the ability to complete more complex movements and steps make more intense training possible. The child is more able to apply verbal corrections. Basic movement patterns that are well established may be hard to correct later, therefore it is important to establish correct movement that can be built on, rather than complex movements which are performed badly and become ingrained. The jump height and stamina will be improving. Temperature regulation and sweating does not fully mature until after puberty. Children may forget to drink so need to be reminded to do so.

Cognitive

At this stage children are able to work out problems in their heads and apply corrections in different situations. They are still unable to consider the long term consequences of present actions, e.g. the consequences of dancing on an injury, causing it to become chronic. The child is able to describe conflicting feelings about the same event, "I am excited about dong the exam but nervous as well".

Psycho-social

Children are interacting and coming into contact with more people and a wider range of viewpoints. They are beginning to be capable of more formal reasoning, and the ability to take different aspects of a situation into account. They become able to use different strategies to remember things, such as mental rehearsal or categorising / association in order to remember sequences of steps. They are also becoming more aware of their own mental processes, and this helps the storage of knowledge and new information which can be checked against what they already know (learning a more complex version of a step that was learnt earlier for example).

Adolescence

Early adolescence is considered to be from 10-14 years, middle from 14-18 years and late adolescence from 18-21 years. These stages are the transition from childhood to adulthood, and are associated with periods of rapid growth, development of secondary sexual characteristics and a gradually increasing independence from the parental home.

Physical

Puberty sees changes in growth of height and weight, and changes in body proportions. Boys have higher levels of androgens, the principal one being testosterone, while girls have higher levels of oestrogen. Reaching a certain weight seems to trigger hormonal activity, which is why dancers may mature later than the average. There is about a seven year range for the onset of puberty both in girls and boys, which tends to begin earlier in girls and may take about four years to complete.

The physical changes that take place in both sexes include growth spurts, the development of pubic hair and muscular growth. Differences in the way the body matures between the sexes are: in females, the pelvis widens, fat is deposited on the hips, breast development; whilst in males, the shoulders become wider and the legs longer relative to the trunk, and there are changes in the way the face grows, with the voice becoming deeper. These changes can lead to temporary gawkiness and short sightedness. The maturation of the reproductive organs leads to the beginning of ovulation and menstruation in girls and the production of sperm in boys. Puberty tends to occur earlier than a century ago – possibly because of better nutrition and heavier body weights on average. Most boys and girls have reached their full height by 18 years old.

Improving physical fitness includes increasing muscular strength and endurance. This in turn helps improve bone density and also helps control weight, and decrease anxiety and stress. Physical fitness can also improve self-confidence. A sedentary lifestyle can lead to obesity, heart disease and cancer.

Whilst generally adolescents are healthy, they are often preoccupied by their health needs. Injuries can occur but are generally less in non-contact moderate activities such as dance. There are also injuries / pathologies associated with growth which are unique to adolescence.

Adolescents need about nine hours sleep and a lack of adequate rest may lead to poor school performance.

Cognitive development

Thinking becomes more flexible so that adolescents are able to consider things in terms of what *might* be and not just what *is*. They are able to understand other people's points of view and enjoy using irony, puns and metaphors. Adolescents have an extensive vocabulary and will debate issues using terms such as *however, otherwise, anyway, therefore,* and *probably*. At times they will indulge in teenage slang.

There are various theories regarding cognitive development. See Chapter 1 for further details. Piaget's theory is that adolescents enter a higher level of cognitive development which is known as 'formal operations' (Papalia, 2009, pp. 402-404). This allows abstract reasoning and sophisticated moral judgements and the ability to plan more realistically for the future. Piaget's theories are still accepted but are considered not to give enough weight to aspects of mature intelligence such as experience, intuition and wisdom.

Kohlberg's theory is of three levels of moral reasoning (Papalia, 2009, pp. 407-410). The last is the 'post-conventional morality' or morality of autonomous moral principles. This is when people are able to make individual judgements on the basis of rightness, fairness and justice and is usually reached sometime during adolescence.

In spite of increasing maturity, adolescents may still be strangely immature at times. They may be rude to adults, have difficulty in making up their minds and can be quite selfish.

Elkind (1984, 1986) suggested possible reasons for adolescent immaturity which are due to conflicts in the way young people think:

- Idealism and criticalness – the idea of a perfect world versus the real world.
- Argumentativeness – enjoying the chance to try out the new reasoning abilities.
- Indecisiveness – the ability to hold many alternatives in mind, but difficulty in choosing one.
- Apparent hypocrisy – expressing an ideal but not being prepared to make the necessary sacrifices to live up to it.
- Self-consciousness and imaginary audience – being aware of thinking and others thinking.
- Specialness and invulnerability – the feeling that they are special and that their experience is unique.

Different ethnic and cultural groups may value different aspects of maturity which can add to the confusion that adolescents may experience.

Psycho-social

Erikson (1950) described a period during which the adolescent is involved in the search for identity in order to become a coherent conception of the self, made up of goals, values, and beliefs to which the individual is solidly committed. Some sort of identity confusion is normal and may not be resolved until in the 20s.

Three major issues need to be considered: occupation, adoption of values to believe in and live by, and the development of satisfying sexual identity. This occurs when the young person makes choices regarding values, and people to be loyal to, rather than just accepting their parents' views (Erikson, in Papalia, 2009 pp. 425-428).

Identity formation is complicated for those in minority groups, and different groups struggle with different issues depending on culture and ethnicity. Generally, the adolescent will gain self-esteem with age. Relationships with siblings and parents will alter as the adolescents spend more time with peers and less time within the family. Even so the family tends to remain a secure base. Peer groups are a source of affection, sympathy, understanding and moral guidance – a safe place to share opinions, admit weaknesses and get help with problems. Amongst girls confidences and emotional support seem more important, whilst boys share activities such as sports or creative interests. Generally boys prefer competing with friends, whilst girls prefer helping each other.

Rebellion and risk taking behaviours, although more common at this stage, are not as prevalent as expected.

Some adolescents are able to cope with multiple outside school tasks and still achieve at school. However whilst a job outside school can be a positive, more than 15 hours of work a week seems to become a negative.

Case Study 4

When preparing a dance workshop for a group of adolescents (14-15 years old) what should be considered in order to get the best from them, and for them to feel that the class was worthwhile?

REFLECTION

1. Consider Elkind's list. How might you assist adolescent dancers in your sessions or deal with issues that might arise?

2. Select one age range for further study in respect of physical and cognitive development. Try to identify three new pieces of information that you did not previously know about this age of child or young person. Consider how this new understanding might assist in planning and delivery of dance sessions.

Bibliography

Elkind, D. 1984 *All grown up and no place to go.* Reading, MA: Addison-Wesley.

Elkind, D. 1986 *The miseducation of children: Superkids at Risk.* New York: Knopf.

Erikson, E. H. 1950 *Childhood and Society.* New York: Norton.

Luckstead, E. 1992 *Medical Care of the Adolescent Athlete.* USA: Practice Management Information Corporation.

Papalia, D. Wendokos Olds, S. and Duskin Feldman, R. 2009 *Human Development.* [9th edition] New York: McGraw-Hill.

Chapter 15

Dance Training (part 2): Training Principles, Hydration, Nutrition

Lorna Sanders

Introduction

The information in this chapter builds on the preceding one. An overview of training principles, hydration and nutrition is provided so that further research can be more confidently undertaken.

Training Principles

Muscle cells are fast twitch (used for anaerobic and short bursts of maximal output) or slow twitch (used for aerobic, endurance, sub maximal output). To understand training principles there is a need to explore the energy production systems.

Anaerobic System

Literally, this means without air. Each muscle cell has stored a small amount of fuel ready to be broken down to produce the energy for contraction. Muscle cells are unique in the body in that they will tolerate temporary deprivation of oxygen. Anaerobic chemical reaction occurs without oxygen and produces lactic acid as a result. This type of energy cannot be sustained for long. Frequent rest is required because the oxygen, in effect, is in deficit. It needs to be paid back to the muscles and if lactic acid builds up there will also be a temporary failure to contract. The anaerobic system provides a quick supply of energy: for example, it is important at the start of any action or for short duration bursts of strenuous activity and / or maximal output of muscle strength.

Aerobic System

This provides a more enduring supply of energy to sustain longer steady bursts of less than maximal outputs. Fuel is broken down in the presence of oxygen. The cardio-vascular system keeps up with the muscle cell's demands for oxygen and waste product removal, although if continued for very lengthy periods lactic acid will still build up in the muscle. Oxygen processing is increased in the body. Breathing becomes deeper and more efficient and the heart pumps more deeply with each stroke. The metabolic rate increases and will eventually burn stored fat in order to keep fuelling the energy production.

As with all forms of fitness, 'improvement in cardiovascular fitness is related to the manipulation of [...] frequency, duration, intensity' (Kirkendall and Calabrese, 1983, p. 536). The following descriptions make reference to Clippinger (1988), unless otherwise stated.

Training Principles

Frequency: This is perhaps the easier point to understand, since it refers to the amount of exercise or training that occurs. It could be as simple as more classes. For example, once a week attendance at dance class becomes twice a week and gradually increases in number.

Duration: This would increase the amount of time involved. For example, an hour might be extended by half an hour; a six week course may be extended to ten weeks.

Intensity: This would increase the difficulty in various ways. There are several strategies to employ here. See Case Study 1.

Case Study 1	**Increase the intensity by:**
Increase the amount of resistance	For example: working against gravity; work against body weight by holding for longer.
Increase the distance the load / weight is moved	For example: work with longer levers (straight legs as opposed to flexed); jump higher.
Decrease the rest intervals	For example: reduce the time to move to the alternate side; reduce the time spent in intervening exercises.
Increase the number of repetitions	For example: repeat the exercise itself; repeat a component within an exercise; increase the number of repeats before a rest interval or intervening exercise is taken.
Decrease the amount of time taken for movement to be performed	For example: increase speed and / or power of the exercise.
Apply the strategies to an action of your choice in order to progress the training intensity. For example; taking a simple bent leg raise as the basis – lifting the leg higher and more slowly (adds resistance); lift it straight not flexed (load is moved further away from body); go straight into the lateral repeat (decrease rest) and immediately into a brief arm combination before repeating leg exercise again twice through (brief rest and then increase repeats); perform at double time (decrease amount of time taken).	

Overload and specificity which target the muscle groups concerned are needed to develop progression / improvement in fitness, strength and flexibility. Stretching is covered in Chapter 16 so strength is the focus of discussion here.

Increasing the intensity to approximately 50% overload is considered to build endurance, of which strength is a component. For strength training of a specific muscle group, high intensity overload begins gradually with fewer repetitions but at close to the maximum capacity. Rest is then needed and this can be undertaken by working a different muscle group and then performing another set of increased repetitions on the original muscles. Rest avoids overuse injury and allows lactic acid removal, thus preventing early fatigue and improving motor memory by allowing movement patterns to become embedded. Rest can also involve the variation of subsequent exercise routines. Overly repeated class structures, offering exactly the same exercises to perform day after day, along with poor hip / knee / ankle alignment, have been linked with shin splints (Lawson, 1991).

It is important to develop balanced strength in all muscles, hence it is necessary to work not only the prime movers but also the antagonists and the associated synergists which stabilise the part being moved (see Chapter 14). In order to maintain flexibility in the muscles undergoing strength training, it is also necessary to mobilise and exercise the joint through its full range of motion.

In terms of intensity in aerobic fitness, it is necessary to raise the pulse until it reaches the training zone and to continue keeping it there for a minimum of twenty minutes. The 'training zone heart rate should exceed the sum of the resting heart rate and 60% of the difference between resting and maximal heart rates, age-related maxima being estimated as 220 less the age in years' (Koutedakis and Sharp, 1999, p. 160). This somewhat complex sounding formula is simplified below:

Case Study 2

To work out what your training zone is you will need to work out your Maximum Heart Rate (MHR is 220 minus your age) and your Resting Heart Rate (RHR needs your pulse to be taken when you are calm and inactive). For example a 40 year old will have a MHR of 220 – 40 = 180. And they might have a RHR of 60 beats per minute.

To work out their training zone:

Deduct the MHR from the RHR	180 - 60 = 120 beats
Calculate 60% of 120 e.g. using a calculator:	120 x 0.6 = 72
Add the RHR to 72	72 + 60 = 132 beats per minute

You would need to work continuously for 20 minutes with a pulse of around 132 beats to increase your endurance fitness.

- Work out your training zone. Then experiment with some simple pulse raising activity for 20 minutes (see Chapter 16); take your RHR before you start; take your pulse at intermittent points to check whether it is in the training zone and again at the end.

Bear in mind: heat can cause a higher RHR; children will have a higher RHR; and young people do not always perceive steady and prolonged activity as aerobic, so you need to be cautious about the challenge offered to them and ensure good hydration.

When considering how to apply the training principles of frequency, duration and intensity in order to overload selected muscle groups, it is necessary to take care of the individual needs of participants and to understand the anatomical and physiological structures of children and young people. Chapter 14 introduced these and Bramley (2002) includes useful summary charts. Koutedakis and Sharp (1999) is also an excellent source of information on child development and their specific needs. It is not possible in a chapter of this length to give all the information that you might require so further research is strongly recommended. See the end of Chapter 16 for details of a Level 5 qualification in Safe and Effective Practice.

Figure 1 below summarises some general principles and points to bear in mind in respect of the individuality of approach that is needed to training.

General Principles for Dance Training

Be aware of individual differences in adolescence, maturation and gender	Look at the biological stage reached not the chronological age; note key differences between boys and girls in terms of growth rate, body structure, physical capability and the different training responses required for strength and flexibility, and anaerobic / aerobic capacity at different stages.
Progress should be gradual	Need for basic skills and fitness first; avoid large amounts of training / rehearsals before late adolescence; avoid sudden increases in work load.
Children and pre-adolescents need specific care	Basic skills are the focus and can be augmented with short sessions of specific fitness training in strength and endurance.
Never interfere with normal growth rate	Avoid any focus on weight issues (puppy fat is part of the growth process)
Growth spurt causes muscle tightening	Mainly affects hamstrings and calf muscles. Gentle stretching maintains flexibility during the growth

Figure 1: Adapted from Koutedakis and Sharp (1999, p. 287)

Hydration and Nutrition

An adult body uses on average about 1,500 calories a day to support basic physiological functions alone, such as maintaining body heat and the slight contraction that all healthy muscle retains throughout life (muscle tone). We all have different requirements depending on our muscle mass, genetic make up, health, age and gender. An active adult needs around 3000 calories. See Mastin (2009) for a formula to work out the specific and detailed requirements for a dancer.

Carbohydrates – sugar, vegetables, cereals, fruits

This should be around 60% of total food consumption. It is the most efficient fuel because excess is stored as glycogen (this is metabolised into glucose, released into the blood as blood sugar and burned during exercise). If not enough glycogen is stored in the muscles and the liver, we feel tired, have headaches, low blood sugar levels and poor repair of tissue. Diets low in calories can also be low in nutrition so the need for a slender dancer can be problematic if they are also training hard and undergoing growth spurts.

The available stores of glycogen in the body last for only 90 minutes of strenuous activity and need to be replaced quickly (Koutedakis and Sharp, 1999). The body uses fat to fuel low intensity exercise, sparing carbohydrates for higher intensity activity and endurance. It is important to avoid triggering high insulin production which causes carbohydrate to be used quickly (encouraged by eating foods such as chocolate / sweets): this is the sugar rush experienced when high blood sugar levels peak. When these are then reduced rapidly by insulin, this can leave you feeling tired and depleted. Eating complex carbohydrate a minimum of two hours before class is effective so that the stomach has the chance to digest it.

Fats – in meat, fish, eggs, dairy, beans, certain vegetables (eg soya, olives, avocado)

It is recommended that fats are approximately 30-35% of the total daily food intake. They also bring with them fat soluble vitamins and essential fatty acids needed for overall health. They are useful for fuelling continuous low intensity exercise and for making us feel full so that we do not overeat. Too much causes weight gain however.

Protein – meat, fish, dairy, beans

Protein is made of amino acids and there are many different types. It is so essential, the body is able to manufacture all but eight of these acids from other sources. Protein should form around 12% of an adult's diet and more in growing children. It is needed for muscle and tissue development / repair; excess is excreted by the kidneys or stored as body fat.

Vitamins and Minerals – in most foods and particularly vegetables

Vitamins are needed for metabolic functioning and dancers do not need much more in quantity than others. Although some like to take supplements, it is considered to be better if they come from a balanced diet which consumes each of the four food groups: dairy, meat, vegetables / fruit, bread / cereals.

Minerals are needed for bones and for producing enzymes and hormones in the body. Bones are living tissue and they store calcium, phosphorus and other minerals. Bone is continually being deposited and reabsorbed throughout life so ongoing supplies of minerals are needed. Poor diet and conditions such as anorexia can result in brittle bones. Vitamin D is needed for calcium absorption. Bone will also be deposited where stress is felt, hence bunion and bursa formations in the feet of dancers (Vincent, 1980). An adult needs around 800 mg of calcium and 1200 for teenagers, and similar amounts in phosphorus. Iron supports haemoglobin production for red blood cells and is thus essential for energy production – anaemia (low haemoglobin levels in the blood) results in fatigue.

Water

Hydration is important: muscles are approximately 72-75% water and dehydration limits endurance. All physiological processes are dependent on water; it flushes the waste products away from the kidneys, is key to sweat production and thermal regulation of the body, and supports blood volume for example. Thirst is the body's way of indicating that you are *already* dehydrated. Koutedakis and Sharp (1999) recommend that 300 mls of water are drunk about 30 minutes prior to exercise to give the body time to absorb it. Then a top-up of 150-250 mls is needed at regular 10-minute intervals during class.

If the day is hot and / or you are sweating this soon results in loss of blood volume and has a resultant deleterious effect on the regulation of body temperature. Men sweat more so they can suffer dehydration more quickly and fit people sweat sooner too because the aerobic system is more efficient. Children sweat less than adults and their body shape means they heat up more quickly, hence they need to drink regularly. When dehydration sets in the heart beats faster as the body tries to regulate temperature by sending more blood to the surface where heat can be radiated away. This puts an increased stress on the heart which may already be working hard. Water should also be taken after class to avoid muscle cramp, fatigue, exhaustion, and injury through dehydration.

Summary

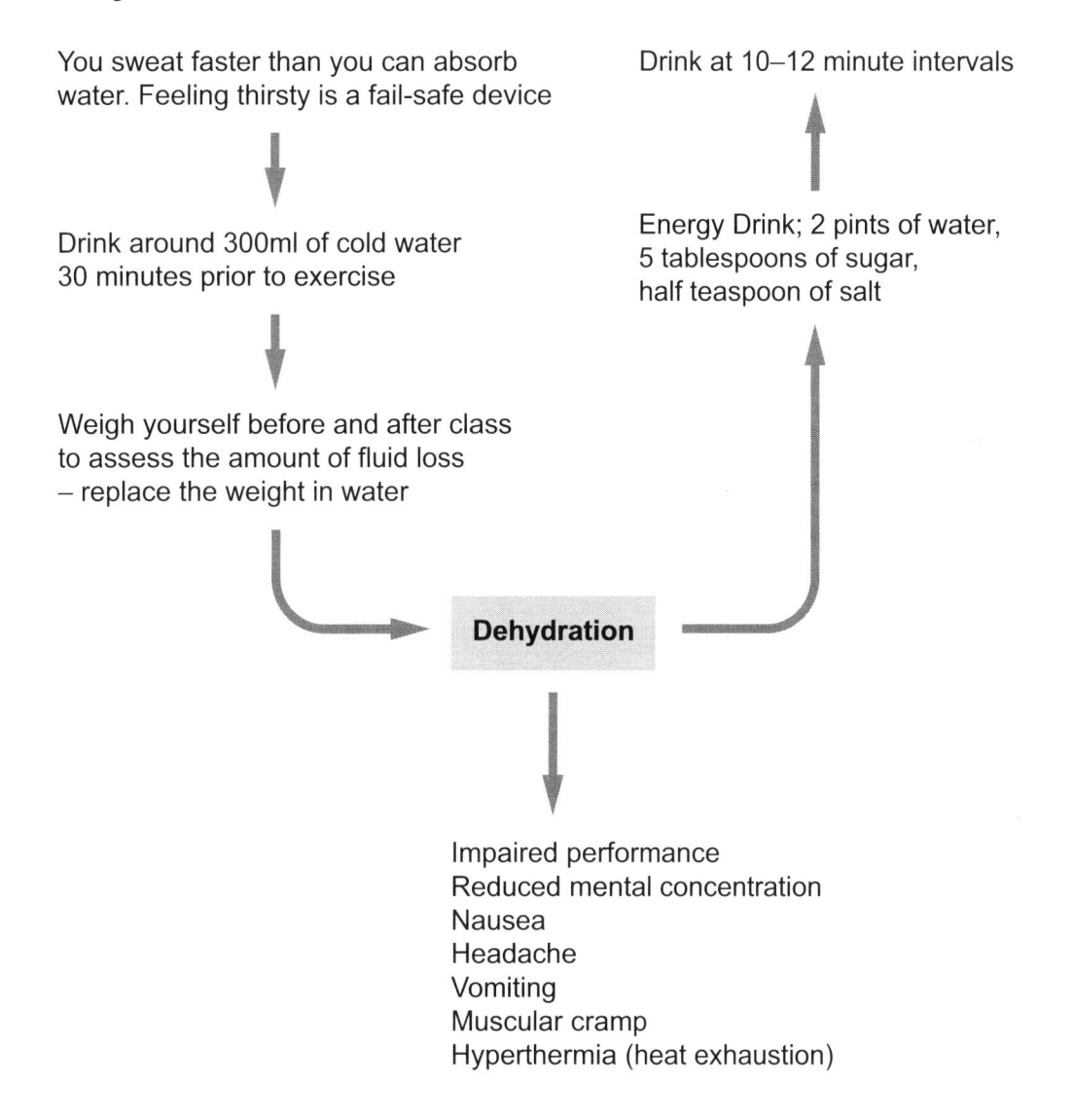

You sweat faster than you can absorb water. Feeling thirsty is a fail-safe device

↓

Drink around 300ml of cold water 30 minutes prior to exercise

↓

Weigh yourself before and after class to assess the amount of fluid loss – replace the weight in water

→ **Dehydration** ←

Drink at 10–12 minute intervals

↑

Energy Drink; 2 pints of water, 5 tablespoons of sugar, half teaspoon of salt

↑

↓

Impaired performance
Reduced mental concentration
Nausea
Headache
Vomiting
Muscular cramp
Hyperthermia (heat exhaustion)

Case Study 3

The **Food Standards Agency** has published a colourful and informative illustration of the balance needed in different food groups – The Eatwell Plate can be downloaded from: www.food.gov.uk/multimedia/pdfs/eatwellplatelarge/pdf

- Ask participants to consider their diet for one week.

For details of nutrition and diet, further research should be undertaken in Mastin (2009).

Unit 2 - Professional Knowledge of Dance Teaching

REFLECTION

1. It was stated that balanced strength in all muscles is needed. Select one muscle group to work on. Identify the prime mover(s) and the antagonist(s) and the associated synergists which stabilise the part being moved. What exercise might you do to strengthen the prime mover first and then work on the antagonist? What would you do to strengthen the synergists? Useful resources: Blakey (2000) and Calais-Germain (1993).

2. How do you advise your participants to avoid the sugar rush? What foods should you avoid one hour prior to class? What food might make a suitable small snack?

3. Eating complex carbohydrate a minimum of two hours before class is recommended. What foods are complex carbohydrates?

4. For a one-hour class how much water would you recommend your participants to bring with them to drink?

5. A participant who is normally highly engaged and motivated lacks energy during class. Evaluate how many different reasons there might be that might have caused this.

Bibliography

Blakey, P. 2000 *The Muscle Book* Stafford: Bibliotek.

Bramley 1. 2002 *Dance Teaching Essentials*. London: Dance UK.

Calais-Germain, B. 1993 *Dance Anatomy and Kinesiology* Seattle: Eastland Press.

Clippinger, K. 1988 Chapter 5: Principles of Dance Training. In Clarkson, P. and Skrinar, M. *Science of Dance Training*. Champaign, Illinois: Human Kinetics, pp. 45-90.

Kirkendall, D. and Calabrese, L. 1983 Physiological Aspects of Dance. In Sammarco, J. (ed) *Clinics in Sports Medicine: injuries to dancers*. 2, 3, November, Philadelphia: W.B Saunders, pp. 525-537.

Koutedakis, Y. and Sharp, C. 1999 *The Fit and Healthy Dancer*. Chichester: Wiley and Sons.

Lawson, J. 1991 The Shin Splints Epidemic. *The Dancing Times*, November, p. 137.

Mastin, Z. 2009 *Nutrition for the Dancer*. Alton: Dance Books.

McCormack, M. 1990 Dance Study Supplement 5: A Level Anatomy. *The Dancing Times*, February, pp. *i-viii* (available to purchase from www.dancing-times.co.uk)

Vincent, L.M. 1980 *The Dancer's Book of Health*. London: Dance Books.

Chapter 16
Dance Training (part 3): Safe Practice
Lorna Sanders

Introduction

Safe practice covers a large area. What is offered in this chapter is an introduction to the issues. It is recommended that further study of the sources in the bibliography is undertaken. Legal requirements (health and safety, safeguarding, for example) overlap with safe practice but are not addressed. Chapter 18 is devoted to those issues.

Safe Studio Environment: Physical Space

Of significant importance is the suitability of the floor. Foley (undated) gives separate consideration to the surface and its underlying structures. The dance style and the type of footwear may require different surface finishes or treatments for the amount of grip needed. For bare feet, a smooth surface is needed but some floor coverings, advertised as non slip, are slightly roughened and would be uncomfortable (Dance UK, undated).

The underlying floor structure tends to be safer if it has some *give* in it, usually referred to as sprung. Foley identifies two types: *point elastic*, in which the immediate floor area under the supporting leg cushions the impact; and *area elastic*, in which a wider area spreads the force. By these means the dancer's weight is dispersed into and through the floor during weight transference, otherwise further pressure is loaded onto tendons, ligaments, joints and bones. Although the body is built for shock absorption under normal conditions (for example spinal curves provide a natural springing), in repetitive dance training a floor with an unyielding substructure of concrete can increase the physical stress. Exacerbated by any technical deficiency or lack of strength in the body, working on this type of surface increases fatigue during a lesson and can lead to a range of injuries, such as shin splints and bursas.

Chapter 18 outlines the legal framework for risk assessment of the studio / venue. If you are employed by an organisation they will have a Health and Safety Policy and Risk Assessment procedures. The following checklist for identifying the suitability of the dancing space is adapted from Bramley (2002) and Siddall (2010). It is provided to get you thinking about the spaces you work in and some of the hazards that are typically met with. It is also necessary to apply common sense and attend to the more specific needs of the group and the dance style.

> **Case Study 1**
>
> - **Warm:** 21°C minimum but warmer, around 24°, is better.
> - **Well ventilated:** not stuffy or draughty; safe window height.
> - **Well lit**
> - **Sprung floor:** or wooden with some give, not too unyielding.
> - **Clean, non slippery surface:** not highly polished, wet, dirty, buckled / ridged / bumpy.
> - **No obstacles:** for example, electric cables; pillars; placing of wall mounted heaters /air conditioners; unsafely stored furniture and equipment / dance kit / bags / water bottles; type and placement of mirrors; hazard from inward opening doors.
> - **Ceiling with sufficient height for the activity:** 4.5m high is recommended; issue of low hanging lights or cables.
> - **Fire exits:** unrestricted, accessible and clearly marked; fire extinguishers accessible and safely stowed.
> - **Safety-checked electrical equipment:** electrical sockets covered if necessary.
> - **Sufficient space:** venue may have regulations covering numbers in the space but evaluate this further in terms of appropriateness for dance style, purpose and group. Minimum dimension is 10m wide and 14m long. Provide approximately 3 square metres of space for each primary school age participant; and 5 square metres for ages 11 and upwards.
> - **First aid equipment:** in the space? Accessible nearby? Telephone?

Take each of the bullet points in Case Study 1 and consider how you could work around the difficulties that might be presented to minimise potential dangers. For example: if the room is cold, participants could keep extra layers of safe clothing on; you could adapt the warm up to make the pulse raising section longer; you could avoid exercises that involve sitting or lying on the floor; you could minimise pauses in the activity and re-warm briefly from time to time if the activity level has dropped for any reason; and if the room is stuffy you might use attention-promoting strategies such as shortening tasks and changing them frequently, encouraging the drinking of water, and giving less detailed information to avoid tiring cognitive processing abilities.

Safety is always your responsibility and if an aspect of the space is completely unsafe in the circumstances the lesson should not continue, but we often work in less than ideal circumstances. Bramley (2002) states: 'the space should be appropriate for dance. Where this is not possible, then the dance activity must be appropriate to the space' (p. 35).

Safe Studio Environment: Psychological / Emotional Needs

Emotional well being is significant to the sense of safety that participants feel. In Chapter 1, Maslow's Hierarchy of Needs indicated the importance of this aspect. While abuse is clearly illegal, language and feedback need to be positive to avoid carrying detrimental implications.

Of particular sensitivity in the dance class is body image and the importance placed on this for developing good self-esteem:

> young people, by definition do not have a fully developed sense of self...at that stage of life, identity is strongly invested in the body and the developing sense of mastery of it. For teenage girls particularly, the sense of self is near identical to their sense of their bodies and physical selves. Physical training for young people, therefore, has the potential either to enhance and develop their confidence and self-esteem, or to undermine and damage it.
>
> (Buckroyd, 2000, pp. 2-3)

A study by Barr (2009) confirms this impact: "the importance [...] to those students could not be ignored. Feedback was closely linked to their feelings about the classroom environment and [...] the teacher's construction and delivery of feedback correlated to their sense of self" (p. 41). In other words, not only were attitudes to learning affected, but emotionally unsafe environments resulted in negative feelings related to self worth.

The following checklist gives suggestions for providing an optimum emotional environment (adapted from Bramley (2002) and Buckroyd (2000).

Case Study 2

- Use of positive forms of speech and imagery.
- Recognise achievement *and* effort.
- Provide specifically focused and particular feedback.
- Develop an attitude of trust: avoid highlighting inadequacies, use problem solving approaches.
- Project a calm, good-tempered teacher presence which is tolerant of physical errors and compassionate.
- Give structure which focuses the work and provide goals that are shared with the class.
- Facilitate two-way communication and develop an interactive style between teacher and student, and between students (e.g. allow them to share ideas, contribute to goal planning, be involved in decision-making, agree rules for classroom conduct).
- Be aware of and manage the feelings of the participants.
- Be fair and consistent; discourage pecking orders from developing.

Consider each of these bullet points in terms of how you establish good working relationships with participants and how you "encourage a positive, supportive and mutually respectful working atmosphere" (Bramley, 2002, p. 35).

Safe Studio Environment: Physiological Needs

Warm up

It might be assumed that the dance activity itself would be adequate to the purpose but unless it is specifically designed to meet the need, this is not the case. Warm up prepares the body 'enabling you to safely and effectively carry out the very first dance movements' (Laws *et al*, undated). While a reduced risk of injury is a significant reason for warming up, there are several important physiological changes that occur. Increases in the cardio-vascular rate (breathing and pulse rate) result in an increased blood supply to the muscles which brings additional nutrients and heat. Hormones released into the blood dilate the artery walls to allow a greater volume of blood to flow and this is diverted away from the digestive organs towards the working muscles. Oxygen in the blood increases and is also exchanged for carbon dioxide more readily.

Warm up kick starts the energy production cycle. The increase in core temperature speeds up chemical reactions and metabolism to generate energy more rapidly. Increased heat is also needed in the working muscle itself and 'the only efficient way to reach this temperature in the muscle is by working it' (Trotter, 1990, p. 1). Heat produces smoother, faster muscle contractions and 'for each degree of temperature increase, the speed of metabolism in the muscle cell accelerates by about 13% (Koutedakis and Sharp, 1999, pp. 164-5). This also avoids early fatigue since the removal of waste products, such as lactic acid and carbon dioxide, is enhanced by the increased blood flow.

Activity results in an increase in the amount and viscosity of the synovial fluid within the joint capsule, which bathes the cartilage and provides improved shock absorbing qualities, protecting the bones from impact. Heat also results in softer, more pliable muscle tissue which can be stretched more safely. There is some disagreement about the type of stretching that is most effective but all agree that this is not about flexibility training. Rist (1991) recommends gentle, steady stretching and not ballistic bouncing in warm up. Some favour dynamic stretching, often termed mobilising the joints, in which slower, controlled, continuous movements of the joint take the associated muscles through their normal full range, for example lighter intensity swings and lunges (Laws *et al*, undated). Others suggest gentle static stretching, held (no more than 10 seconds) in a comfortable position (Van Gyn, 1986 and Marsh, 1990). This pre-stretches the muscle and diminishes the stretch reflex (the process by which muscle fibres resist a sudden strong stretch when cold), allowing a bigger range of movement to be undertaken later.

Nerve impulses travel faster in warm tissue and co-ordination is thereby enhanced. Stimulating the energy pathways also awakens the neurological responses and enhances the proprioceptive sense, attuning us to the feeling in our bodies and preparing alert, focused responses.

Typically, a warm up might last around twenty minutes and is important for asthmatic dancers. However, the optimal length depends on fitness, age, type of dance activity and length of class. Material should gradually progress in intensity 'from simple to complex, easy to difficult and from large to small muscle groups' (Koutedakis and Sharp, 1999, p. 167).

The following stages in warm up are adapted from Koutedakis and Sharp (1999):

- **STAGE 1 (5 minutes)**
    pulse raising activity

- **STAGE 2 (10 minutes)**
    general mobilising of all major joints and light intensity stretching with continued pulse raising. Blakey (1994) gives a preferred order for stretching:
    1. upper and lower back
    2. both sides
    3. arms before stretching the chest
    4. buttocks before the groin
    5. calves before hamstring
    6. shins before the quadriceps

- **STAGE 3 (5 minutes)**

    mobilising further the more specific muscles and movement patterns required for the class and the dance style.

Case Study 3

- How long do you spend on warming up your participants?
- What activity or exercises do you include in your warm ups?
- Consider if the activity progresses through the stages. Pulse raising could be as simple as walking into jogging. Mobilising could be stretching / curling of the spine; lunges; knee bends; rhythmical swinging; isolations such as circling of joints; followed by stretching.

Warm up can also provide opportunity for teaching class rituals, discipline, and developing generic skills such as use of space.

To achieve the benefits of warm up summarised below (adapted from Koutedakis and Sharp, 1999; and Trotter, 1990), you need to raise the core temperature by 2 degrees.

Summary of Physiological Benefits

Reduced muscle viscosity (more pliable) and pre-stretched	Improved joint mobility and less likelihood of injury
Increased rate of chemical reaction in the muscle and increased speed of nerve impulses	Muscle contraction optimised; neuromuscular co-ordination improves
Increased anaerobic outputs; also improved ability of blood to carry oxygen; more oxygen extracted from lungs with each breath	Sustain higher performance levels; less quickly fatigued
Increased volume and viscosity of synovial fluid in joint capsule	Improved shock absorption capacity
Increased ability to deal with lactic acid removal and other waste products of metabolism; fuel / nutrients provided.	Less quickly fatigued; muscle contraction optimised (lactic acid build up would eventually prevent contraction)

Summary of Psychological Benefits

Reaction time for visual and auditory stimuli improves	More alert to new physical information, more co-ordinated
Improved self discipline and motivation	Prepared mentally for challenge; brings attention to the dance activity
Improved mental preparation, concentration and focus	More alert to instruction
Decreased emotional stress and anxiety	More relaxed and able to learn or to focus on performance

Mind-body connections and references are improved	Enhanced proprioceptive feedback; aware of posture and any unnecessary tension

Cool Down

At the end of the lesson, it is important to assist the participants to recover to a state of rest and attain physiological balance. Cool down should 're-mobilise the joints, gradually bring down the heart rate and stretch muscles that have been used in the preceding activity' (Laws *et al*, undated).

There is a need to promote *active recovery*. The cardiovascular system needs a gradual return to normal while good circulation continues, because any sudden stopping of activity can lead to the pooling of blood in the legs. The venous return of blood to the heart is assisted by muscular pressure on the veins in the legs (arteries contain valves which aid the onward flow but veins do not) and if not enough blood returns to be pumped on around to the head it can cause dizziness and even fainting. Light stretches can also continue the effect of the muscle action for this purpose.

The assisted venous return of the blood helps circulation and also assists the removal of waste products, such as lactic acid, thus minimising cramp and post exercise muscle soreness. (Delayed onset muscular soreness can be caused by a range of issues, including the continued presence of lactic acid and micro tears in the connective tissue which covers the muscle spindles). Mobilising and stretching also allow muscles to recover faster after exercise because it encourages the transport of amino acids to the muscle cells to aid repair. The hormone, noradrenaline, which is produced during exercise is also removed by the continued circulation. If this remains in raised amounts it can cause an irregular heart beat after exercise (Koutedakis and Sharp, 1999).

A sudden cessation of activity can also overload the body's temperature regulation system in hot conditions; as blood is pumped around the surface of the skin it cools down and circulation needs to be sustained for this to be effective. At what point you might put on extra layers of clothing needs consideration. Eventually, by progressively slowing down the activity, the breathing rate diminishes, the heart slows down and blood flow is gradually rebalanced in its distribution between the working muscles and the organs of the body.

It is recommended that cool down lasts as long as warm up if possible, but should be no shorter than five to ten minutes depending on the intensity of the dance class just experienced. Cool down should be structured in reverse order to the warm up. The joints and muscles focused on in class need to be re-mobilised. Stretches can be held for 60 seconds and the range of movement can be increased for flexibility gains as the muscles are warm. At this point either static or PNF stretching is suitable (proprioceptive neuromuscular facilitation). PNF relaxes the elongated muscle group first so as to bypass the stretch reflex and progress the muscle to a longer position (Marsh, 1990).

The pulse then needs to be further reduced by progressively slowing it and some recommend that cool down ends with lighter stretches to return the working muscles to their resting length (Van Gyn, 1986). It is also thought that cool down of this type assists the connective tissue and muscles to maintain any flexibility gains (Koutedakis and Sharp, 1999). The final consideration would be to breathe, refocus and relax to retain emotional balance. This psychological benefit can be important if the participant has judged their work as poor during class. Cool down also provides opportunity for analysis and calm appraisal of performance as well as reinforcement of what has been learned.

> **Case Study 4**
> - How long do you spend on cooling down your participants?
> - What activity or exercises do you include?
> - How are these related to the cool down stages indicated above?

Safe Practice: dance injuries and treatment

Ryan and Stephens (1988) identify the following as contributing to injury:
- Inadequate warm up
- Ineffective training techniques
- Poor pre season conditioning
- Rehearsal and performance schedules
- Improper teaching of technique
- Developmental muscular imbalance
- Starting dance training too late

Apart from the final point, the practitioner can do a great deal in terms of prevention. Bramley and Parker (2005) find that professional dancers perceived fatigue and overwork as the most common cause of injury, indicating that early training in how to alleviate these might assist.

Risk factors in causing overuse injuries to add to the above list include: abrupt changes in intensity, duration or frequency of training; improperly fitting shoes that give inadequate support or are not made of sufficient impact-absorbing material for the dance style; inappropriate floor surfaces; and poor alignment of pelvis and spine, in particular excessive pelvic tilt (flexion and extension of the lumbar spine), in other words the bottom tucked under or sticking out with a hollow back (Lyle, in Sammarco, 1983, pp. 474-475). Posture and technique thus play a significant role.

It is not possible to outline the many injuries that might occur during a dance lesson. See Koutedakis and Sharp (1999); Arnhiem (1991); Howse and McCormack (2009), Knight (2011) for example. For advice on first aid, see the commonly listed PRICE sequence for treating immediate injury, as in Sefcovic and Critchfield (2010) for example. There is a free, short film (*How to Prevent Injury in Dance*) produced by Dancetothis.com, available from YouTube and www.yde.org.uk

If safe practice and exercise physiology are areas with which you are unfamiliar it would be beneficial for you to undertake study of the *Certificate in Safe and Effective Practice*, a Level 5 qualification offered by Trinity College London in partnership with the International Association of Dance Medicine and Science (IADMS). Contact dance@trinitycollege.co.uk for further information.

The following resources offer useful ways of keeping up to date with the latest thinking in the area:
- IADMS website (www.iadms.org) produces a regular free to download *Bulletin for Teachers* (back copies are available too)
- Trinity Laban Conservatoire of Music and Dance's Dance Medicine and Science department (at www.trinitylaban.ac.uk), offer research reports free to download - Connolly, MK. *et al*, 2010 *Dance 4 your life research report*; Blazy L, and Amstell S. 2010 *NRG2 Youth Dance and Health Research Report*; and The *CAT Research Project Report* jointly funded

by Department of Education and Leverhulme Trust (a three-year longitudinal dance science project at Trinity Laban, examining the processes of developing talent in dancers aged 10-18 years).

REFLECTION

1. Consider the summary of Psychological Benefits of Warm Up. Do you notice the impact of this at the start of sessions? Read the benefits of cool down and make your own chart (use the summary of benefits of warm up as a model).

2. Research different types of stretching: dynamic, static, PNF, ballistic (see for example Laws *et al*, undated; and Blakey, 1994). Consider what types of stretching might be effective for your uses.

3. When did you last experience an injury in a dance lesson (either yourself or one of your participants)? Consider why this was. Did any of the bullet points in the final section of the chapter indicate areas that might be of concern?

Bibliography

Arnhiem, D. 1991 *Dance Injuries: their prevention and care*. [3rd edition] Princeton: Dance Horizons.

Barr, S 2009 Examining the technique class: re-examining feedback. *Research in Dance Education*, 10, 1, March, pp.33-44.

Blakey, P. 1994 *Stretching without Pain*. Stafford: Bibliotek for Twin Eagles

Bramley, I. (ed) 2002 *Dance Teaching Essentials*. London: Dance UK.

Bramley, I, and Parker, D. (eds) 2005 *Fit to Dance* (2). London: Dance UK.

Buckroyd, J. 2000 *The Student Dancer*. London: Dance Books.

Clarkson, P. M. and Skrinar, M.(eds) 1998 *Science of Dance Training*. Champaign, Illinois: Human Kinetics.

Dance UK undated *Improving Dance Floors*. webpage available at: http://www.danceuk.org/healthier-dancer-programme

Foley, M. undated *The Importance of Floors*, Information Sheet, number 6. Dance UK.

Howse, J and McCormack, M. 2009 *Anatomy, Dance Technique and Injury Prevention*. [4th edition] London: Methuen Drama.

Kimmerle, M. and Côté-Laurence, P. 2003 *Teaching Dance Skills: A Motor Learning and Development Approach*. USA: J. Michael Ryan.

Knight, I. 2011 *A Guide to Living with Hypermobility Syndrome*. Singing Dragon Books.

Koutedakis, Y. and Sharp, C. 1999 *The Fit and Healthy Dancer*. Chichester: Wiley and Sons.

Laws, H. Marsh, C. and Wyon, M. undated *Warming Up and Cooling Down*. Information Sheet 3, Dance UK.

Marsh, C. 1990 Gentle Stretching for Gentle Bones. *Dancing Times*, January, pp.358-359.

McCormack, M. 2010 *Teaching the Hypermobile Dancer*. IADMS Bulletin for Teachers, 2, 1, pp. 5-8. http://www.iadms.org/displaycommon.cfm?an=1&subarticlenbr=186

Rist, R. 1991 Dance Science (part 1). *Dancing Times*, December, p. 243.

Ryan, A. J. and Stephens, R. 1988 *The Dancer's Complete Guide to Health Care and a Long Career.* Chicago: Bonus Books.

Sammarco, J. (ed) 1983 *Clinics in Sports Medicine: injuries to dancers.* 2, 3, November, Philadelphia: W.B Saunders.

Sefcovic, N and Critchfield, B. 2010 First Aid for Dancers. *International Association of Dance Medicine and Science*, Resource Paper, www.iadms.org

Siddall, J. 2010 *Dance In and Beyond Schools.* London: Youth Dance England.

Siddall, J. 2010 *Dance Spaces*, Resource, www.yde.org.uk

Trotter, H. 1990 *Safe Dance Project.* Jamison: Australian Association for Dance Education.

Van Gyn, G, H. Contemporary stretching Techniques. In Shell, C. 1986 (ed) *The Dancer as Athlete.* Champaign: Illinois, pp. 109-116.

Chapter 17
The Legislative Framework (Part 1)
Jeanette Siddall

Introduction

Between Autumn 2010 and Summer 2011 there was a raft of changes in public policy. In education, initiatives included the introduction of Free Schools and plans for the English Baccalaureate, reviews of Teachers Standards, the National Curriculum, Music Education, Cultural Education, a new *Education Bill* reached its final committee stage in the House of Lords in August 2011, and the *Protection of Freedoms Act* came into force in 2012.

Legislation touches everyday life in numerous ways that we need to become conscious of and to which we must respond.

Case Study 1

Keep a log of all the ways that legislation impacts on your life in one day. Think about how it affects:
- Your work life.
- Travelling.
- Leisure and social activities.

Legislation sometimes reflects wider social changes but it can also encourage social change, such as the *Equality Act* (2010) that replaced a legislative framework designed to fight discrimination with one that promoted equality of opportunity. The legislative process is thus the main means by which the values, priorities and ambitions of a government are expressed and realised, so any change in government will result in legislative change and practitioners will always need to keep themselves fully informed. Legislation goes through various stages of discussion and amendment, however the progress of a Bill can be followed on the Parliament website (www.parliament.uk/business/bills-and-legislation/draft-bills/). Once Royal Assent is given, the Bill becomes an *Act of Parliament* and is law. Its implementation is then the responsibility of the appropriate government department.

This chapter explores some changes in education as an example of how legislation might point to wider policy trends. This aims to encourage a critical approach to thinking about policy and legislative change. It then looks at ways in which policy frameworks, current in 2012 (the time of writing), can affect the teaching and learning environment.

Examples of change in education policy 2010/11

Quotation marks denote phrases taken directly from the Department for Education website (www.education.gov.uk).As you read through the outlines, look for any common themes or policy directions.

Free Schools

The first Free Schools opened in September 2011, just fifteen months after proposals were invited. They are non-profit making, independent, state-funded schools, set up by local proposers who might be teachers, parents, charities, businesses, universities or faith groups. Free Schools can be set up for any reason and in any appropriate building, in response to local demand for "a greater variety of schools". The current variety includes independent and specialist schools, Technical Academies, new University Technical Colleges for which there were originally 37 applications, Studio Schools and Academies. Free Schools will be subject to Ofsted inspections but will have a high degree of "autonomy", for example their teachers will not necessarily need to have Qualified Teacher Status. The "success" of Academies and the experience of Charter Schools in America are both quoted as exemplifying how autonomy over "what is taught and how a school is managed" has "transformed the life chances of pupils". See the Department for Education website for further information about Free Schools and the other new varieties of schools.

Teaching and the curriculum

A major review of the National Curriculum (NC), announced in January 2011, had the following remit: to "replace the current substandard curriculum with one based on the best school systems in the world"; to consider "what subjects should be compulsory at what age"; and "what children should be taught in each subject at each age". Public consultation on the phase one recommendations (including new Programmes of Study for English, Mathematics, Science and Physical Education) took place in early 2012, originally for implementation from September 2012 (but were delayed). Other subjects were to follow, with a view to the whole of the new NC becoming statutory from September 2014. A new review however of the NC is ongoing (February – April 2013).

The English Baccalaureate was not a new qualification but a performance measure that was introduced in the 2010 performance tables. It recognised the success of pupils who attained GCSEs or iGCSEs at grades A*-C in five subjects (English, Mathematics, History or Geography, the Sciences and a Language). As a reason for more rigour, the Department for Education cited the increase in "young people from deprived backgrounds" taking "vocational qualifications", many of which "do not carry real weight for entry to higher education or for getting a job". Plans to replace GCSEs with the EBacc were abandoned however in February 2013 after much lobbying and arts subjects are again included as part of the measurement by which schools are judged.

The *First Report of the Review of Teachers Standards* was published in July 2011 and accepted by the Secretary of State for Education. It proposed a new set of standards for what teachers within the formal education sector do and for their personal and professional conduct, to be established from September 2012.

A new *Education Act* was passed in November 2011 with measures that include:

- extending the Secretary of State's powers to intervene where schools are under-performing
- introducing smarter school inspections to focus on four core elements – pupil achievement, teaching, leadership, and behaviour and safety
- comparing UK examination standards against the highest performing countries internationally.

There is also a focus on reducing bureaucracy; improving behaviour and discipline; giving teachers powers to search for items that "disrupt learning" (further clarified in the 2012 *Protection of Freedom Act*); and allowing schools the final say in expelling violent pupils, making it easier to impose detentions, and protecting teachers from unfair allegations by pupils.

Cultural Education

In February 2011 the Secretary of State for Education responded to Darren Henley's *Review of Music* in schools to provide £82.5 million for music services across England to "make opportunity more equal" and "enhance the prestige and esteem of music teaching as a career route for professional musicians". A *National Plan for Music Education* was published in November 2011.

In April 2011, the government announced a review of cultural education, again led by Darren Henley. In October 2011 it announced a cessation of funding to Creative Partnerships to take effect from the end of that 2010/11 academic year. Arts Council England also reviewed the organisations it funds on a regular basis, designating some as 'Bridge' organisations with additional responsibility to deliver arts education across a particular geographical area in collaboration with other arts organisations. As part of the same process, the Arts Council ceased funding Youth Dance England. Bridge organisations are in development and practitioners should keep abreast of any potential impact on their work.

Case Study 2

Have any policy changes impacted on your working environment in the last year? Think about:

- How you found out about the change.
- The impact it had on your employers / commissioners.
- The impact it had on those you work with.
- The benefits and disadvantages you encountered because of the change.
- The impact it had on your practice.

Policy Directions in 2012 - 2013

Austerity

It is possible to see a number of these initiatives as consistent with a wider austerity in public expenditure. The Arts Council reviewed arts organisations in the context of a significant cut in its budget, and some of the teaching and curriculum initiatives included a reduction in the number of government agencies. One effect of austerity can also be a more generic less specialist approach, such as the shift from arts education to cultural education. The Cultural Learning Alliance was formed to provide a "collective voice working to ensure that all children and young people have meaningful access to culture in this difficult economic climate"; it brings together the arts, including music, film, literature, museums and science with funders, and education and youth agencies. See www.culturallearningalliance.org.uk. What subjects would you include in 'culture', and why?

Localism

Free Schools can be seen as part of a wider concern to extend democracy and shift power from central government to local communities, as highlighted by the Localism Bill (introduced to Parliament in December 2010). When legislation is echoed across several areas, it adds weight to the idea that a larger, more significant policy direction is operating. Extending democracy and power to local communities is a powerful rationale; but it could also be argued that there is a tension between allowing local groups to run schools in the way they see fit and consultations over the National Curriculum which appear to emphasise the importance of some subjects over others. Or, it could be argued that such measures are necessary to ensure a diversity of education providers deliver appropriate life chances to every child.

Case Study 3

How might 'localism' affect the teaching and learning environments in which you work? Think about:

- The benefits of extending democracy and powers to local communities.
- How such benefits could enhance the environments in which you work or live.
- Who might benefit and who might be left out of the benefits.
- Any problems or disadvantages you can see in the policy.
- The balance between local and national – what kind of decisions might be best made locally or nationally, how do the local and the national connect.
- Young people you teach or those you know who would benefit from opportunities only available beyond the local.

Implications for the teaching and learning environment

None of the cited examples of policy change have been specifically concerned with dance, but dance may be the victim of unintended consequences. For example, the arts are currently not included in the English Baccalaureate; if schools are only measured on examination results in certain subjects they will necessarily prioritise time, teachers and money to support those subjects. It is possible to see localism operating in the Arts Council's decision not to include Youth Dance England or Dance UK in the Portfolio of organisations it announced in April 2011. Extending democracy to local level reduces the argument for national organisations or strategic authorities.

Dance teaching and learning often takes place in the context of wider agendas and with objectives related to promoting instrumental benefits such as improving health, social engagement or personal development. The legislative framework and policy directions that underpin wider legislation, therefore, necessarily impact on the environment in which dance teaching and learning takes place. A positive example of this can be seen in the investment in dance that followed Tony Hall's *Dance Review* (2007) (see link to this document at www.yde.org.uk) which made it possible for Youth Dance England to establish its national performance framework, *U.Dance*, the School Dance Coordinator pilot programme, and national programmes such as *Young Creatives*, *National Young Dance Ambassadors*, *Stride!*, and also conferences and publications that together enhanced opportunities for young people and raised the profile of youth dance.

There are winners and losers in any policy change. The loss of *Creative Partnerships* will be devastating for some, while the Arts Council's establishment of 'bridge' organisations will benefit others. Change is disruptive and distracting; it can be energising and debilitating; and also have implications for the future. For example, Youth Dance England's national programmes are developing the teachers, artists, audiences and policy-makers of tomorrow.

REFLECTION

1. How can you be proactive in the process of policy and legislative change? Think about:
   - How you can remain informed and up to date about proposed changes.
   - How you can take a view and reflect on the potential benefits and disadvantages of proposed change.

2. How can you contribute to advocacy for dance, and for dance teaching and learning?

3. How can you influence policy and legislative change? Look at Youth Dance England's *Ten Year Vision for Children and Young People's Dance 2010-2020* (see www.yde.org.uk/publications)

4. Health and Talent Development continue to be important agendas. Where do you contribute to dance and health or dance and talent development? See bibliography below. Chapter 12 also gives sources of Heath projects.

Bibliography

Blazy, L. and Amstell, S. 2010 *Youth Dance and Health Report (NRG2). Trinity Laban Research Report with Hampshire Dance.* (free to download from www.trinitylaban.ac.uk/dance-science)

Burkhardt, J. and Brennan, C. 2012 The Effects of Recreational Dance Interventions on the Health and Well-being of Children and Young People: A Systematic Review. *Arts and Health*, 4, 2, pp.148-161.

Murcia, C. Kreutz, G. Clift, S. Bongard, S. 2010 Shall we dance? An exploration of the perceived benefits of dancing on well-being. *Arts and Heath*, 2, 2, pp.149-169.

Redding, E. Nordin-Bates, S. and Walker, I. 2011 *Passion, Pathways and Potential in Dance: an interdisciplinary longitudinal study into Dance Talent Development. Trinity Laban Research Report.* (free to download from www.trinitylaban.ac.uk/dance-science)

Siddall, J. 2010 *Dance In and Beyond Schools.* London: Youth Dance England.

Chapter 18

The Legislative Framework (Part 2): Legal Requirements for Dance Practitioners

Anna Leatherdale

Introduction

As a dance practitioner working with young people in any one of a range of contexts you need to be aware of the legislative framework that governs and guides the work that you do. Legislation is likely to affect your own behaviour as a practitioner and have an effect on your interaction with young people or their parents and carers. Laws are introduced to guide individuals and institutions in society by highlighting rights and responsibilities. Dance practitioners are subject to a wide range of legislation covering issues as diverse as tax, insurance and child protection. Your responsibilities in respect of tax and national insurance are likely to be altered frequently so are not dealt with here. For the other areas of regulation outlined below, current at the time of writing, it is important to ensure that you remain up to date in the future.

Protection and Equality

The *United Nations Convention on the Rights of the Child* (1989), ratified by the UK government in 1991, led in the UK to the development of the *Human Rights Act* (1998), *Protection of Children Act* (1999) and the *Criminal Justice and Courts Act* (2000). The latter incorporated a number of previous Acts but, crucially for a dance practitioner, governs the requirement to check the criminal history of anyone seeking to work with children and young people. Criminal Records Bureau (CRB) checks were introduced to stop people with a criminal record of abusing children gaining jobs in child-related employment.

There are two levels of CRB checks: standard checks and the enhanced checks required for people involved in the regular care, training or supervision of anyone under 18. Enhanced checks show current and 'spent' convictions, cautions, reprimands and warnings held on the Police National Computer. Currently, for those working regularly with children enhanced CRB checks should be renewed once every three years. Most organisations employing a dance practitioner, such as schools, local authorities, play groups or arts venues, will expect the practitioner to have an enhanced CRB check before they will allow them to work with children or process information about them. *The Protection of Freedoms Act* (2012) has ushered in a radical overhaul of the criminal records regime. The Criminal Records Bureau and the Independent Safeguarding Authority were merged in December 2012 into a new Disclosure and Barring Service and further legislative changes will come into force during 2013 and 2014.

Article 12 of *The United Nations Convention on the Rights of the Child* also introduced a requirement to listen to the opinions of children and young people on issues affecting them. This includes listening to their views about education provision and opportunities provided by the youth service. Those working in the youth sector therefore also have a requirement to consult with children and young people about the services that they provide. In the context of dance this can mean discussions with the young people about any aspect of the dance programme delivery – from class content to discussions about the venue, timing of classes and methods of evaluation.

Other aspects of the Convention also affect the work of dance practitioners, for example, Article 31 gives children the right to relax and play and take part in cultural, artistic and recreational activities, while Article 29 places a requirement on governments to help to develop a child's or young person's talents and abilities to their fullest potential. It also states that education should help children and young people to develop respect for themselves, their parents, the environment and the culture, language and values of others.

Education Act (2002)

This Act was created in response to the UK's adoption of the *Human Rights Convention*. The key aspect introduced in relation to this Act is the requirement of safeguarding children and young people from abuse or neglect. It sets out the roles and responsibilities of teachers and those with delegated responsibility for child protection. It requires anyone working with children and young people to share information or concerns in relation to a child's safety and well-being.

At a practical level this means that a dance practitioner working within a youth group setting must know about and implement the child protection procedures set out by the agency organising the youth provision or, if setting up an independent group, the practitioner must understand their responsibility in relation to safeguarding and know how to contact their local authority's child protection officer or the NSPCC if they have concerns about abuse or neglect. A range of organisations including the NSPCC's Child Protection in Sport Unit (CPSU), Arts Council England, Foundation for Community Dance and Youth Dance England provide information and advice on the development of child protection procedures and safeguarding issues. Child protection policies generally provide guidance on a range of things from recruiting volunteers and staff, gaining parental consent for a child's participation in an activity, having photographs taken and used for a variety of purposes, through to procedures that must be followed if neglect or abuse is suspected.

Case Study 1

A child you are teaching on a regular basis always arrives at your class looking grimy, listless and complaining of being hungry. What are your responsibilities? Who can you turn to for help and advice?

Digital abuse is an area of growing concern and dance practitioners need to consider the use of photography and videoing during their sessions. This includes the use of phones or cameras by participants who take photos of their peers during a class or session, since cyber bullying and 'sexting' (using phones to take sexual images of young people for distribution to a wider audience) is becoming increasingly common. The UK Council for Child Internet Safety (www.education.gov.uk/ukccis) launched new guidelines for organisations and Internet Service Providers to make sure parents and children get quality and consistent messages about internet safety. Advice for teachers on these issues can also be found on a number of websites including www.thinkyouknow.co.uk and www.saferinternet.org.uk.

In June 2010 the Government commissioned Professor Eileen Munro to conduct an independent review with the aim of improving child protection. Professor Munro's report and fifteen recommendations were published in May 2011. These aim to shift child protection procedures to a more child-focused and less 'tick-box' approach. As a result the Government issued changes to the statutory guidance and undertook a public consultation on these in 2012.

Practitioners working in the fields of the arts and sports have become increasingly uncertain about what is or is not permissible in relation to physical contact with children and young people. Guidance provided by the NSPCC's Child Protection in Sports Unit recognises that 'It is sometimes appropriate and necessary to have direct physical contact with children in order to develop their skills in a safe environment'. However physical contact with a child must always be driven by the child's needs and welfare – not the adults. Establishing correct placement as part of a dance class, the prevention or treatment of an injury, or to prevent a young person from harming themselves or others, are all circumstances in which physical contact between the participant and the teacher might be called for. Dance practitioners should seek training and advice in order to ensure that they and their pupils remain safe and confident in relation to the use of physical contact.

The Children Act (2004)

This amends the 1989 Act and it came about largely as a result of the inquiry into the child abuse case of Victoria Climbié. The Act introduced a single system for safeguarding children and young people across a wide range of disciplines including education, health, social services, criminal justice and adoption services. The Act aims to protect children and young people by joining up information about them, and services used by them, with a view to improving their quality of life. The Act set out five key outcomes to ensure that all children have the support they need to:

- Stay healthy.
- Be safe.
- Enjoy and achieve.
- Make a positive contribution.
- Achieve economic well-being.

This formed the basis of the Government's policy: *Every Child Matters* (ECM), published in September 2003. The Act and the policy both required Local Authorities to find out how best to serve the needs of children and young people and required Local Authorities to include children and young people in the conversations to determine these needs. ECM remains current policy at the time of writing although government ministers now tend to refer to its requirements as *Change for Children* and this is likely to be reviewed in the future.

Case Study 2

Select one of the key *Every Child Matters* outcomes. Consider how dance activity might meet this outcome.

The Equality Act (2010)

Replacing all previous legislation promoting equality of opportunity, this Act makes it illegal to discriminate against anyone on the grounds of disability, race, sex, sexual orientation, marital status, age, religion / belief, being pregnant (or having a child), or being transsexual. The legislation allows positive action that specifically enables anyone identifying with one or more of the groups listed above to access services. So, for example, the Act allows for an all-male dance group or a Muslim girls dance group on the grounds that members might not have the opportunity to access dance if an exclusive group was not created for them.

The move towards non-discriminatory practice is well developed in the arts sector and within dance where professional companies like Candoco, StopGAP, Salamanda Tandem and Tin Arts have led in the development of inclusive practice. See *The Arts Included* (download free from Arts Council England). Practitioners still need to question their own assumptions and attitudes to ensure that activities have not been inherited from a time when more exclusive attitudes towards the arts prevailed. Use of language is one of the most common means of perpetuating stereotypes and inequalities and can inadvertently cause offence (see Chapter 7). Dividing activities or exercises by gender (skipping for girls, marching for boys) is also something that might not be appropriate.

Case Study 3

Think about your own practice and the language that you use on a regular basis. Identify the stereotypes you may have inadvertently adopted or brought with you from your own training. Think about the *Equality Act* and consider the ways in which you could adapt your practice to make your sessions more inclusive.

The Data Protection Act (1998)

This Act requires anyone holding personal information about anyone in a business capacity to conform to a set of eight principles that safeguard relevance, accuracy, and the security of the information held. If as a dance practitioner you hold information about the personal details of pupils and their parents or carers (ie phone numbers, addresses, medical or dietary information etc) or if you hold information about suppliers, other organisations or community groups, you need to become a registered data controller with the Office of the Information Commissioner. Registration needs to be renewed annually on payment of an annual fee.

Case Study 4

What sort of information are you keeping about the young people that come to your sessions?

Do you know if any of the children you work with have allergies? How do you record this information? Is this information kept in a secure manner?

Do you know in which country your computer service provider stores your emails?

Health and Safety at Work Act (1974)

This protects people at work and the health and safety of others that may be affected by the activities of people who are working. It is a duty of every employer **and self-employed person** to conduct their work in such a way as to ensure that they and others (whether or not employed by them) are not exposed to risks to their health and safety. The Act therefore requires all workers and volunteers to consider the safety and welfare of themselves and those around them. According to the Act, potential hazards include: the environment where the activity takes place (e.g. flooring), methods of handling, storing and transporting things (e.g. moving a ballet barre), lack of provision of information or instruction about health and safety issues (e.g. where to find the nearest fire exit) and lack of adequate facilities (e.g. access to drinking water on a hot day).

Case Study 5

Do you know where the fire exits are?

Do you know who else is using the building while participants are waiting for your class to start?

Where is the nearest telephone or first aid kit?

Where will you find the nearest person capable of administering paediatric first-aid?

If you are storing equipment, is it stored safely?

Are there trip hazards to or from your teaching space?

As a dance practitioner you need to consider not only the welfare of the children you are teaching, but that of the parents or carers that bring the children to the sessions or any other person who might potentially be affected by your practice (e.g. the caretaker). Conducting a risk assessment in relation to each class or workshop you deliver will help you to identify potential hazards.

Licences

Children and Young Person's Act (1933) and (1963)

This legislation was drawn up to safeguard the health and safety of young people working as professional entertainers or artists, however owing to the increase in the number of opportunities that children and young people now have for performance this law may also, at times, be applied to youth dance activities. Each Local Authority in England is responsible for producing guidelines and issuing Child Performers Licences in relation to the Act with the result that there are variations between different local authorities. The decision on whether or not a licence is required rests with the local authority in which the child or young person lives (rather than the one in which they are going to perform).

In general a licence is not required if:

- The child, young person or adult on their behalf receives no payment (other than expenses).
- The child or young person is not going to be absent from school.
- The child or young person has not taken part in a performance on more than three days in the six months preceding the application for the licence.
- The performance is being organised by an agency or person approved by the local authority.

However, as it is the responsibility of the person organising the performance to obtain a licence, dance practitioners should seek advice as to whether a licence might be required. Youth Dance England has information on this topic or advice can be sought from your local authority.

Copyright, Designs and Patents Acts (1988)

Copyright is a property right that can relate to literary, dramatic, artistic or musical work. Almost every track of recorded music is protected by two rights: copyright of the musical and lyrical composition and another copyright of the actual sound recording. In order to play recorded music in a public place (including the use of recorded music to accompany a dance lesson or workshop) consent has to be in place in the form of a licence so as to comply with the Act.

See the resource list at the end of the chapter for websites where further details can be obtained about the following licences.

Performing Rights Society (PRS) licence

The Performing Rights Society for Music (PRS for Music) is the UK association of composers, songwriters and music publishers. PRS for Music usually issue licences to the companies or groups responsible for locations in which music will be performed (eg community halls, youth clubs, theatres). Schools are only exempt from requiring a licence providing that the music production relates specifically to the use of music as part of the national curriculum and is only performed to teachers and their pupils, and the performance is given by a teacher or pupil. Any other use of music in school does require a licence. Dance practitioners should check that the building in which they intend to play music has a PRS licence, or they will need to obtain this for themselves.

PRS ProDub Licence

The PRS also supply a ProDub Licence. This licence is required if you want to transfer tracks from your CD (or record) collection into any sort of digital format (for your laptop or MP3 player for example) that you will subsequently use in your own professional practice. PRS operate a tiered flexible payment system, with prices varying depending on the number of tracks that you want to copy over from one format to another.

Public Performance Licence

Phonographic Performance Limited (PPL) is the company that licenses the use of recorded music in the UK on behalf of performers and record companies. Individuals or companies that play recorded music in public pay an annual licence fee to PPL which then distributes revenue to musicians and record companies. Dance teachers and dancing schools using recorded music as an accompaniment to tuition require a licence – as do people teaching exercise to music. Licence fees are calculated in relation to the number of likely participants in classes over the course of a year.

REFLECTION

1. Consider the list of Licences involving music and its recording and playing. Do you need to explore this further? Do you hold the appropriate licences?

2. How do you prepare for performances if your participants are performing in public? Do you have adequate permissions? Do you have enough adults assisting? Have you checked the amount of performances, for example, given by participants who might dance with other groups?

3. Read *The United Nations Convention on the Rights of the Child*. How does your practice or your personal values and beliefs address some of the issues raised?

Bibliography:

Child Protection in Sport Unit, undated *Physical Contact and Young People in Sport*. NSPCC: www.nspcc.org.uk

Council for Dance Education and Training, undated, *Code of Conduct*. CDET.

Department for Education, 2010: *Working Together to Safeguard Children: A guide to inter-agency working to safeguard and promote the welfare of children*. https://www.education.gov.uk/publications/standard/publicationdetail/page1/DFES-Safeguarding

Foundation for Community Dance, 2002 *Child Protection issues and the Criminal Records Bureau*, Information Sheet. www.communitydance.org.uk.

Gordon, R. 1993 *Firstcheck: a step by step guide for organisations to safeguard Children*. NSPCC.

Hadley, J. 2005 *Keeping the Arts Safe*. Arts Council England.

Health and Safety Executive, 2008 *Employer's Liability (Compulsory Insurance) Act 1969, A Guide for Employers*. http://www.hse.gov.uk/pubns/law.pdf

Munro Review 2010, http://www.education.gov.uk/munroreview/index.shtml.

Siddall, J. 2010 *Dance in and Beyond Schools*. Youth Dance England.

Tariff for the Public Use of Sound Recordings. Phonographic Performance Ltd, www.ppluk.com Phonographic Performance Licences (PPL).

UNICEF, Undated *Fact Sheet: A summary of the rights under the Convention on the Rights of the Child*. www.unicef.org.uk

Youth Dance England, 2009 *Protection of Children, Young People and Vulnerable Adults*. www.yde.org.uk

Youth Dance England, 2011 *Facts on Child Performers Licences For Youth Dance Performances* www.yde.org.uk

Websites:

Internet and digital safety:
 www.saferinternet.org.uk
 www.thinkyouknow.co.uk
 www.childnet-int.org

Phonographic Performance Limited:
 www.ppluk.com/en/music-users/Why-you-need-a-licence/www.legislation.gov.uk

The Office of the Information Commissioner:
 www.ico.gov.uk

Performing Rights Society for Music (PRS for Music):
 www.prsformusic.com

Children's Rights Alliance for England:
 www.crae.org.uk/rights/uncrc.html

Disclosure and Barring Service:
 www.homeoffice.gov.uk/dbs

Chapter 19

The Professional Context (part 1): Working Well With Others

Sue Davies

Introduction

Who might want my teaching skills? What is the niche for my kind of work? How do I find the right kind of work for me? How do I work with other people (employers, collaborators, stakeholders, or partners) more effectively? As the arts sector undergoes changes due to funding cuts in the arts, education and local authority sectors, freelance and employed dance practitioners alike will have to sharpen their skills in promoting and developing their work.

Increasingly dance practitioners are moving into other sectors such as health, criminal justice, and social care along with established sectors of the arts and education (Amans, 2008, p.161). The role of the dance practitioner has always been to work in a creative way but now creativity is needed increasingly outside of the dance space too. Practitioners need to be able to create opportunities for dance development as well as provide dance teaching for employers who buy their services. Clearly then this proactive role requires other skills besides art form expertise and knowledge.

In this chapter we will look at the skills needed to promote your work. A useful range of processes informed by theories from marketing and business can help freelance and employed dance practitioners develop the ability to promote their work. The tasks and case studies help with writing a position statement about you and your work, and look at the fundamentals in writing a pitch for work, planning projects and recognising effective partnerships.

KEY IDEAS

In this chapter two positions will be explored and practised that are fundamental to working effectively with others.

1) KNOW YOURSELF AND YOUR INDIVIDUAL WAY OF WORKING

- What is my work, how is it different to other dance practitioners?
- What is my kind of teaching approach?
- What are my strengths as a dance practitioner?

These are hard questions to answer at any stage but more so at the start of your career. It is particularly hard to answer the questions as a dance practitioner because you embody the very thing that you are trying to describe. In this chapter you will explore some processes that can help you identify your unique voice: or in marketing language, your brand and unique selling points (USP). These processes will go some way to helping you answer the three questions but also feedback, evaluation and mentoring all play a key part in providing you with information to base your answers on.

2) SHIFT POSITION AND VIEW YOUR WORK FROM ANOTHER PERSPECTIVE

- Why should booker X want to contract me?
- How does my work make a difference to their work?

It is essential to develop the ability to view your work from the participant, employer, partner, funder, or commissioner's perspective. By shifting your position you will quite literally get a different perspective on your work, what it is and why it is valuable, in other words the benefits your dance practice offers different people in different positions.

The ability to see your work from another's perspective is a key skill that can improve all kinds of working relationships. This ability is critical for such practical matters as negotiating contracts, developing projects with other partners, writing copy for publicity, applying for jobs and talking to people about your work etc.

Before launching into techniques of writing a pitch for a project or funding application, it is essential to undertake some planning activities first.

1. KNOW YOURSELF: What is your baseline?

In order to promote your work you need to know where you are now and take stock of what you have done and where you want to go. It is particularly important for independent practitioners to do this as there is no obvious support system (e.g. appraisal) for reviewing the targets and goals that employed practitioners may have. Not doing so can lead to taking on work that does not fit with your own goals and values. In turn, this often leads to problems such as stress or even poor work.

Case Study 1

Take some quiet time to answer the questions below. Do this task when not under pressure. A useful technique is to write some answers and come back to them a few days later and ask yourself is this really what I think and refine your answers if needed.

- Where am I now in terms of my work as a dance practitioner?
- Where do I want to go from here? (1-3 years ahead rather than next month)
- How will I get there? (What do I need to do more of, or to change?)
- What could stop me / help me get there? (Factors including personal and professional)

SWOT Analysis (Strengths / Weaknesses / Opportunities / Threats)

There are many reasons for doing a SWOT analysis. Firstly, it is a useful tool for standing back and thinking about your work. In the context of selling your work, it can help you to not only sort out who might be interested, i.e. identifying your market, but can also help to inform you of what to include in your pitch. In Case Study 2, write your thoughts in each box to clarify your strengths and weaknesses as a dance practitioner and then the opportunities and threats you face now and in the medium term (next year or two).

Your Strengths and Weaknesses: these relate to your work and how you are as a dance practitioner. This refers not just to your standard of skills and knowledge but also your experience, your reputation, your credentials, your partners and networks. These are the assets that you bring to the job market.

External Opportunities and Threats: these relate to the external world in which you live and work. Identifying these can help with looking for work opportunities, for developing projects and changing how and where you work in the future.

Case Study 2	SWOT Analysis
Your STRENGTHS	Your WEAKNESSES
External OPPORTUNITIES	External THREATS

Your Vision, Mission and Values

To write a strong pitch you must be clear about what is special about your work. This can be hard to do because you are talking about yourself or you may not have thought about yourself in this way before, so it is very useful to show what you write to a third party who knows you well and in whom you trust. Often they can see things differently and more positively!

One way of tackling this is to think about a particular group you work with first and identify your vision, mission and values for that group. Then broaden your thinking to find your overall vision, mission and values for your work more widely. All this will inform how you write and talk about your work in a clear and assertive way. Also it can help you to identify which situations you might not want to teach in because there are big differences between your vision and values and those of the third party involved.

> **Your Vision:** this is where you see your work going – a future state that others will be inspired by.
>
> **Your Mission:** this describes what you do and how – what drives your work, what is important about it.
>
> **Your Values:** this explains how you do things – your particular way of teaching (e.g. inclusive, creative, collaborative).

Case Study 3 - Complete the following:
Vision:
Mission:
Values:

Setting your AIMS and OBJECTIVES

This task will help you work out what in particular you offer and how you provide it. It will help with writing your pitch and make what you say clear and understandable to the reader. Initially, consider a specific current workshop, class, or a project for practising this task. Then stand back and try to find the common thread that links your different jobs. What are the common aims for your practice rather than project aims?

> **AIMS:** these are general statements written in broad terms about your dance teaching work.
>
> **OBJECTIVES:** these are the outcomes of your dance teaching and should be SMART (specific, measurable, attainable, relevant / realistic, time-related), in other words, not vague.

Case Study 4

AIM:

OBJECTIVES:

AIM:

OBJECTIVES:

etc.

These first four case studies have all focused on you and your individual way of working as a dance practitioner. All the tasks will inform how you write, for example, your CV (see Chapter 20), your position statement for applications, and any project proposals for work. The aim has been to help you identify your particular way of working, which in turn is what you are promoting to others (participants, employers, partners etc).

In this next section, the spotlight moves from you to the perspective of those who might want to work with you.

2. YOUR WORK FROM ANOTHER PERSPECTIVE

> Talk to the right people
> About the right things
> In the right way
> At the right time
>
> (www.heathermaitland.co.uk)

Essentially this is what marketing covers. At its core, marketing is a process by which you, the dance practitioner, help others to see HOW to work with you. It may seem obvious but not all people know and understand the value of dance the same way that you might.

If one side of the coin is WHAT you have to offer or sell, then the flipside of the coin is WHO should be the target of your work, or who are the right people to talk to about your work now? Do you know who are the best bets for your work? If yes, how do you know that, and if not, this section will help you to find your niche or target market.

This next task will help you to begin to identify who your work might suit and who might want to book such work. Often practitioners cannot say who their work is aimed at specifically which makes it very hard, particularly for a booker, to know who to promote it to. It is not useful to say dance workshops are for 'everyone' or for 'young people', not least because neither you, nor a booker, will have enough resources to sell to all young people or everyone; you will have to make choices because of resources.

Your Target Groups (i.e. Who are the right people?)

Case Study 5	
What kind of person would want to attend your class / workshop or project? Be SPECIFIC i.e. age range, geographic area, income, employment status, specific interest group, appeal to male / female etc.	List (NOT "young people" but age / area etc.)
Who books workshops for this sector or target group? Be SPECIFIC and REALISTIC i.e. tie in your selection with your vision, aims, SWOT, resources etc.	List (NOT "schools" but which schools / who to contact)
WARM LIST OF CONTACTS i.e. actual contacts who know your work or have booked you already.	LIST
COLD LIST OF CONTACTS i.e. potential contacts who you have researched for their policy, past programme, resources etc.	LIST

This information should form the basis of your own plan for developing work and constructing your own database of contacts to which you can keep adding.

Different target groups are interested in different things about your teaching. Again this may seem obvious but often pitches, proposals, workshop flyers etc. do not make clear what the BENEFITS are for the booker, or for the participant, from their perspective. (Think of a flyer for a performance which you have read and then you thought "I have no idea what the show is like", and did not book a ticket).

A participant would want to know the benefits of participating in your session:
- What is the class / workshop like?
- What will I do?
- How will I feel when I do it?

Focusing on the benefits or experience for the participant will be the right thing to address in your publicity or project proposal for example.

From the perspective of the booker they want to know the answer to the same questions, plus how it will help them to achieve their objectives. Just telling them your workshop is available is not enough.

> Good information is crucial. Flash colour print is not enough. We don't have time to work it all out for ourselves, so you need to tell us why it is relevant to us personally.
>
> (Teacher, 1998, *Building better relationships with schools*, n.p)

The **Qualifications and Curriculum Development Authority** (QCDA is now defunct but its web archive is available, see listing at end of chapter) have suggested the following model for information about arts workshops, which is familiar to teachers (Rose, 1998):

- **FOCUS** – What is the event about? What does it concentrate on?
- **ACTIVITY** – What will the participants actually do during the event?
- **OUTCOME** – After the event, what will the participants have experienced and learned?

CHECKLIST: Writing a pitch

1. Before you start writing, decide:
   - Who are you talking to? (Specific person, job title, their brief?)
   - What are they like? (Staffing, resources, current practice for contracting work?)
   - What are they interested in? (Their policy, mission, standard of work etc)
   - What is an appropriate tone of voice to use? (How do they write about themselves?)

2. Now think about your list of selling points and benefits, i.e. for participant and organisation.

3. Imagine that you are face to face with someone from your target group. What would you say to them to persuade them to book your teaching?

4. Start to jot down ideas. Concentrate on communicating the most important benefits and then backing it up with facts. Think what you want to say, then say it as simply as possible.

5. Do not use the first ideas that spring to mind. Leave your draft overnight – or even for a few days.

6. Test your copy. Try it out on your colleagues who will spot the obvious mistakes. Then show it to people from the target group, e.g. a contact on your warm list whom you trust.

(Source: Swindon Dance / Dancers' Recess materials
Creative Touring Part 3 or how to sell your work, led by Heather Maitland)

GUIDELINES: Writing a project proposal

POSITION STATMENT

- The aim of this section is to give the reader a sense of you, your work and its values.
- Vision and Mission for your work with dance and young people.
- Describe what your achievements are for this kind of work.
- If experienced, say when and where worked as relevant to this proposal.
- Core aims for your dance teaching.
- Describe the need for your work.
- Focus on the benefits of dance for participants and for the employer.

PROJECT BRIEF

Here the potential commissioner is given a real sense of the project so that they take ACTION (call you for a meeting to discuss the pitch, book the project, consider funding it).

Project Description – nuts and bolts description, who, what, where etc.

Aims and Objectives of the Project – give clear aims for the project and how these will be achieved. Short bullet points are useful.

Timescale and Timetable – give a sense of how and when the project will be offered.

Management of Project – who will run the project?

Personnel – include a short biography or attach dance teaching CV version (give evidence of your credibility for leading the project).

Project funding – describe costs and how they will be met.

Monitoring and Evaluation – how will you record what happens; what feedback methods will be used?

Equal Opportunities Statement – how you work in terms of values and legislation standards.

Effective Partnership working and project management:

Working well with others

There are many ways in which you may be working with others. Various terms are used interchangeably to describe collaborations: including project group, network, consortium, scheme and partnerships (Maitland and Roberts, 2006). At its essence, joint working is to achieve goals that no individual or organisation can achieve on their own.

Some of these partnerships are formal with specific agreements, such as a Memorandum of Understanding, or a Service Level Agreement, or they may be more informal where partners come together for a time-specific project (Amans, 2008).

> Partnerships are not about organisations working together but about interaction between people. They change over time so they are more of a process than an outcome.
>
> (Tuckman, 1965, pp. 384-399)

Rose (1998), Maitland (2004), and Maitland and Roberts (2006) all make the point that if joint working is to succeed it is essential that you are clear not only about your own aims and objectives but also those of your partner. As partnerships are about interaction between people, Rose (1998) suggests that the web of relationships created is best thought of as a triangle where all sides benefit from working together:

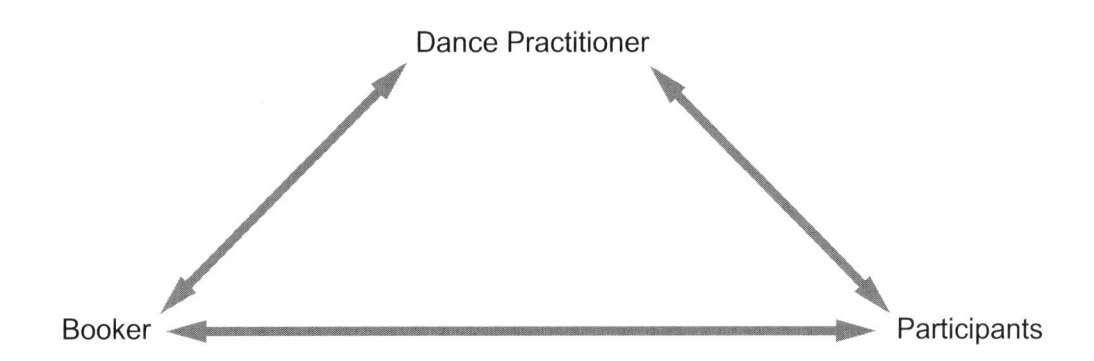

```
                    Dance Practitioner
                      /\
                     /  \
                    /    \
                   /      \
              Booker <------> Participants
```

What are the benefits on each side of the triangle when working together?

- A dance practitioner working with a booker can benefit by

_____

_____

- A booker working with a dance practitioner can benefit by

_____

_____

- Participating group or individual can benefit by

_____

_____

The triangle model is also useful when clarifying the roles and responsibilities of each partner. An effective partnership depends on all those involved understanding their own role and respecting the responsibilities and agendas of the other partners (Woolf, 2000).

Sample Partnership Agreement: Planning a workshop (Source: Rose, 1998)

What needs doing?	Who does it?	Deadline	Is it done?
e.g. Agree workshop dates	Venue and Artist	16/03/2012	

Sample Guidelines: School and Artist partnership (Source: Orfali, 2004)

ISSUES	List what should be covered so partners can work together
Project Brief	
Contract	
Budget	
Matching school needs with artist	
Selection process	
Preliminary Research	
Evaluation	

CHECK LIST: Planning and Researching Your Project

Checklist	Guidance	Your Action Notes
SET OBJECTIVES	Identify your objectives for the project. Remember to make them SMART ones.	
BUDGET	Set your budget including income and expenditure, fees etc.	
TIMING	Consider planning cycle of bookers / partners i.e. realistic lead in time. Draft a timeline of tasks (weekly, monthly). What deadlines are there?	
RESEARCH COMPETITION	What do other similar workshops / events cost? When are they? What offered? Use information to decide your own unique selling points.	
LEGALITIES	What are the legal requirements to consider?	
RISK MANAGEMENT	What risks are there for me? How can I minimise my risk?	

REFLECTION

1. Referring to your warm list of contacts, why should a particular booker use you for a project? Can you answer this?

2. Can you think of an example where your role as a dance practitioner has not been understood by a venue or booker and what issues this brought up? How might you rethink your approach?

3. Download Felicity Woolf (2000) – see below. Consider the examples of practice. What can you learn from these?

4. See Lord et al (2012). What can you learn about how to present a quality product to a potential booker?

Bibliography

Amans, D. (ed) 2008 *Introduction to Community Dance Practice*. Basingstoke: Palgrave.

Burns, S. 2007 *Fundraising Toolkit* Foundation for Community Dance and Youth Dance England.

Hukins, C. 2004 *Events Planning: Quick Guides*. Kent: Edenbridge.

Lord, P. Sharp, C. Lee, B. Cooper, L. and Grayson, H. 2012 *Raising the Standard of Work By, With and For Children and Young People: Research and Consultation to Understand Principles of Quality.* Slough: National Foundation for Educational Research.

Maitland, H. 2004 *Marketing and Touring – A practical guide to marketing an event on tour* London: Arts Council England.*

Maitland, H. and Roberts, A. 2006 *Greater than the sum of its parts – A joined up guide to working in groups*. London: Arts Council England.*

Orfali, A. 2004 *Artists working in partnerships with schools. Quality indicators and advice for planning, commissioning and delivery.* North East: Arts Council England.*

Rose, C, Bedell, S. and Roberts, A. 1998 *Building Better Relationships with Schools*. Cambridge: ETA.

Stradling, H. and Goodacre, J. 2007 *Turning the Tide: Designing & Managing a Participatory Arts Regeneration Project*. Cambridge: Momentum Arts.

Tuckman, B. 1965 *Developmental sequence in small groups*. Psychological Bulletin, 63, pp. 384-399.

Woolf, F. 2000 *From Policy to Partnership: Developing the arts in schools* London: QCA and ACE, p.13-23.*

Websites:

* free to download from www.artscouncil.org.uk/publications.

Information Sheet: *Planning a Marketing Campaign* Foundation for Community Dance Jan 2011 from www.communitydance.org.uk.

QCDA: http://webarchive.nationalarchives.gov.uk/20110813032310/http:/www.qcda.gov.uk/

National Foundation for Educational Research: www.nfer.ac.uk.

Chapter 20

The Professional Context (part 2): You and Your Career

Sue Davies

Introduction

What do I need to learn now in order to continue to work as a dance practitioner? How do I go on learning throughout my career? How do I decide what Continuing Professional Development (CPD) to do when there is so much choice / too little time / too costly? How do I get the work I want? What am I really qualified to do now with my experience? What should / can I do next? Depending on what stage you are in your career, you may be asking yourself some, or even all, of these questions.

This chapter will look at a process that can help you to answer these questions. It will consider the skills and techniques needed in career development that help you to manage your own career. Rather than having a pinball approach to career management, i.e. reacting to what comes along (Reactive) or directed by others (Passive), the model is one of self-management or self-empowerment (Hopson and Scally, 2009). Career management is not about forcing you to plan your life away but it aims to help you gain more control over what happens to you.

For many practitioners, their intensive vocational dance training is a way of getting started in a dance career. For most, dancing is their passion, their principal motivator for a career in dance. However, the world continues to change at a pace and therefore to sustain your career you need to go on learning after your initial dance training. Lifelong learning or CPD is a pathway to success in a competitive and dynamic work context.

As the informal dance sector matures, the professionalisation of the dance practitioner's role means that the practitioner has to consider not only what is taught, but also how to teach and how the work context affects their practice. Recent work by the Foundation for Community Dance to develop a code of practice for its diverse membership, along with the publication of National Occupational Standards for Dance Leadership (NOS) (*Animated*, Winter, 2011), are indicative of the sector looking to establish standards of practice and to provide a framework or map for professional development. A dual professionalism (in dance and in teaching skills) is needed to sustain a career as a dance practitioner and is demanded by many employers in both the formal and informal sectors.

What is CPD?

As a process, CPD has been around for some twenty years in management. Increasingly professional bodies in other sectors such as medicine, law, architecture or teaching, have developed CPD policies for their members, including mandatory requirements for membership. Originally CPD was used to help make sure a person fitted their career environment, i.e. an organisation assessed an individual's skills / knowledge / aptitude in relation to a job and then sent them off for training in order to get a better 'fit' or match between the individual and the job. It was the employers' role to shape staff development. Now CPD is seen as a lifelong learning process helping you to build your own career. The power and the responsibility for CPD has shifted to the individual, whether employed or freelance. Careers are now seen as owned by the person not the employer.

> CPD comprises more than just courses, workshops or formal study; it is the critical reflection on different learning experiences and resulting action planning that demonstrates development as a [dance] teacher.
>
> (Institute for Learning, 2009)

> [CPD is] the systematic maintenance, improvement and broadening of knowledge, understanding and skills and the development of the personal qualities necessary to undertake your duties throughout your working life.
>
> (CPD Certification Service, 2011)

CPD is therefore a mix of skills enhancement and development of personal / professional competence. CPD is a conscious process of structured learning rather than *ad hoc*. The individual is actively learning: in control. For freelance practitioners this model is more relevant than one where the employer directs learning to meet the organisation's needs.

Benefits of CPD

CPD can help dance practitioners keep up-to-date as it includes everything you learn that enables you to do a better job. By taking a more structured, active role in planning CPD you can maximise the value of learning for yourself in terms of your own self-esteem, your employability and your future career choices. In turn, it is also of benefit to the people you work with, and those who employ you will have increased confidence in your ability to work professionally and effectively. As your level of performance increases, your job satisfaction improves: a kind of virtuous circle of development is created.

Managing your own CPD

If you do not know where you are going, you will probably end up somewhere else (Hopson and Scally, 2009). At its simplest, the CPD cycle is made up of four activities:

REFLECTION – PLANNING – ACTION – EVALUATION

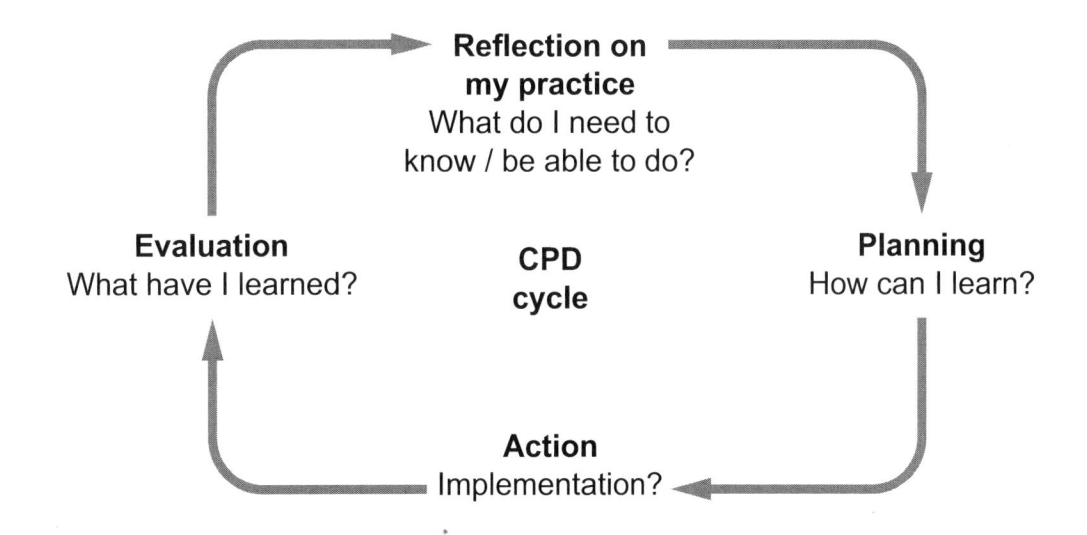

CPD cycle

- **Reflection on my practice** — What do I need to know / be able to do?
- **Planning** — How can I learn?
- **Action** — Implementation?
- **Evaluation** — What have I learned?

There are various tasks that can help you to achieve each of these activities in the CPD cycle.

Where am I now?

When needing to make changes, do a SWOT analysis of your situation (chapter 19). This is a way of thinking about your own strengths and weaknesses. Secondly, it can help you think how you are affected positively and negatively by changes happening externally.

Case Study 1: SWOT Analysis	
Your Strengths **What are your skills?** **What do you do well?** My artistic / teaching skills and knowledge. My transferable skills (other work skills not dance specific).	**Your Weaknesses** **Where are your skills / knowledge lacking?** **What would you like to improve?** From your point of view? From the point of view of other people? i.e. colleagues and participants (feedback / evaluation)
Strengths (your notes)	Weaknesses (your notes)
Opportunities **What are the opportunities facing you?** **What are the interesting new trends?** Changes in youth dance market. Emerging new specialisms. Funding partnerships.	**Threats** **What obstacles do you face?** **Is your professional role changing?** Funding changes. Legislative changes. Different skills needed when working freelance. Limited opportunities for progression. Threat of redundancy.
Opportunities (your notes)	Threats (your notes)

Case Study 2

For CPD to be useful it is essential to have some clear goals that relate to both what you know, what you can do, and what you have experienced so far with the kinds of knowledge, skills and experiences needed for your future work goals.

Or putting it more simply:

$$A - B = C \text{ (your CPD goals)}$$

Answer the questions in the table below.

A	B	C
What Skills and Knowledge do I need in order to work more successfully as a dance practitioner e.g. in a new context, or at a different level?	What Skills and Knowledge have I already gained as a dance practitioner?	What Skills and Knowledge do I need to learn which take account of what I have (B) and have not got (i.e. what to learn?) (C)?
List what might be needed below	**List what you have already below**	**List any gaps in skills and knowledge below**
e.g. consider aspects in detail such as: Dance Skills Teaching Skills Communication Skills Knowledge of Sector Personal Effectiveness		

There are various other ways of undertaking your own dance skills audit in more depth. A useful model is provided by Amans (2008, p.142), she provides a tool to find your strengths and areas to develop as a community / informal sector dance practitioner. She also makes the point that your goals for CPD must also be Specific, Measurable, Achievable, Realistic, Timed (SMART) ones (see further information on this in Chapter 10).

UNIT 2 - PROFESSIONAL KNOWLEDGE OF DANCE TEACHING

| **Case Study 3** | **Prioritising your CPD** |

Using a model of dual professionalism for CPD, dance and teaching, (see www.ifl.ac.uk for fuller explanation) as a starting point, think through your priorities for planning CPD in any one year. This model helps you to make choices and to use your time and resources well.

In the model below, the number 1 relates to CPD which develops your subject specialism in dance for young people, and 2 relates to CPD which develops your teaching and learning in the context of children and young people outside formal education. In the heart of the diagram are the CPD activities that are not only dance-led but are also about teaching young people.

If you are a student on a DDTAL course your main driver has presumably been to find a course that developed your capabilities as a dance teacher of young people outside formal education. The DDTAL course therefore meets all your CPD needs and sits in the centre of the diagram, or is top of your list of CPD priorities at present.

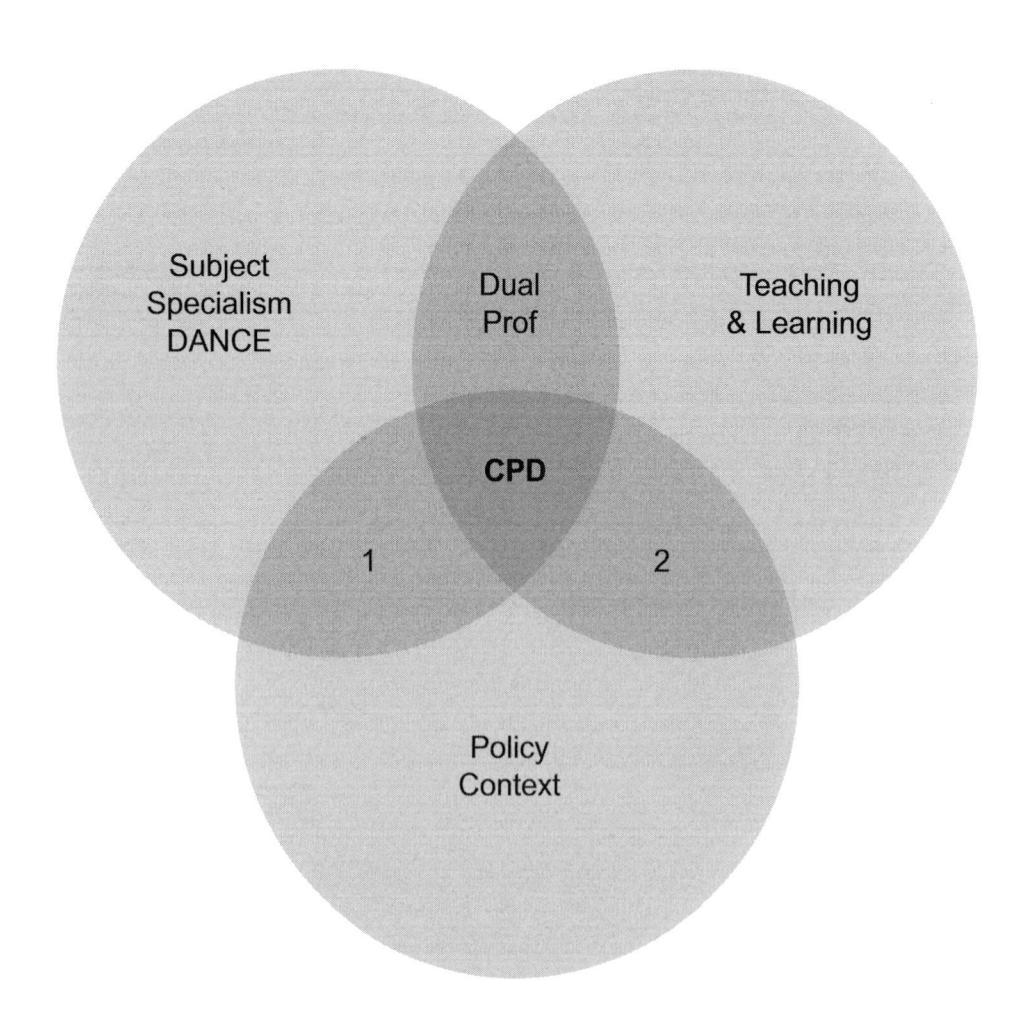

Venn diagram with three overlapping circles labelled "Subject Specialism DANCE", "Teaching & Learning", and "Policy Context". The overlap of the top two circles is labelled "Dual Prof". The central overlap of all three is labelled "CPD". The overlap of Subject Specialism and Policy Context is labelled "1", and the overlap of Teaching & Learning and Policy Context is labelled "2".

After doing these case studies you will be in a better position to identify your CPD goals based on where you are now and where you would like to be (in 1 or 2 years, or further if major career change is desired). Usually four or five goals are plenty.

Writing your own CPD plan

In the CPD cycle, the planning phase is about taking the time to consider how you can learn best, bearing in mind your goals, and combining these with what you consider to be the most effective way for developing your practice as a dance practitioner.

It is important to remember that from the host of learning activities possible you pick those that suit your learning style (see Chapter 1) and experience along with your goals.

Although CPD is a planned rather than *ad hoc* process, this does not limit the range of activities to formal learning off-the-job courses, seminars or workshops. The possible activities might also include: learning from experience, independent learning, one-to-one learning, peer to peer, or group learning; and work-based learning (Amans, 2008).

CPD is an individual choice and needs to be relevant to the learning you want to achieve. There are, however, criteria which teaching associations (Institute for Learning, 2009) use that are useful in checking your chosen activities against. An activity will count as CPD if:

- You can critically reflect on what you have learned.
- You can show how you have applied this to your practice.
- You can show how this has impacted on your learners' experience and success.

The sample CPD Plan below can be used to practise making your own plan. Having established up to four or five goals for development in the next 1-2 years you can use the plan to make more concrete SMART goals. It is important to be realistic in your plans so that you have the possibility of achieving the change that you want.

Many plans fail, not because of lack of money or time, but because of lack of time spent thinking them through. Without support, it can be hard to do this type of reflective thinking so a useful strategy for independent practitioners is to involve someone else to read through / discuss your draft plans with. The act of talking can often help to clarify the gaps in plans and ideas. Here is a sample CPD Plan:

CPD Plan - From (date) to (date)

Current Position: where am I now? (Use the reflections from Case Studies 1, 2 and 3 to contextualise the CPD planning) *Write your position statement*

Planned outcome: Where do I want to be by the end of this period? What do I want to be doing? (e.g. May be 'more of the same' or having made a change in career) *Write your outcome*

What do I want / need to learn? Why is this goal needed? (goals)	Potential benefit and impact on my practice.	1. What will I do to achieve this? (methods / courses) 2. What resources or support will I need?	What will my success criteria be? (review and measure)	1. Action Plan to achieve goal. 2. Target dates for review and completion

Make a table using the previous model as a template so you can click into the boxes to expand them.

Note this table is for analysing your needs, it is not suggested as the final format for presenting your CPD Plan for Unit 2 DDTAL Assessment. This will need further research into actual courses, time scales and costs for example.

Reflecting on your learning

In the CPD cycle, evaluation of what you have learnt will be helped if you try to keep a record of what you do and what you have taken away from the experience. This can be as simple as keeping your own journal and recording your reflections, through to sharing your learning in peer support networks or discussion in appraisal sessions.

Your reflections will include thinking about what you have learnt and in turn how it has changed your practice.

Finally, your reflections should be matched up against your CPD plan's original goals to see where you are now. The CPD cycle then starts again.

You and your career

We started in this chapter by looking at careers and their development. Recent theories of career development now place the individual as central in constructing their own career (Savickas, 1993). In this way, career development is person-centred rather than organisation-focused.

Each career story is unique and takes account of not only personality, but also the experiences, preferences, interests and values that you hold. This is a much broader, richer picture of a career than one defined by a linear progression through a career determined by others. The two pictures below represent these different perspectives.

When you think about your career which picture is nearest to your thoughts?

TWO MODELS OF CAREER PROGRESSION

1.
Linear
Hierarchical
Incremental steps mapped out in front
Move from low to high position
Externally determined (i.e. the ladder already exists)

2.
Different branches in different directions
All branches connected to the central core / trunk
Grows in three dimensions
Growing in complexity as tree matures
Is unique
Growing in strength and resilience

The model of the tree is a much more holistic model for a career:

- It provides an image that is developmental and is not random, as all the experiences (branches) are grown from the central trunk.
- It reinforces the point that a career stems from the individual's own strengths and individuality.

In this final section of the chapter, we explore some aspects of professional practice that help others see the particular qualities you bring to the workplace. The challenge to managing your career successfully is to know yourself, your strengths and priorities, and to communicate this well to the others you work with or teach. See www.cpduk.co.uk for further detail of the CPD planning process for freelance individuals.

Writing your CV (or what does your CV say about you?)

Your CV, in many circumstances, will be the first contact an employer has with you. Therefore it is important to provide a professional snap shot of who you are, and what you contribute through your teaching and can bring to a new project, organisation or work situation. A CV should not list everything you have done. It is an opportunity to show those aspects of yourself and your history that are relevant to the job that you are applying for.

Some useful tips:
- Maximum length - 2 pages.
- Use internet-friendly font e.g. Arial.
- Do not use heavy graphics, tables, images that may corrupt when you email.
- Check your spelling.
- Make the content relevant to the job context – be selective and specific.
- Provide 2 referees who know your work well and have agreed to be a referee.

From a scan of *The Guardian*'s career resources online (http://careers.guardian.co.uk/cv-templates) there appears to be some common content headings, although there is some variance between a graduate CV and an experienced freelance worker CV.

Profile (position statement)	Work History	Qualifications	Awards & Memberships	Interests
30-40 word statement that highlights *relevant* expertise, transferable skills and qualifications. Describe what you are like to work with e.g. self-management skills.	List 3 work histories starting with the most recent. Highlight transferable skills and experience that relate to the new job or context.	List highest qualifications and any relevant courses.	List awards and memberships that are relevant to future work context	List interests that relate to the job you hope to move into. **Only use if the CV is light on relevant work history**

> **Case Study 4**
>
> Identifying, listing and describing your skills is not an easy task. Talking about ourselves in a clear open way is often difficult. However, it is critical to job-search success and you need to invest time in finding the best way to talk about yourself. This task will help you write your profile and your work history.
> - List by title a project or job you have held. Start with the most recent and work backwards.
> - Write a detailed description of four to five major duties you had.
> - Think of the skills needed to accomplish each duty listed – job related.
> - Write them down on paper.
> - Repeat the steps for the other work that is relevant for an application, CV or in an interview.
> - By the end you will have a long list, edit it down to those that match your job goal(s).

Professional Conduct in the Workplace

In Chapter 19, it was seen how important it is to know your own vision, goals and beliefs for your work as this informs your mission and distinguishes your way of working as a dance practitioner.

In the context of managing your career it is important to identify your own professional code of conduct. Useful starting points for considering this are the professional dance organisations that have developed Codes of Conduct and Professional Practice for their members. The **Foundation for Community Dance**, after much research of their members' practice, published their *Code of Conduct* in 2009. Since its introduction members are able to indicate their positive support of the Code by indicating their agreement to it on their membership status.

> This code of conduct translates the core values of community dance into standards of ethical and responsible practice to which community dance professionals adhere. It enables them to be clear and upfront about how they go about their work, their ethical stance on how they approach their work, and the expectations people can have of them in terms of their professional behaviour, actions and attitudes.
>
> (*Animated*, Winter, 2009, n.p.)

See www.empd.org for an example code of ethics for individual dance teachers.

REFLECTION

1. Compare the Code above with the list Bramley provides under the sub-header 'What qualities do dance teachers need?' in *Dance Teaching Essentials* (2002), p. 19, published by Dance UK. What similarities do you notice?

Foundation for Community Dance	Council for Dance Education and Training	Royal Academy of Dance
• Professional Competence • Responsibility • Safety • Working with people • Commitment to Code of Conduct	• Integrity • Objectivity • Competency • Courtesy and consideration • Confidentiality • Health & Safety	• Integrity • Competence • Professionalism • Compliance
What behaviour and attitudes do you expect of yourself when teaching?	What behaviour and attitudes do you expect of people you teach and work with?	What do you feel responsible for and what do you have to be responsible for when teaching?

2. Find a job advertisement in a context similar to where you currently work. It should not be something you wish to apply for but something you would fully understand. Imagine yourself to be the prospective employer who placed the advertisement. What kind of experiences and skills would you require of applicants? How would you know what kind of person an applicant is from their CV? You have 10 applicants all with good experience and qualifications but only time to interview five of them. How would you whittle them down?

3. Ask a colleague to look over your CV and give you an opinion on it.

Bibliography

Amans, D 2008 *Introduction to Community Dance Practice*. Basingstoke: Palgrave.

Bartlett, K. and Stenton, C. 2009 *Definitions, core values and a code of conduct for community dance*. Animated: Winter.

Bolles, Richard 2011 *What Colour is your Parachute? A practical manual for job-hunters and career-changers*. New York: Ten Speed Press.

Hopson, B. and Scally, M. 2009 *Build your own rainbow: A workbook for career and life Management*. Cirencester: Management Books 2000 Ltd.

Savickas, M.L. 1993 Career Counselling in the postmodern era. *Journal of Cognitive Psychotherapy: An International Quarterly*, 7, (3), pp. 205-215.

Websites (available at the time of writing):

Institute for Learning 2009 *Brilliant teaching and training in FE and skills: A guide to effective CPD for teachers, trainers and Practitioners*. Online publication: www.ifl.ac.uk

Museum Association 2011 *How to write a CPD plan: Building a successful career in Museums*. Online publication: www.museumsassociation.org/cpdresources

UNIT 3

CRITICAL REFLECTION ON DANCE TEACHING

Chapter 21
Critique not Criticism: Observing Teaching
Lorna Sanders

Introduction

Good quality teaching within all sectors of dance education is assisted by reflective practice. It can encompass a range of strategies but, most frequently, it inculcates evaluative processes that you apply to yourself (reflecting on whether the planning of your dance sessions is effective for example). Advice about how to use a Reflective Journal for these purposes is provided in Chapter 24 and for more detailed discussion of evaluation see Chapter 10.

Understanding how to observe the practice of other teachers and to learn from this experience is important. It requires a specific type of reflection in order to avoid being judgemental. Although advice on reflection can be found in many sources, see the list in Amans (2010) for example, it is useful to understand the origins of the principles since these have an impact on the observation strategies proposed in this chapter.

Key Theorists

Donald Schön (1987, 1991) is the most significant theorist in the area of reflective practice and the idea that professionalism is based in this is also his. He drew on John Dewey's earlier notions of *reflective inquiry*. Dewey (1902, 1910, 1916, 1938) is an important philosopher whose work underpins much of our thinking about how people learn because he popularised ideas such as the importance of democratic principles within education and the emphasis this places on active learning. Our current notions of the importance of teaching strategies such as problem solving and discovery learning trace back, in large part, to Dewey's thinking and influence.

Schön's developments began as a way of marrying what had then been considered to be two very different types of knowledge: academic knowledge (*knowing about*); and practical knowledge based in competence and mastery of skills (*knowing how*). Although these notions were prevalent in the 19th and early 20th centuries, they can still be seen to have an impact today:

Academic Knowledge (theoretical understanding)	Practical Knowledge (competence-based understanding)
Leads to notions of …… Elitism of academia: • facts / theories / evidence are most important • higher status of scientific proof / objective understanding A stereotypical accusation is that an academic can think / know about something in great detail; they can write about it but not be able to do it in any real sense (no practical application). *They are thinkers not doers.*	Leads to notions of …… Mystique of art: • intuition, artists are born not made • the lower status of aesthetic feelings / subjective understanding A stereotypical accusation is that a practitioner or artist can do it but cannot be articulate about what they have done – analysis would spoil the essence of the created art object in some way. *They are doers not thinkers*

Case Study 1

Those who can, do; those who can't, teach.

This common aphorism, often levelled against teachers as a criticism, is indicative of attitudes that once saw knowing how and knowing about as very different types of understanding.

- Consider your position in respect of theoretical (*knowing about*) and practical knowledge (*knowing how*).
- Do you consider one type to be more important than another, or not? Why? What underpins your opinion?
- How might this lead you to value different types of understandings and skills?
- Have you been able to observe another practitioner at work in the past? How might your values, concerning knowledge as an issue and what this is, have had an impact on the judgements you made about the practitioner and what they valued?

Academic knowledge was typically seen as invested in universities and theoretical knowing was considered to be for elite thinkers. Practical knowledge was valued for its foundation within skills / competence and this was invested in craft guilds and apprenticeship schemes. These existed, in the main, outside of universities. In the second half of the 20th century, governments of different political persuasions tried to break down what was called the Academic / Vocational divide. Our current idea of studying dance at university and approaching it through a mix of theoretical and practical aspects is thus relatively new in historical terms.

Reconsidering problem-solving (or the problem with problems):

Teachers were (and to some extent still are) seen as instrumental problem solvers. This means that their role is to select from a range of pre-determined strategies in order to solve the problems with which they are faced. One of their professional skills, therefore, lay in identifying those strategies most appropriate to the particular circumstances. This process only requires the matching of solutions to problems; this might be done quite creatively but it was not considered to be inventing the techniques that were to be applied. For example, a teacher may select an approach(s) from a selection of previously learned behaviour management tactics in order to solve a child's inappropriate responses. If it proves ineffective, they select again from among the tactics. Schön pointed out however that as situations became ever more complex in the modern world, this mechanistic, instrumental view of practice was increasingly challenged: identifying which of the routine applications to apply in problematic situations was more difficult than supposed and problem-solving needed to be more widely characterised.

To do this, Schön asked four significant questions in respect of the professions in general:
- What is the kind of knowing in which competent practitioners engage?
- In what sense is there intellectual rigour in professional practice?
- What is the point of reflective practice?
- What is it to be a professional?

> **Case Study 2**
>
> Take each of Schön's questions and reflect on how you would answer these in respect of teaching dance.

Schön's Knowing-in-Action

Rather than seeing understanding as segregated, *knowing about* and *knowing how*, Schön integrates these into a single concept that he termed *knowing-in-action*. This implied a characterisation of professional competence as involving thoughtful-action, in every sense of the term. Schön also identified a further skill, *reflection-in-action*, an ongoing holistic, problem solving process where action and evaluation come together consciously in the moment to provide 'the capacity to cope with unique, uncertain, and conflicted situations of practice' (Schön, 1991, p. *viii-ix*). In other words, layers of interpretation are brought to bear when dealing with problems, thus *reflection-in-action* involves **creativity** as well as physical, cognitive, social and emotional skills. We apply this whether we are leading dance sessions, or reflecting on our own practice and that of others.

Problem Solving? Even the terms we use to describe this mode of enquiry thinking are challenged by Schön. Problems in professional practice are not singular, as when we say we have 'a' problem. For Schön, a problem is a site of multiple conflicting elements which need to be discerned; there is usually not just one aspect of a situation that will resolve the whole issue. We are not here considering the more simple problems of life but the more complex ones of professional concern. Schön (1991) points out that 'the situations of practice are not problems to be solved but problematic situations characterised by uncertainty, disorder, indeterminacy' (p. 15-16).

Problematic situations, therefore, are best seen as a nexus of events where a range of issues interact in complex webs. Analytic techniques, interpretation and inventiveness are needed to deal with these: Schön calls this 'an art of practice' (p. 17). In this, we account for the processes central to our practice; explain the competences necessary; and no longer take for granted that something works just because it has always tended to.

Thus, reflective practice at all levels of operation must not be considered as **self-criticism** but is about inquiring into and analysing the thoughtful choices of ourselves and others.

What is Critique?

As with reflecting on your own practice, critiquing sessions delivered by other practitioners needs to be a *reflective conversation* between your own thinking and the particular features you observe. It is vital to remember that unconscious values and personal beliefs can have an impact on how we identify those aspects to which we will attend in the first place, as well as on how we interpret what we observe. A checklist is provided later to broaden what aspects of teaching and learning we might consider when undertaking observations.

Criticism results when:

- Your personal values intervene in the process in such a manner that you make a judgement of worth of the practitioner and / or the observed session.
- You jump to conclusions about what you have observed.
- You make statements which are opinions and these tend to be overly general.
- You base your opinion on partial evidence.
- You do not take account of the history of the group with the practitioner which you may not necessarily know / understand.
- You make judgemental statements that reveal more about your personal values than about the quality of the learning that you have observed.

Critique results when:

- You attend to the peculiarities of the specific situation and do not generalise.
- You become a good detective in that you explore different reasons to account for what you observe in the session.
- You remember that Schön indicated that problems are not singular but involve multiple aspects and you seek to identify and explore these.
- You consider your own thinking and not just evaluate the perceived outcome of the session.
- You make analytical statements which consider alternative explanations and which result in open-ended questions being posed for further research.

Case Study 3

Orlich (2004, p. 307) suggests that critical thinking is composed of the following:
- Identifying issues.
- Identifying relationships between the elements.
- Deducing implications.
- Inferring motives.
- Combining elements to create new patterns of thought.
- Making original interpretations.

Take an aspect of a session that you have observed which puzzled / interested you. Remember that Schön indicates that problems have multiple elements within them and this links well with Orlich's first point. Analyse what you observed by considering it in relation to each of the bullet points.

continued on next page

> To help you, the following questions clarify Orlich's list:
> - What aspects of the situation I am observing are significant to me? And why do I notice these in particular?
> - How do these aspects seem related to each other? E.g. Cause and effect? Chance?
> - What is implied by the relationships I perceive between the observed elements?
> - What seem to be the motives of the parties involved?
> - Can I reconsider how the relationships between the elements are operating? E.g. can what I perceived as a cause actually be an effect of something else? Is there an aspect of the situation I did not notice before which might change the relationships?
> - How can I think differently about what I have observed and apply this thinking to my own practice?

Evaluation and Critical Thinking

To add to this discussion of critical thinking in respect of observing sessions, we can also look at Schön's explanation of what is involved in applying evaluation. A simplified model follows.

Evaluate *how* your prior knowledge is brought to bear when you observe another practitioner: for example, do you treat each observation as offering unique problematic situations and look for both the familiar and the unfamiliar aspects of these; or do you draw conclusions by comparing it too quickly with similar experiences, attending only to what seems similar (familiar) and assuming it is caused by the same aspects.

Evaluate *what* prior knowledge you bring to bear: a rich repertoire of understanding provides more ideas to work with and consider.

Evaluate values and the impact on outcomes – do I like what I get as an answer to this issue? How does it fit with my fundamental values? Did I notice if the system in play has institutional aspects that are out of the practitioner's control?

Evaluate the adaptability shown – did I notice the opportunities for a variety of answers?

Evaluate the reflective questions – did the questions I set myself for the observation, or which arose in my mind during it, lead to simple, direct answers (not helpful) or to more complex higher-order thinking about implications, motives, assumptions? Could they involve types of the following (adapted from Schön 1991):

> … this is puzzling, how can I understand it?
> … this is unexpected, how can I capitalise on it?
> … this is surprisingly successful, what was the practitioner really doing?
> … this is a failure, how did I come to this conclusion?
> … this is the outcome I expected, what can I infer from this?

A Process for Observation and Evidence Gathering

A simple table is now offered as a way of summarising the content of this chapter. GOSPEL was introduced in Chapter 5 as a way of identifying positive feedback processes. It can be useful here too.

When observing a peer's dance session, avoid:	When observing a peer's dance session, you should try to:
Generalisations.	Consider the specific context of this specific session and group.
Over-layering with personal values.	Keep in mind that your values will affect what you choose to see and how you choose to think about it.
Simplistic assumptions.	Keep in mind that cause and effect are rarely linked simply and you need to be a good detective – explore different explanations for what occurs.
Predictions about what might happen in a different session.	Keep focused on the specific instances of this session.
Evidence which is focused solely on the teacher; what they did, what they said.	Keep your focus on the participants and how they are learning and responding. You rarely get a chance to see learning happening which you can interrogate in such detail. Place yourself where you have the best view of the participants rather than the practitioner. Your evidence gathering will be more balanced. Sitting directly at the front and back of the studio space is intrusive and best avoided if possible.
Linking to a narrow notion of learning which is based on how you think your own participants, or even yourself, might have responded.	Keep focused on the participants and how they are learning in this moment. If you or your participants had been in this session, the practitioner would not be teaching it like this. Do not speculate. There can be many right ways of teaching.

The important thing to remember in observing is that you are not there to criticise or judge in a negative sense. You are observing to see:

> What children and teachers do in certain situations and with certain children.
> How certain actions and situations produce certain responses.
> How policies and theories work in practice.
> What you can learn from the situation.

(Medwell, 2005, p. 37)

A Lesson Observation Checklist

You will not be able to comment on all of the issues in the checklist that follows during every observation opportunity, the questions are there as types of information to gather evidence for and as guidance to broaden what you might be looking at in a session. A generic list is provided so some questions will also be less applicable in different situations. For a practice observation try something simpler for the first attempt and identify only a few areas to observe.

Advice:

- Focused observation is important. Keep your list of questions in mind during the observation but do not worry if you cannot find evidence for all of them.

- Thick description may be useful (write down what you observe during the session in some detail).
- Be as unobtrusive as possible during the session, give the participants every opportunity to forget that you are there.
- Confidentiality: although you need an account which places the context for the information, you do not need to name the teacher or any participants.
- In your journal when writing up your observation, lay out your material under headings and pay attention to the ordering of this. It is sensible to keep to the same order for all your observations:
    - you may find it useful to save the checklist as a template so you can type into the boxes which will expand as you enter your information. This way you will retain the order of the information from one observation to the next.

Areas of dance education, as stated by Siddall (2010) these are dancing, creating, performing, watching, arise in different amounts and for different purposes in lessons. They will not be equally present in all. However, dance is a whole domain which incorporates them all. For example, in a lesson which focuses on technical training there will be moments of creating and watching, even if only informally, such as when a participant waiting to perform watches the preceding dancers. Try to notice the impact (planned for and unplanned) of the four areas.

And finally, appreciation (one of the skills most obviously used in watching) is perhaps the one least noticed in observations. It has practical applications as well as theoretical ones. For example, appreciation is involved in the following: the participant might discuss the choice of unison as their chosen choreographic device in a creative lesson or explain why certain movements express different characters; they may understand through physical demonstration that a particular dynamic quality is needed for a certain movement or that flicking the head quickly in a pirouette assists the turn; while performing a set phrase they might have their attention drawn to aspects of its choreographic structure, such as the contrast and highlight given by the large leap at the end of a phrase which can be given greater emphasis by their committed performance or use of the eyes. Try to notice how appreciative aspects reinforce enjoyment and learning.

Lesson Observation Checklist	
VENUE / DATE / DURATION OF SESSION:	**TYPE OF ACTIVITY:** e.g. ballet technique class; contemporary dance creative workshop; CAT youth group.
BRIEF DESCRIPTION: lesson number in the unit of work / name of syllabus or other; links to curriculum, purpose of the activity	**PARTICIPANT PROFILE:** e.g. number in session, age, gender, special needs, previous experience
IDENTIFY RESOURCES:	
LESSON PLAN: What aims did the plan convey (as observed in the session if you did not have access to it)? Reference to other curriculum documents / syllabi / or other as needed? How did the plan (if you had access to it) identify expected learning outcomes for the session? How did the plan link with previous ones and to the next lesson? How did the plan sequence short term, medium term and long term planning?	

STARTING THE LESSON

What is the effect of how the teacher welcomed the group? How do participants respond to the management of their behaviour and expectations on entering the room?

What is the effect of the management of promptness of start?

How do participants respond to how learning outcomes / expectations are made evident to them?

How is previous experience, prior learning / recall of previous knowledge checked?

If there are other adults, what do they do / how are they managed?

WARM UP

How do participants respond to the construction, presentation, management of the warm up?

How does it link to the content of the rest of the lesson?

How does it meet the physiological needs of the class?

How does it meet the socio / cultural / psychological needs of the class?

DELIVERY AND TEACHING OF THE LESSON

How do participants respond to how learning objectives and key teaching points are clarified?

What teaching methods, strategies, styles are evident? What is the effect of these on learning?

How are demonstration and instruction used? What are the effects of these on learning?

How do the participants respond to the manner in which the practitioner uses their voice and presents him / herself? What effect does this have on learning?

How do the participants respond to attention management strategies?

How do the participants respond to where the practitioner positions themselves during class? What effect does this have?

What is the balance of practitioner to participant talk? What impact is there on learning?

How do participants respond to being given opportunities to question?

What type of questions do the participants ask? What effect does the practitioner's response have on their learning?

CONTENT AND ASSESSMENT

How does the lesson content / knowledge / skills link to overall aims?

How does the lesson progress through structured activities?

How are the four areas of dance education integrated (dancing, creating, performing, watching)? To what effect?

What kind of subject specific vocabulary is used and to what effect?

What assessment or evaluation criteria are in evidence? Who has access to these during the lesson and to what effect? How do they link to the Learning Outcomes / Objectives?

How are safe practice and legal requirements managed before, during and after the session?

DIFFERENTIATION AND INCLUSION
How is a variety of participant activity included (solo, group work etc.)? To what effect?
How is differentiation used and how do participants respond to this? What effect does this have on their learning?
How do participants respond to the general management of inclusion?
How do participants respond to the catering for their individual physical, psychological, social and cultural needs?

RESOURCES, LINKS TO CURRICULUM, ICT SKILLS / PROCESSES
What is the impact of these on learning?
How are resources managed for inclusion?
How are context specific issues dealt with and to what effect eg cross-curricular links, skills and processes used for particular contexts, links to repertoire, skills for life or wider learning?

MOTIVATION AND LEARNING
How do the participants respond when the practitioner checks that learning is taking place?
What is the participants' response to how different learning styles are taken into account?
What type of feedback was used? What effect did this have on learning?
How does lesson content and structure maintain participant focus / concentration / motivation?
How are transitions between activities managed? Signals / cues / instructions?
How does the pace of the lesson impact on learning? How does the practitioner judge when an activity has been engaged in for long enough?
What is the participants' response to behaviour management strategies? What is the effect of rewards (e.g. praise, eye contact) and sanctions (e.g. frown, name, ignoring)?
How do participants respond to the responsibility given in respect of their learning?

CONCLUDING THE LESSON
How do the participants respond to being asked to share / show their work?
How do participants respond to cool down activities? How is cool down managed?
What effect does the conclusion or plenary of the session have on the participants?
What learning does the practitioner revisit and to what effect?
What learning outcomes are achieved?
How do participants know how well they have done?
Was any homework / extension activity suggested?

REFLECTION

1. Consider how you usually tend to solve problems. Identify an occasion when you needed to solve a complex problem (it does not need to be in teaching) but it would be useful if you were not particularly happy about the decisions you took. Try to recall the actual parameters of the problem and how you phrased it as a problem to yourself. What steps did you take in thinking about this problem. What steps did you take to solve it?

2. Now consider the same problem again. Revisit Orlich's list for Case Study 3. Apply his bullet points to your problem and see if you can identify a different way of thinking about it and different responses to solving the issues.

3. Identify a specific interest / issue / problem that has arisen as a result of your own practice or which you have recently encountered in reading or studying. Construct a range of specifically focused questions around this for observation of a lesson. Then identify further research you might undertake to further the inquiry into this issue.

Bibliography

Amans, D. 2010 *Passport to Practice*. London: Foundation for Community Dance.

Dewey, L. 1902 *The Child and the Curriculum*. Chicago: University of Chicago Press.

Dewey, J. 1910 *How We Think*. Boston and London: D.C. Heath.

Dewey, J. 1916 *Democracy and Education*. New York: MacMillan.

Dewey, J. 1938 *Experience and Education*. New York: Collier and MacMillan.

Medwell, J. 2005 *Successful Teaching Placement*. Exeter: Learning Matters

Orlich, D. 2004 *Teaching Strategies*. [7th edition] Boston: Houghton Mifflin.

Schön, D. A. 1987 *Educating the Reflective Practitioner*. San Francisco: Jossey-Bass.

Schön, D. A. 1991 *The Reflective Practitioner*. Aldershot: Arena, Ashgate [originally published London: Maurice Temple Smith, 1983].

Siddall, J. 2010 *Dance In and Beyond Schools*. Youth Dance England.

Chapter 22
Good Practice in Dance Teaching
Linda Jasper

Introduction

What is good practice in relation to teaching children and young people dance? Is there a common understanding of what it is? Does the understanding of what is good practice change depending on the context in which young people experience it? For example, is good practice the same in a school, a youth club, a Pupil Referral Unit or a county youth dance company?

In order to reflect on your own and other people's practice it is useful to look at it through the lenses of various theories and models that different writers / practitioners have presented.

Is there a common consensus of what good dance practice is?

As chapter 25 further illustrates, perhaps what individuals' define as 'good' practice is the recognition of shared values and intentions between the teacher and young people / other practitioners. In other words, if between those taking part there is consensus that the experience is valuable to them then good practice is taking place. But this can lead to a view of good practice that is limited by the experience of the people involved. How do they know if there is other practice that they might consider to be 'better'? Teachers usually strive to improve and develop their practice and comparing other people's practice / models / ideas with their own is a valuable place to start to recognise good practice in their own and other people's work.

Is good practice with young people different from that when working with adults?

People develop physically, intellectually, psychologically and socially at a faster rate when they are young than at any other stage of their life. There is therefore an imperative to offer them experiences that will help them to develop positively, which might not be as pressing as when they are adults and are then in a better position to assess the value of the experiences in which they are involved. One could argue that the teacher has much greater power to influence and affect the development of a young person than an adult. In this respect the teacher has the responsibility to make sure that what young people are experiencing is the best they can deliver in response to their needs.

This level of responsibility for young people is reflected in law: young people are minors, dependents in law and as such there is much legislation to protect their interests (see Chapter 18). Governments want all young people to fulfil their potential and to play a positive and active role in society: http://www.education.gov.uk/childrenandyoungpeople/youngpeople.

The *Every Child Matters* (ECM) manifesto (arising from *The Children's Act* 2004) is used as a way of assessing all Children's Services: for example it is used by Ofsted when inspecting schools and social services. The manifesto encourages services to help children:

- Be healthy.
- Make a positive contribution.
- Stay safe.
- Achieve economic well-being.
- Enjoy and Achieve.

> **Case Study 1**
>
> These aims are very broad but indicate what is expected for all children to experience through publicly funded services.
> - Are these aims relevant to your dance teaching?
> - Can you connect these five aims to your mission statement and aims of Teaching Plans when working with children and young people? Select one of your Teaching Plans to investigate more specifically.

Definitions of good dance practice

Jeanette Siddall in *Dance In and Beyond Schools* (2010, p. 18) addresses the question, 'What is high quality dance experience for children and young people?'

- Inclusive – programmes and activities are relevant, challenging and achievable for every child and young person; prejudice and stereotyping is challenged.
- Coherent – young people experience the roles of creator, performer, leader and critic through the activities of dancing, creating, performing and watching in a range of contexts and dance styles / genres. They make connections with other dance opportunities, art forms, subjects and contexts.
- Purposeful – creative responses, autonomy and decision-making are encouraged. There are clear learning outcomes, young people take responsibility and make informed choices about their future engagement with dance.
- Progressive – young people progress in and through dance. They are encouraged to achieve their potential, broaden their horizons and raise their aspirations.

These statements by Siddall have certain things in common with the aims of ECM in that they place the child / young person's needs at the centre of the experience; that they are involved in activity that is positive and developmental; and that it is available to all.

> **Case Study 2**
>
> - Do you agree with Siddall's outline of high quality dance? Would you change / add to any of the areas?
> - How does this relate to your aims when planning, delivering and evaluating dance teaching?
> - Do you think there are contexts where these aims might not be relevant or need to be modified?

Approaches to achieving good dance practice

Perspective 1: Dance as Art model

For many people working with young people, particularly in education settings, the 'dance as art' model is central to their practice as it allows young people to learn and develop their skills, knowledge and expertise in a wide range of dance experiences and nurtures the young person as an artist. The three interrelated aspects of creating, performing and appreciating have been central to dance educationalists' work. Jacqueline Smith Autard's publications advocate this approach (*The Art of Dance In Education*, 2001) and the National Dance Teachers Association in their document: *Maximising Opportunity: Policy Paper* 2004, state:

> It is now widely accepted that the interrelated study of composition, performance and appreciation provides a coherent conceptual framework for the study of dance.

(www.ndta.org.uk)

This model is not genre specific, in that it can be applied to a wide range of dance forms including African dance, ballet, ballroom, contemporary, jazz, kathak etc. It makes demands on teachers to be knowledgeable in a range of dance areas. It is quite likely that this model is used by specialist dance teachers working in and beyond schools who have an understanding of dance as artistic and cultural practice.

Peter Brinson (1991) also advocates for young people to be exposed to dance education as an art form. He states that: 'the realm of dance is education of the body and the imagination' (p. 69). He argues that dance's contribution to young people's education lies in its uniqueness in using kinaesthetic and enactic modes and allows for the 'exploration of values, rationality and creativity which accompany both modes in their unique uses of the body and the imagination' (p. 71). He and Peter Abbs argue that dance should be taught as an art form alongside the other arts in the school curriculum and that dance teachers are not using dance to its fullest extent to educate young people.

> There is a great need for a broad and vital understanding of dance in our society: of dance seen as an artistic form of expression crossing all cultures with a long, variegated past and a rich present. Strangely such a broad understanding is absent among our arts teachers, and it must be said, even among a significant number of dance teachers and dance practitioners.

(Peter Abbs, in Brinson, 1991, Preface p. *xi*)

Brinson goes on to encourage dance teachers to be more aspirational in their practice:

> The dance class, therefore, is a place for excellence and for thinking. It becomes an exercise in observation and experiment, in thesis and antithesis, as much as any science lesson. The special characteristic of this exercise, as with all practice of the arts, is synthesis and integration to create where most other disciplines emphasise analysis and dissection to create [...] the knowledge communicated by the arts [has] to do with intuition and feeling, direct action and experience, aesthetic, religious and moral areas of knowing communicated through movement.

(p. 78)

He sees the location of dance within Physical Education in schools as not conducive to deliver this model of dance education: it 'not only cannot provide adequate opportunities to experience the kinaesthetic mode, but also omits the enactive mode and the exploration of values, rationality and creativity which accompany both modes in their unique uses of the body and imagination' (p. 71).

He comments on the lack of time and resources allocated to dance as a part of the PE curriculum and also the approach taken, with its emphasis on the physical, limiting the full experience that individuals can gain through dance.

Case Study 3

Do you agree with Abbs' observation that dance teachers can have a limited understanding "*of dance seen as an artistic form of expression crossing all cultures with a long, variegated past and a rich present*"? Explain why.

Do you meet / see Brinson's expectations of the dance class for "*excellence and thinking*" and "*observation and experiment*" in your own and other's work?

If you do, say when and where you see these elements being fulfilled in your practice. If you don't, say why these features might not be important / appropriate to different contexts / practice?

How would this dance as art model apply to the following settings?

Sports and Recreation:
In settings such as sports and fitness centres there is more of an emphasis on the dancing (performing) than creating work and viewing / contextualising other dance works. Dance is seen as a means of encouraging individuals to exercise, especially girls who often are not attracted to competitive sport, focusing on using dance to improve health and fitness.

Youth club:
In youth work the activity programmed is usually a medium for personal and social education. For example, the drop in youth centre where a selection of activity is devised for and with young people that addresses aims such as: developing cooperation between members, gaining leading / organising skills, educating about substance abuse / sexual health etc. Dance in this context would be only one of a variety of activities that the young people engage in. Dance is used mainly as a vehicle for addressing other aims / objectives – rather than exploring the form itself.

Young Offender Institutions:
Dance work with young people at risk is often focused on instilling self discipline, increasing self awareness and cooperation between individuals etc. Dance is used as a vehicle to bring about personal change by addressing individuals' behaviour.

In these settings we can talk about an education *through* dance (extrinsic) rather than an education *in* dance (intrinsic) that has been advocated by Autard and others. Often dance teachers justify and advocate for dance by focussing on its extrinsic values, especially when trying to convince head teachers, funders, and parents about its value. However, in practice it is sometimes difficult to discern the difference between intrinsic and extrinsic intentions. Participation in dance brings about benefits such as improved body awareness, communication with others, ability to problem solve etc. But the more overt setting of aims / intentions to bring about changes in behaviour, without reference to what dance can be to young people, could be ignoring its inherent value:

dance is a unique form of human expression. One could argue that dance *is* education (as in the title of Brinson's book).

Whether it is an education in or through dance, it can be used by teachers to realise different outcomes depending on the young people and the context in which they are dancing. What is assessed to be good practice therefore, to a large extent, depends on the context in which you are working. The emphasis on what you deliver will change depending on the setting you are working in.

Perspective 2: Experiencing different roles in dance

Another way of viewing practice in dance is to consider the roles that a young person can experience when engaged in dance. Young people can take on the roles of Performer, Creator, Viewer / critic and Leader (Siddall, 2010, p. 19). The latter role, Leader, recognises the importance of providing young people with opportunities to lead projects, performances and take responsibility for themselves and others in and through dance. This is the model that Youth Dance England has used to devise its national programmes such as: *U.Dance* (national performance framework that stimulates dance performances local, county, region and national levels), *Young Creatives* (young choreographers programme), *Stride!* (Young leaders programme) and *National Young Dance Ambassadors* (see www.yde.org.uk/Programmes). These programmes do not need to be delivered in any particular setting or genre but are applicable across a number of contexts, depending on the aims of the teachers and requirements of the young people involved.

Case Study 4

How far does your practice, and that of others that you observe, fit the 'dance as art' model? Is this more relevant to certain contexts, than others?

- Would a focus on the different roles in which young people engage in dance result in a different approach to your teaching and learning outcomes?
- When do you use extrinsic or intrinsic aims when planning, delivering and evaluating dance teaching?

Perspective 3: What is good practice in community dance?

Community Dance has been a major area of dance development in the UK since the late 1970s. The Foundation for Community Dance defined Community Dance practice as:

> Community dance is about artists working with people, it's about people enjoying dancing, expressing themselves creatively, learning new things and connecting to other cultures and each other.
>
> (Foundation for Community Dance website: 2006)

Community Dance was introduced in the publicly funded sector to increase access to dance for everybody, especially activity led by professional artists. In Brinson (1991, Chapter 5. *Whose Arts, Whose Community?*) an overview is provided of the development of community dance that identifies its origins and what ideas and beliefs have shaped the practice.

Community Dance is thus person centred, concerned with personal development and affirmation of the individual: 'More than in professional dance world, community dance is about learning and growth, both as individuals and in community with others' (Thomson, 1996, n.p).

To encapsulate Community Dance practice many have said: 'the product is the process'. The process that the individual experiences is of paramount importance rather than the end result (e.g. a performance or an examination). Amans (2008) gives a list of the 'process orientated values of community dance since its inception in the 1970s (p. 10):

- A focus on participants.
- Collaborative relationships.
- Inclusive practice.
- Opportunities for positive experiences.
- Celebration of diversity.

As in ECM the importance of the individual and their experience is of uttermost importance and, in addition, the importance of building relationships within communities of interested people (e.g. a dance club, youth dance company) and also the communities in which people live (e.g. youth action group, local carnival) etc.

In Amans (2008), Rosemary Lee (choreographer, director, film maker and performer) discusses her approach to working as a choreographer within community dance settings. She describes the responsibilities of leadership (leadership – meaning in community dance contexts, professionals who are leading / teaching / facilitating dance activity with people) as described in the title of her chapter *'Aiming for Stewardship Not Ownership'*. The role of the leader in community dance settings is seen more as a facilitator, assisting the participants to express their own ideas and contribute equally with each other, and the leader, to create their dance experience. This is a very different view from the teacher as 'the font of all knowledge' and defines good practice as when the leader / teacher supports individuals to find their 'own voice' and shape their own experiences. (See Chapter 7).

In championing access for all and challenging the notion of who can dance, what dance and where, inclusive practice and diversity are central to community practice. The practice is not genre-specific and as the community dance 'movement' progressed, its influence broadened so that its values can be seen within a wide spectrum of dance participation and education experiences. However, community dance tends to be associated with dance practice that takes place beyond formal education in community settings, such as: local communities, dance, health and youth centres, hospitals and prisons.

Good practice in Integrated Dance

In the UK there has been a significant development in integrated dance practice, that brings together disabled and non disabled dancers, which has in many ways been most visible in the creation of the professional integrated dance company: Candoco. Adam Benjamin (2002), who was the co-founder of the company with Celeste Dandeker, has written about what he believes is good practice in working with groups that include non-disabled and disabled dancers.

The aim of his book might be summarised thus: *"to know how our bodies work, to understand and be comfortable with how they may differ, and to seek in everybody, the fullest possible expression of what it means to be human."*

He advocates for the use of improvisation as an art form that can allow for true integration between dancers and also for difference to be valued. In order to accommodate difference he argues that problem solving is key to addressing the needs of individuals, from creating structures for courses to the delivery of dance practice.

Case Study 5

Assess how far your own or others' practice relates to community dance principles by asking the following questions:

- How far am I concerned with individual young people's development in my dance practice?
- Am I interested in building a community through dance?
- How far do I want to be inclusive or exclusive in my practice? And would this differ in the different settings in which I work?

Perspective 4: Process and Product

Dance Practice can be analysed against the Process and Product continuum. Thomson (1996) observes that most community dance practice is focused on process / intention, whereas professional dance companies focus on product / form. There are times, however, when teaching certain types of groups, where the focus might change or could be constant depending on the settings. For example, a teacher might be leading a selected county youth dance company on producing a piece for performance at the end of a week's residential period, whereas the same teacher might also work on sessions with a youth dance group over a whole term where different material is explored in each session and which does not lead to a performance.

Process / Intention ⟷ Product / Form

Case Study 6

Where would you put your practice on this line (if the mid point is equal focus)?

- If and when do you see the focus changing?
- How useful is this line when observing other practitioners' practice?
- Do you see patterns emerging depending on the setting, young people's age/ experience etc?

What is good practice when presenting dance performances?

Dance is realised in its performance product – 'performance' being used here generally to include every aspect from a young person dancing in his bedroom to a performance in a theatre in front of a public audience. Many young people's experience of dance culminates in a performance in front of peers or a public event. The question: 'What is good practice in presenting dance performances' was discussed by Chris Thomson (1996):

Dance is a performance art and involves display in social contexts to other people. Many projects, end of term sessions end in a performance. It is seen as a way of providing a stimulus for working towards a final product, a way of celebration of the experience of the project, and a channel for including friends, family and wider community in sharing the achievements and experiences of the participants. What would be considered when structuring a performance?

1. Why is this dance being presented? (What do I want the performers and the audience to get out of the experience?)

2. Where does the work sit on the continuum from process / intention to product / form? (What do I want the performers and the audience to get out of the experience?)

3. Given the answers to 1) and 2) where and how should it be presented ?
(e.g. with reference to such elements as venue, position / layout of audience, formality/informality, programme notes/introduction / post-show discussion, etc.)

4. What relationship does the audience have to the performers? What relationship would I like them to have? What should I do to help this new relationship come into being?

5. Is this presentation to be appreciated (or appreciated and evaluated?)
   a) for what it shows or celebrates about the progress / learning / growth this group has made? (i.e. in relation to the group's previous achievements)
   b) in relation to other comparable community dance works / community dancing?
   c) in relation to other comparable dance works, including professionally produced / performed ones.

6. What should we do to make sure the work is adequately contextualised for the audience (especially if 5a) or 5b) above apply?)

Case Study 7

Consider the function(s) of performances in your own and other practitioners' work:
- When do performances take place and to what purpose?
- What have generally been the relationship(s) between performers and audiences?

The role of the teacher in delivering good practice?

> Teaching is not necessarily the same as education. [...] Traditionally the purpose of teaching dance was simply [...] to teach people *how* to dance, to pass on and improve physical and interpretative skills.
>
> (Siddall, 1997, n.p.)

In community dance, for example, there is a challenge to the notion of traditional teaching roles. The person leading this experience is a 'steward of the individual's experience rather than the 'owner': using their skills and knowledge to help participants find their own way of experiencing dance. This view of the role of the teacher focuses not on *what* is taught, but rather *how*. You could argue that any genre or choreographic or improvisation approach could be taught in many ways. The *what* needs to be appropriate in terms of material and level for the young people, but the *how* achieves the intended outcomes. The outcomes, therefore, need to be related to the teaching methodologies and approaches you use. It takes more than just knowledge / skill in a particular dance genre to be a good teacher.

Content: age appropriate?

The teacher is in a role of *locus parentis* and this role brings responsibilities for the young people with whom we work. Popular culture and media, which can link dance with sexually implicit or violent material, places the dance teacher in a difficult situation when accommodating young people's wishes to dance in ways that reflect this content. Young people sometimes want to use movements, music / lyrics and costumes that are outside of their understanding. The exploitation of young people in any form does not fit with the responsibility we have for protecting and nurturing. Young people do not always question what they are being asked to do by their peers and teachers or the celebrities' performances that they wish to emulate. Good practice, where the young person's best interest is placed at the centre of the experience, must consider their maturation and understanding of the material that they want to perform. Content and presentation needs to be age / maturation appropriate. Commenting on gender politics through dance is very different from imitating overtly sexual material without understanding of its purpose or effect.

Why Dance?

Good practice in dance teaching must utilise the unique qualities of the form itself. The final question is then, why dance? If we are discussing a person centred approach what is it that dance can bring to them that other activities cannot?

If we are to propose that dance is important for young people's development then we need to consider the nature of dance, making a case for its unique contribution to their development. Defining dance as a subject has been the work of our leading dance educationalists since the beginning of the 20th century. They have identified it as a discipline distinct from other forms, such as gymnastics, sport and exercise, so that young people could have access to it as part of their education.

Statements about the value and distinctiveness of dance:

> Dance makes the body the instrument of expression, dance removes barriers between an individual and what they want to communicate. Its contribution to education is unique because it combines bodily movement with creativity and imagination.
>
> (Youth Dance England:
> *A Ten Year Vision for Children and Young People's Dance 2010-2020*, p. 5)

> Dance is a distinct area of experience fundamental to human culture and as such has the potential to offer unique learning opportunities within and beyond the school curriculum. As one of the major art forms, its intrinsic value lies in the possibilities it offers for the development of pupils' creative, imaginative, physical, emotional and intellectual capacities. Because of its physical nature, dance provides a means of expression and communication distinct from other art forms and because of its expressive and creative nature it stands apart from other physical activities.
>
> (NDTA: Policy Document. 2004)

The first definition is similar to Brinson's in that it focuses on the body as an instrument of expression and the second makes the case for including dance in a young person's education in and beyond school. Dance is a subject in its own right, and is therefore worthy of its own place within a young person's education in and beyond school.

Summary

Whatever is your approach to achieving good practice in teaching, and it will probably change in response to different groups and contexts, it will be shaped by the values that you believe to be important when working with young people. Most practitioners working with young people, irrespective of the setting, agree on certain basic principles. In short: the best interests of the young person are paramount and the experience must be of value and help them to develop positively. The teaching might be more focused on an end product rather than the process, but the primary intention is to develop the individual. However, we must not lose sight that we are firstly dance practitioners and need to be able to work effectively in and through dance to achieve our aims. Realising our overarching intention to develop young people has to be achieved through applying our expertise and knowledge of dance to the context in which we are working.

REFLECTION

1. Revisit the entries in your Reflective Journal if you are a DDTAL candidate. What aspects of good practice have you been interested in over time? What does this reveal about your concerns and beliefs as a dance practitioner?

2. Consider interviewing a colleague on the topic of what they consider to be good practice. How does it differ from your own position? Why might this be?

3. Consider having the same discussion with some of the young people that you teach. What is revealed to you about their responses?

4. Find the oldest book on dance education that you can gain access to. Does it have anything to say about good practice? (e.g. Laban, R. 1963 [originally published 1948] *Modern Educational Dance*, London: Macdonald and Evans.) How might this differ from today's perspective?

5. Write a paragraph defining your notion of good practice. Limit yourself to around 250 words in order to challenge yourself to identify the essential ingredients for you.

Bibliography

Amans, D. 2008 (ed) *An Introduction to Community Dance Practice*. Basingstoke: Palgrave Macmillan.

Benjamin, A. 2002 *Making an Entrance: Theory and Practice for Disabled and Non-Disabled Dancers*. London: Routledge.

Brinson, P. 1991 *Dance as Education. Towards a National Dance Culture*. London: Falmer Press.

National Dance Teachers Association: Policy Document. 2004 (www.ndta.org.uk).

Siddall, J. 2010 *Dance In and Beyond Schools*. London: Youth Dance England.

Siddall, J. 1997 *Community Dance: Education Plus*. Paper 3. Research papers on Community Dance. Department of Dance Studies, University of Surrey.

Smith-Autard, J. 2001 *The Art of Dance in Education*. London: A and C Black.

Thomson, C. 1996 *Community Dance and Art / Thinking Aloud. In search of a framework for Community Dance*. The Foundation for Community Dance.

Youth Dance England. 2010 *A Ten Year Vision for Children and Young People's Dance 2010-2020*. London: Youth Dance England (www.yde.org.uk).

Chapter 23
Models of Good Teaching
Lorna Sanders

Introduction

There is no single model of good teaching because this will depend upon a wide range of issues, such as the context, the genre, the purposes and the group for example. Notions of what makes good teaching will also vary from culture to culture, and from one point in history to another, because education, and what purposes society attributes to this, is continually changing. Additionally, in the informal and community sectors, dance practitioners might be fulfilling a range of roles: such as artist-in-residence, leader / teacher, mentor, facilitator, or support worker. All these will offer different challenges and hence different approaches to teaching and leading dance activity.

Throughout this book, different chapters have addressed a range of information that underpins what might be considered to be models of good teaching; such as what is needed for effective planning and how children and young people have different leaning strategies. What is offered in this chapter is a summary of different perspectives. These include models from the formal sector of dance education because although in the informal sector there is no requirement to teach in a particular way, these offer useful approaches that can be applied in different contexts. What emerges, to a certain extent, are some shared characteristics across the range of models. Given that good teaching is likely to answer to current thinking, this might be expected. Pedagogy points to certain principles being applied quite widely.

Before we examine the first perspective, it is important to understand our own more specific place at the heart of any model that we choose to apply more personally.

> The practice of education cannot be a mechanical, largely mindless activity; it requires constant decisions and judgments by the teacher, and these he or she cannot make properly without fully appreciating and accepting the underlying rationale of any activity. Teaching, interpreted in a purely technicist sense, may be undertaken in a mechanistic manner. If, however, our concern is with education, in the full sense, much more than this is required, since education is essentially an interactive process. 'The building block is the moral purpose of the individual teacher. Scratch a good teacher and you will find a moral purpose'.
>
> (Kelly, 1999, p. 9, quotation included is Fullan, 1993, p. 10)

Case Study 1

The use of the Reflective Journal can be an important tool in assisting you to articulate your *moral purpose* and your place in the *interactive process* of education (see Chapter 24 for guidance). If you have not already begun to consider the points in italics above, take some time to think these through.

Teaching Models

Perspective 1: Gough (1993)

> Good teaching is concerned with more than knowledge, skills and competencies. It is also about an ability to communicate enthusiasm for the subject and a belief in the right of young people to experience the best possible teaching environment. It requires from the teacher a continuing curiosity regarding the process of teaching and learning.
>
> (Gough, 1993, p. 27)

The Keys to Quality:	adapted from Gough (1993, p. 62)
1. Teaching Process	Take account of: Knowledge and Skills Teaching and Learning Methods Individual Needs
2. Teaching Styles and Strategies	Draw on a variety of approaches, for example: Demonstration Self evaluation Problem solving Collaboration
3. Enhancing Practice	Through: Effective Presentation Vivid Evocative Imagery Active Participation
4. Learning to Dance	The processes involved in: Composing Performing Appreciating
5. Engaging Positive Attitudes	By encouraging young people to have integrity in what they do.
6. Designing the Curriculum	So that it is: Logical Progressive With Clear Criteria for Achievement
7. Evaluating Lessons	In such a way that the teacher can review what has been achieved.
8. Evaluating Progress	Using specific criteria for composition, performing and appreciation.

This model of good practice has eight areas to address to take account of what Gough believes is quality teaching. In her book, she explores each aspect in some detail and is a useful source to consult. Notice how her keys range over different types of issues.

"It is clear from the evidence that excellence does not emerge without appropriate help"

Freeman (1998, p. v)

Consider:
- which key(s) would you deal with at a planning level?
- which key(s) would you deal with during delivery?
- which key(s) do you recognise as concerns which are driven by more overarching theories / models that were introduced to you in Chapter 22?

Perspective 2: Whelan and Neal (2002)

Whelan and Neal construct their advice for effective teaching and learning on behalf of the Youth Sport Trust and the *Sports College programme* which was launched in 1997 as part of the expansion of the specialist schools programme. This was an important government policy which, by moving away from a comprehensive system where all schools had a similar remit, aimed to have schools develop their distinctive strengths and specialisms in order to raise standards.

For Teaching and Learning:
Demonstration of comprehensive subject knowledge and challenging practice through regular CPD.
Confidence in using a range of teaching styles.
Setting high expectations.
Following a structured framework of long, medium and short term planning informed by assessment.
Reviewing practice in learning teams ensuring their planning and teaching is matched to appropriate, focused cycles of lesson observation.
Monitoring pupil progress through individual and effective target setting, identifying fast track pupils and deploying individual education plans when appropriate.
Making the best use of learning assistants, technicians, coaches and young leaders.
Developing a culture of intrinsic motivation within their pupils.
Making effective use of ICT (Information and Communication Technology).
Encouraging collaboration and independent learning.
Recognising pupils' preferred learning styles and adopting appropriate teaching strategies.
Using and creating innovative resources to support teaching and learning.
Seeking to create the most appropriate environment.
Encouraging and empowering independent learning.

As with Gough's model, analyse which areas you would deal with at a planning level; which are applicable for delivery; which are concerns driven by overarching theories.

> **Case Study 2**
>
> You will have noticed some shared concerns between Gough's model and this second perspective. Identify what these are.
> - Why might this be the case? Why these in particular?
> - What is new in the Sports College Model that Gough did not consider?

Perspective 3: Bramley (2002)

Bramley drew together his advice for a wider target readership from all areas of dance education; formal, informal and the vocational sectors.

What qualities do dance teachers need. An effective and successful teacher of dance:

- Has sufficient dance skills, knowledge and understanding to teach the relevant age and ability range.
- Understands and implements the essential principles of safe practice.
- Has a passion for teaching and can impart their enthusiasm for dance.
- Has a clear sense of her / his purpose and value in teaching.
- Calls on a range of teaching methods and strategies to promote and develop skills in dancing and performing, creativity, understanding and appreciation of dance.
- Is a good listener, observer and communicator, and is able to engage and develop good relationships with young people.
- Understands progression routes within and across dance forms.
- Derives personal enjoyment and satisfaction from enabling people to develop and learn through dance.

(Bramley, 2002, p. 19)

> **Case Study 3**
>
> Consider which of Bramley's points are similar to the previous models and which are different in perspective? Why might this be? What shared characteristics are emerging across all three models?

Perspective 4: Amans (2008)

Amans is writing from the perspective of a community dance practitioner and her model is aimed at those who are 'interested in the purpose and defining values of community dance' (2008, p. *xiii*). You might like to consider what these are before reading on. Amans (2010), listed in the Bibliography, is another useful source for this.

Amans emphasises the significance of **people management** in delivery. She couches her recommendations in the form of advice:

- Greet each participant individually (smile, eye contact, touch where appropriate).

- Make sure you arrive in good time so you are available if someone needs to ask you anything / let you know about an injury etc.
- Use people's names and help them learn each other's names.
- Time spent in an icebreaker (such as a name game) will pay dividends later on when you want them to do partner and group work.
- Incorporate some interactive warm up activities which have a social element as well as serving as a physical warm-up.
- An activity in a circle – such as a parachute game or a circle dance – is often useful in helping a group 'gel'.
- Be sensitive to situations where there are participants who are new / different / just don't seem to be very popular with other members of the group. You can manage this effectively if you are careful how partners and groups are selected. Move people around and be prepared to partner someone who needs extra help.

(Amans, 2008, pp. 170-171)

Case Study 4

Consider which of her points are planning and which are delivery-orientated. What domains of learning are emphasised? What does this indicate about Amans' model? What aspects can be transferred to the context within which you teach? Do any of the bullets above link to the shared characteristics that emerged from Case Study 3?

Perspective 5: OFSTED

Excellence in the Cities (1999) was a flagship education policy aiming to improve educational achievement in the inner cities. It initiated the Gifted and Talented Agenda as one of its core strands. My research on behalf of the Dance Network (Youth Sport Trust, National Dance Teachers Association, Specialist Schools and Academies Trust) in developing a *Gifted and Talented Framework of Support* for schools and trialling identification / recognition criteria indicated that all pupils, to some extent, benefitted from the approach and not only the pupils at the more elite level (Sanders 2005). The following perspective, although focused on higher ability, is therefore more widely applicable.

What does good teaching of talented pupils involve?

- A high degree of subject knowledge.
- Understanding of how to plan class work and homework in order to increase the pace, breadth or depth of the coverage of the subject.
- Capacity to envisage and organise unusual projects and approaches which catch pupils' attention and make them want to explore the topic.
- Use of tasks which help pupils to develop perseverance and independence in learning through their own research or investigation, while ensuring that they have the necessary knowledge and skills to tackle the work effectively on their own.
- Use of demanding resources which help pupils to engage with difficult or complex ideas.

- Use of ICT to extend and enhance pupils' work and the opportunity to present the outcomes to others.
- Ability to deploy high-level teaching skills in defining expectations, creating a positive classroom climate for enquiry, asking probing questions, managing time and resources, and assessing progress through the lesson.
- Confidence to try out new ideas, to take risks and to be prepared to respond to leads which look most likely to develop higher levels of thinking by pupils.

(Ofsted, 2001, n.p.)

Clay (1998) identified a similar range of qualities.

> **Case Study 5**
>
> Consider how the above bullet points link with the shared characteristics over all the models. What is new in this perspective and how might this impact on your own practice? How can you apply the principles here to a wide range of abilities?

In 2009 Ofsted reiterated that in the teaching of the gifted and talented more generally schools should 'match teaching to the individual needs of all pupils, including gifted and talented; elicit views from and listen more carefully to what pupils say about their learning, and act on the findings' (p.7). This indicates two relatively new issues within the formal sector that dance education more widely needs to address.

1. Personalised Learning: Hopkins, (ex Chief Advisor to Ministers on School Standards) states that this 'has its roots in the best practices of the teaching profession, and it has the potential to make every young person's learning experience stretching, creative, fun, and successful' (Hopkins, undated, n.p).

Hopkins states that effective teaching strategies are those which emphasise active engagement and 'for teachers, it means a focus on their repertoire of teaching skills, their subject specialisms and their management of the learning experience. Personalised learning requires a range of whole class, group and individual teaching, learning and ICT strategies to transmit knowledge, to instill key learning skills and to accommodate different paces of learning' (Hopkins, undated, n.p). How do these points link to the shared characteristics of the other models?

2. Pupil Voice: the second issue of note is a legacy of the *United Nations Convention on the Rights of the Child* (1989) (see Chapter 18). Giving children and young people opportunity to contribute their opinions and to act on them, has become increasingly important. This begins with listening to them.' Authenticity is about communicating a genuine interest in what pupils have to say: learning to listen, to offer feedback, to discuss lines of action, to explain why certain responses are not possible' (Ruddock, undated, n.p). Ruddock writes in respect of the formal context but her message is widely applicable. The 'benefits of consultation are: membership – so that they feel more included in the school's purposes; respect and self worth – so that they feel positive about themselves; agency – so that they feel able to contribute something to the school (n.p).

Consider how you might address the benefits of membership / inclusion, respect and agency in your own practice.

Perspective 6: Dance Links (2005)

Dance Links was a dance specific strand within the *Physical Education, School Sports and Club Links Strategy* (PESSCL). Its aim was to 'help schools build strong links with dance organisations and individuals' (*Dance Links*, Foreword, 2005, n.p.). The guide was focused towards improving the quality of dance provision by providing criteria for recognising high quality. It 'outlines good practice both within and beyond the curriculum' (p. 1).

Who are the best teachers of dance? They are those who:

- Believe in the value of dance and have a passion for sharing dance with children and young people.
- Understand and meet the different needs of participants of varied abilities, ages, backgrounds and stages of development.
- Use a range of teaching and learning strategies to meet the pupil's individual learning needs and enable them to reach their potential.
- Can successfully integrate composition, performance and appreciation.
- Communicate all aspects of safe dance practice through their own practice.
- Deliver appropriate and challenging dance activities safely and effectively.
- Refresh their practice by taking part in continuing professional development.
- Have knowledge of relevant legislation for working with children and young people.

(*Dance Links*, 2005, p. 7)

How do you address these issues in your practice? What characteristics are shared across all the models in this chapter? What issues seem more specific to different contexts?

Perspective 7: Inclusive Practice

Inclusive practice is a wider concept than disability. The advice below is from Bramley (2002). They are couched as reminders:

- Each individual participates in their own right.
- Establish the best way to communicate with participants, as a foundation for setting and developing movement ideas and developing interaction.
- Ensure each person is heard.
- Participants should speak on their own behalf to encourage responsibility for reactions, thoughts, feelings.
- Work with participants to understand how tasks may work for them.
- Don't be afraid to ask about the level and nature of impairment – it's important to know.
- Reiterate the importance of asking questions if something isn't clear.
- Participants take responsibility for their own bodies.
- Stay open to finding the best way to work.
- Take time to achieve results – this is a journey.

(Bramley, 2002, p. 73)

How do these bullet points link with previous models? See also Chapters 7 and 22 for further information on inclusion.

REFLECTION

1. Read page 31 of the DDTAL syllabus. Consider how the assessment criteria construct a notion of best practice. Consider how this links with the models outlined in the chapter.

2. Bramley states 'Dance Teaching Essentials [...] provides a consensus of current opinion about good practice in dance teaching' (p. 5). In her Foreword to this, Tessa Jowell (Secretary of State, Department for Culture Media and Sport) affirms this is for 'promoting good practice in all areas of dance education' (p. 4). This indicates one route whereby good practice is disseminated but from where might consensus arise do you think? This is a complex question but one that is worth reflecting on.

3. Siddall (2010) provides the most recent summary of what is considered best practice. In particular read her sections 3 and 4 in respect of high quality dance experience and the teacher's role. Looking across all the models presented in this current chapter and the summary by Siddall, consider what characteristics are shared across all.

4. Select one of the models which appeals to you. Consider how it meets your individual values and beliefs about dance education.

5. Research other models of teaching. Often found in articles / books which give advice about teaching – model is a term they might not use, but advice or recommendations come with an often unspoken model or set of underpinning criteria. Consider how they address the issues raised in this chapter. For example: Fay (1997); or Benjamin (2002).

Bibliography

Amans, D. (ed) 2008 *An Introduction to Community Dance Practice*. Basingstoke: Palgrave Macmillan

Amans, D. 2010 *Passport to Practice*. London: Foundation for Community Dance.

Benjamin, A. 2002 *Making An Entrance, Theory and Practice for Disabled and Non-Disabled Dancers*. London: Routledge.

Bramley, I. 2002 *Dance Teaching Essentials*. London: Dance UK.

Bramley, I and Jermyn, H. 2006 *Dance Included: towards good practice in dance and social inclusion*. London: Arts Council England. www.artscouncil.org.uk

Buckroyd, J. 2000 *The Student Dancer: Emotional Aspects of the Teaching and Learning of Dance*. London: Dance Books.

Clay. G. Hertrich, J. Jones, P. Mills, J. and Rose, J. 1998 *The Arts Inspected*. Ofsted. Oxford: Heinemann Educational.

Dance Links 2005 *Dance Links: A guide to delivering high quality dance for children and young people*, DCMS/DfES. Document Ref: PE/DL. November.

Fay, M. 1997 *Mind Over Body: the development of the dancer – the role of the teacher*. London: A and C Black.

Freeman, J. 1998 *Educating the Very Able*. London: Ofsted, The Stationary Office.

Fullan, M. 1993 *Change Forces: probing the depths of education reform*. London: Falmer.

Gough, M. 1993 *in touch with dance*. Lancaster: Whitethorn Books.

Hopkins, D. undated. *Personalised Learning: how can we help every child do even better?* QCA Futures. www.qca.org.uk/futures

Kelly, A.V. 1999 *The Curriculum: Theory and Practice*. [4th edition] London: Paul Chapman.

Ofsted 2001 *Providing for gifted and talented pupils: an evaluation of Excellence in the Cities and other grant funded programmes.* December. www.ofsted.gov.uk

Ofsted 2003-2004 *Provision for gifted and talented pupils in physical education.* HMI 2149, July. www.ofsted.gov.uk

Ofsted 2009 *Gifted and Talented Pupils in Schools.* Ref:090132. December. www.ofsted.gov.uk

Ruddock, J. undated. *Pupil voice is here to stay*. QCA Futures. www.qca.org.uk/futures

Sanders, L. 2005 *Gifted and Talented Dancers: A Resource Booklet for Teachers.* noted in Siddall, J. 2010 *Dance In and Beyond Schools*. Youth Dance England.

Siddall, J. 2010 *Dance In and Beyond Schools*. London: Youth Dance England.

Whelan, J. and Neal, G. 2002 *Best Practice in Sports Colleges.* Loughborough: Youth Sport Trust.

UNIT 4
Dance Teaching in Practice

Chapter 24
The Reflective Journal
Alysoun Tomkins

Introduction

Your reflective journal is a personal document where you follow a line(s) of enquiry concerning your practice.

> Reflection is a thoughtful approach to teaching that helps you examine your professional abilities and better understand what you do. Reflection gives you a context for making positive changes in what you do.
>
> (McCutcheon, 2006, p. 468)

Moon (1999, p. 191) identifies various reasons for keeping a reflective journal but in the context of a reflective practitioner it is 'to enhance professional practice or the professional self in practice.' In order to do this, one must be able to 'translate the products of reflection into the real world of action so that they affect practice and something is done differently' (*ibid*).

Self-reflection can be part of evaluation (see Chapter 10) but in keeping a Reflective Journal one is perhaps taking a step back and widening the perspective so that, rather than evaluating a particular lesson or work plan, you are considering yourself as a practitioner in various contexts, or following a line of enquiry which will inform your practice.

By reviewing your practice and experiences you can learn from them in order to develop and improve your teaching.

A reflective document is a tool for helping you to contemplate what you have done, how you did it, what the outcomes were and how it connects to your present and future practice. There are also some useful suggestions for keeping a Reflective Journal in the DDTAL Syllabus.

Reflection will help you do the following:

- Be more aware of your individual teaching and learning styles.
- Chart your development.
- Develop skills of observation, critical thinking and analysis.
- Identify your strengths and weaknesses.
- Identify barriers to evaluating practice (including emotions and feelings which may hinder your progress).
- Devise strategies to overcome these barriers.
- Develop problem solving skills.
- Identify connections between present and past learning events.
- Anticipate connections with future learning events.
- Challenge your beliefs and attitudes.

- Change your perspectives.
- Avoid repeating mistakes.
- Have greater confidence in your skills and your ability to teach.
- Appreciate the relationships between theory and practice.
- Analyse success so that positive aspects can be applied to future practice.

Reflection in Practice

There are a number of theoretical models that attempt to systematise the reflective process:

1. Kolb (Kolb, cited in Avis, Fisher and Thompson, 2010, p. 93) suggested that the process of learning takes you through four stages, of which reflection is one, and called it a *Learning Cycle*. See Chapter 1 for further information.

If a teacher does not make full use of all four stages, they fail to maximise their learning potential. For example, they may not always reflect on what is happening, they may draw conclusions without reflecting first, or they may not apply the conclusions they draw. In order to be fully effective, your journal should illustrate a complete awareness of the four stages and each learning event you describe should be followed through the entire cycle.

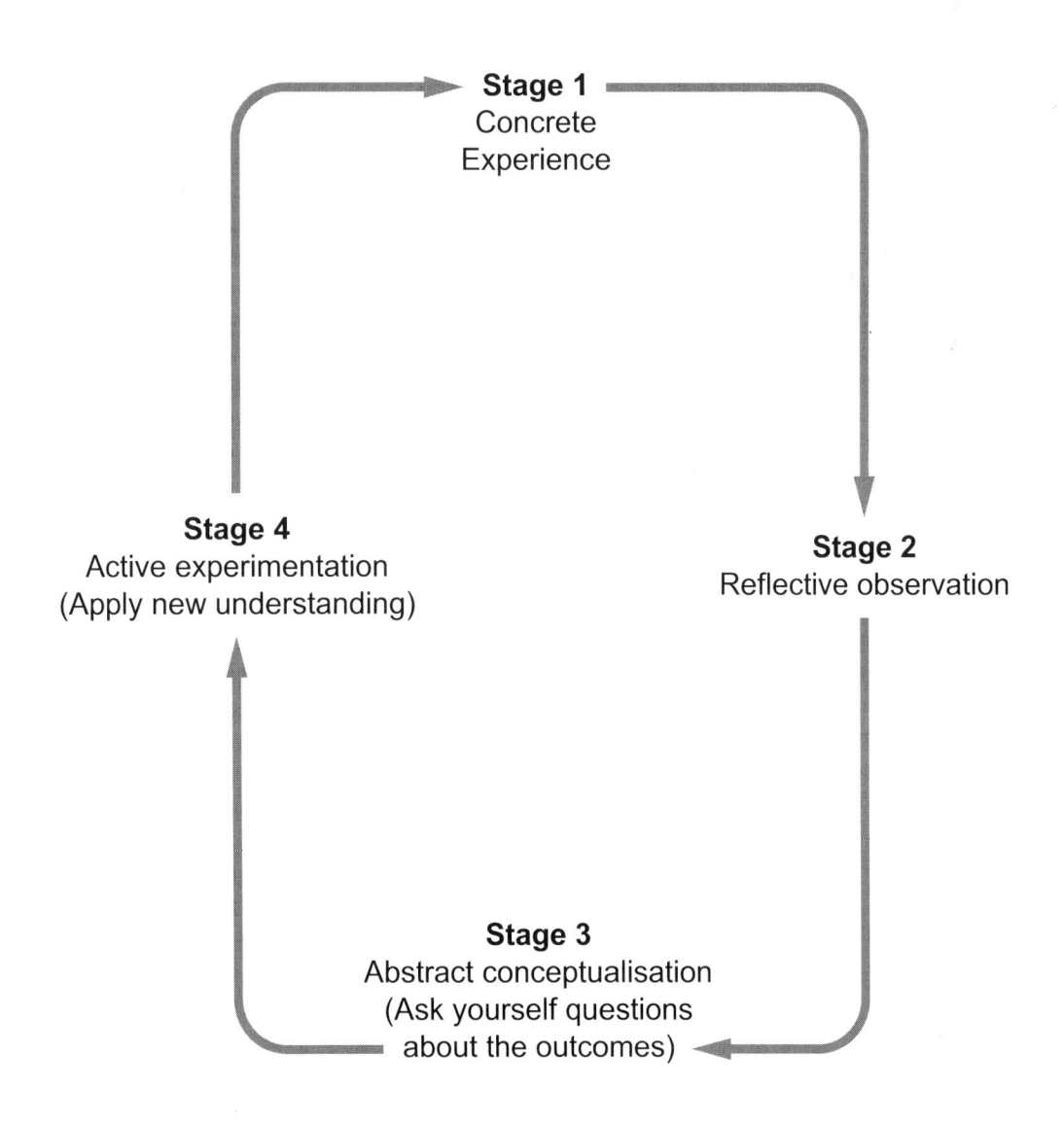

Stage 1
Concrete Experience

Stage 2
Reflective observation

Stage 3
Abstract conceptualisation
(Ask yourself questions about the outcomes)

Stage 4
Active experimentation
(Apply new understanding)

Exactly how this cycle enables us to learn effectively can be seen by examining how we tackle a task such as learning to pirouette:

Concrete Experience: Something occurs in a workshop or lesson?

Reflective Observation: You wonder why this happened.

You contemplate how you feel about it.

You ask yourself if this has happened before and make connections with similar situations.

You ponder on what you should have done differently.

Abstract Conceptualisation: From past experience you know that what occurred can be underpinned in different ways, e.g. other concepts and theories of teaching and learning, etc.

Active Experimentation: You modify your teaching based on new thinking and research.

2. Reynolds and Suter (cited in Avis, Fisher and Thompson, 2010, p. 190) propose a basic model of reflection where reflection and revised practice are ongoing (as in the example above):

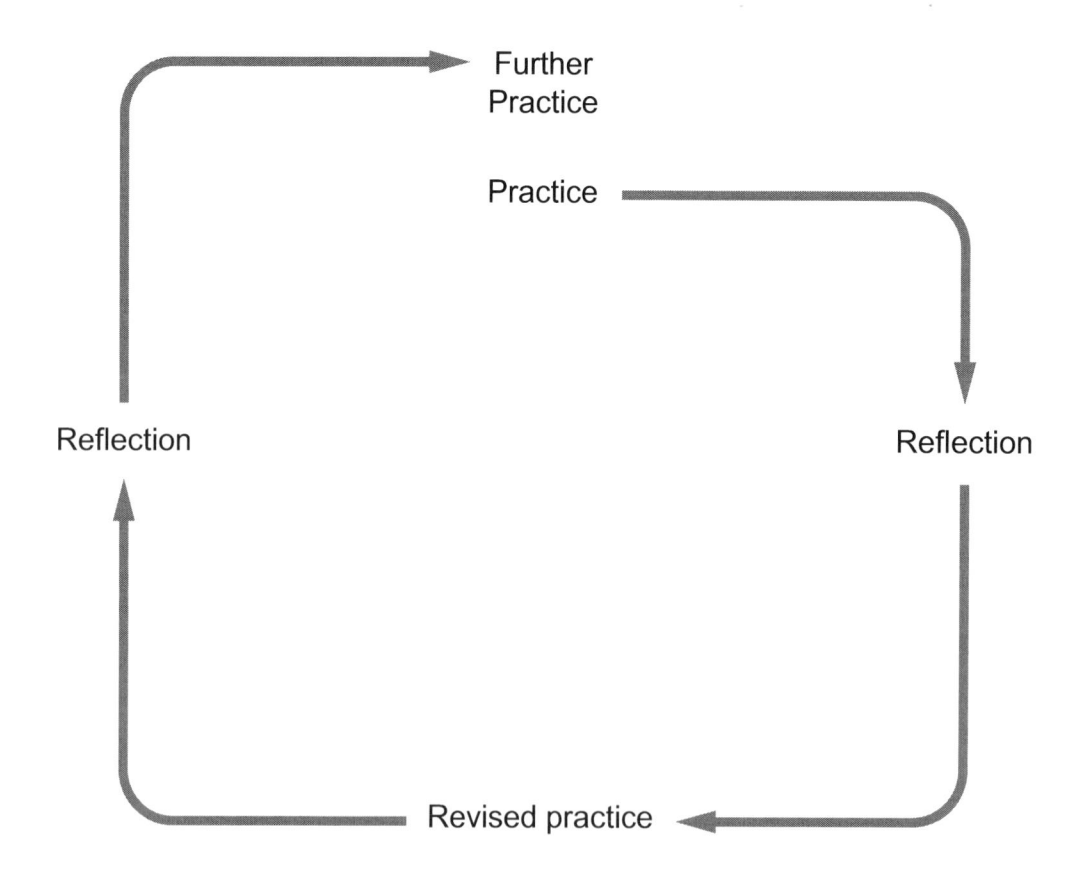

```
              Further
              Practice
                ▲
                │
              Practice ─────┐
                            │
                            ▼
Reflection              Reflection
   ▲                        │
   │                        │
   └──── Revised practice ◄─┘
```

Reynolds and Suter further propose that there are two types of reflection – technical and critical-organisational. They expound this by explaining that *Technical Reflection* can be referred to as 'problem-solving', it is done on a regular basis and deals with the techniques of planning and delivering learning. *Critical – Organisational Reflection* is questioning the decisions and actions of others in managerial positions which affect the success of the teacher's session(s). For example, your planning and delivery of a dance class might have been ideal, but because you had been placed in a small, carpeted room with no ventilation it affected the success of the class.

3. Schön, (cited in Avis, Fisher and Thompson, 2010, p. 194) identified what he called *'reflection in action'* which you and I might refer to as thinking on your feet – if something is not working you change it, and through experimentation in this way you become more able, knowledgeable and competent as a teacher. *'Reflection on action'* takes place after the event and can be achieved through writing about it or discussion with colleagues. (See Chapter 21).

4. According to Boud, Keogh and Walker (cited in Avis, Fisher, Thompson, 2010, p. 94) the reflective process can be broken down into three elementary stages:

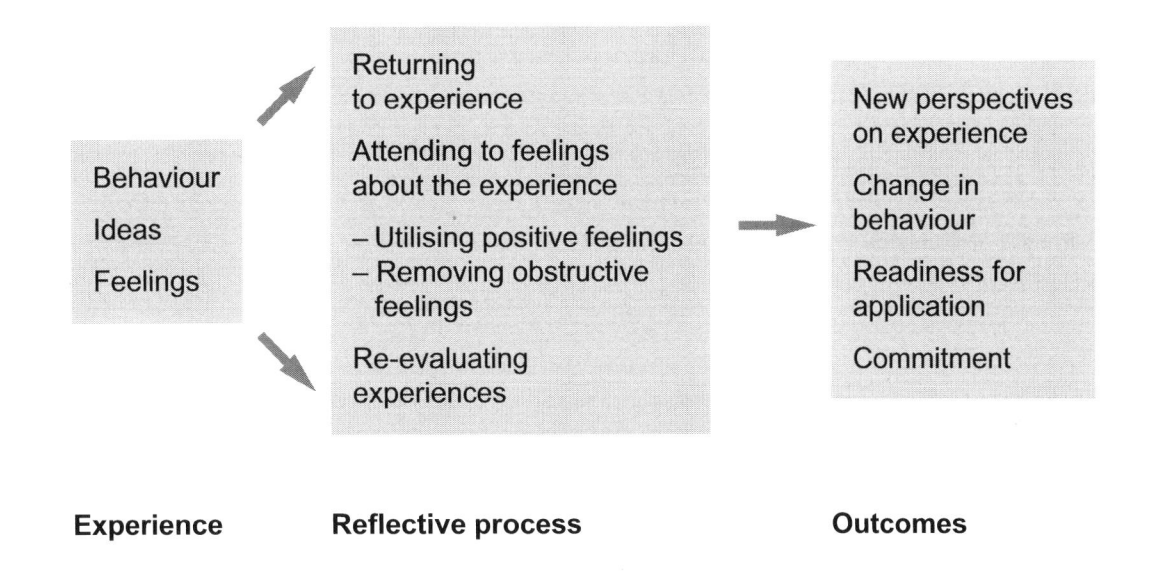

Experience	Reflective process	Outcomes
Behaviour Ideas Feelings	Returning to experience Attending to feelings about the experience – Utilising positive feelings – Removing obstructive feelings Re-evaluating experiences	New perspectives on experience Change in behaviour Readiness for application Commitment

- **The experience**

Returning to the experience(s) allows us to record in a descriptive manner exactly what happened. This provides the data upon which we reflect. Feelings and judgements should also be noted as part of that data.

- **Reflective process**

This stage should involve you in considering how the event affected you on many different levels: emotionally, physically, psychologically or intellectually. Positive and negative feelings should be equally acknowledged. Reconsider and examine the event afresh, clarify your feelings and perceptions and appreciate the event in a wider context - the context of your long-term experience. As well as description you now need to add other elements to your journal: observation, analysis, interpretation and introspection (examination of your own feelings).

- **Outcomes**

This stage involves the consolidation of your reflections and thinking about how you apply them to future experiences. You should extract new knowledge, skills, perceptions, beliefs and attitudes from your experience and you should be fully aware of how these came about and how you will move forward with them. The potential impact of your choice of possible actions should be explored before all the information gathered is integrated and conclusions are drawn.

Barriers To Reflection

The above theories concerning reflective learning all differ slightly (Schön, for example, does not address possible feelings one may experience about the event) but the ethos behind them is similar:

> You do…………..You think about it…………You do it differently

In order for this learning process to be successful, you need to approach it in such a way that it is useful to you. The format of the Reflective Journal is entirely a personal choice and should be based upon your perception of what is achievable. It is the observing, reflecting, thinking, researching, experimenting and discovering new knowledge, understanding and skills which are important. Inevitably, we can all find reasons as to why we are not able to do something:

- Q. *I do not understand or value the essential role of reflection in the learning process.*
- A. It is to learn more about your teaching in order to progress and develop as a practitioner.
- Q. *I am not sufficiently self-disciplined in order to spend the time reflecting and documenting my reflections.*
- A. Build reflection time into your working day/week as you would preparation time.
- Q. *I am unable to identify or admit to weaknesses and failures as well as to strengths and successes.*
- A. Ask someone to watch you teach and talk to them about your teaching experiences. Together draw up a SWOT analysis. Set up a support/discussion group.
- Q. *It is easier for someone to tell me where things are going wrong than for me to take responsibility for my learning.*
- A. One is often teaching alone so to acquire self-critical skills helps us to develop as practitioners.
- Q. *I am comfortable doing what I do and making changes scares me.*
- A. Changes can be small; you do not need to completely change your practice in one go. It is equally important to reflect on something that works well.

The Reflective Document

Hughes (2009) introduces the notion of reflective practice being an internal dialogue – talking to oneself or using an imagined 'other'. In this *autobiographical* form of writing one can move from self-indulgent writing to self-critical reflection. She acknowledges that there will be an emotional component to this style of writing but, as shown above, Boud, Keogh and Walker encourage the acknowledgement and inclusion of feelings as part of the collection of data. Another suggestion Hughes makes is that a teacher writes their reflections from the student's perspective taking into account theories of learning and observations of the students during the sessions. This approach will add another 'voice' to the reflective journal and help move from a purely subjective view to a more objective one. The use of a critical friend who has access to your journal on a regular basis, and with whom you can discuss issues as they arise, offers a further 'voice'.

Moon (1999, p. 75) cites Hatton and Smith's types of reflective writing. These are:

- 'Descriptive reflection' – this relates to Boud, Keogh and Walker's 'Experience' (see above) where the author describes exactly what happened.
- 'Dialogic reflection' – is similar to Hughes' *talking to one self or using an imagined 'other'* where you step back from the event.

- 'Critical reflection' – is when you begin to explore the reasons for the event and put it into a wider context.

It is the final step of the three above which one aims towards, that of critical reflection rather than self-indulgent or descriptive writing.

As stated previously, the Reflective Journal is a personal document which supports your development as a practitioner. It may well be written but equally could include visual material, be taped or video recorded, or it could be multi-presentational. Moon (1999, pp. 194-195) proposes that a Journal might be structured or unstructured.

Unstructured Journal Writing is usually chronological but may not include daily entries. One might make a journal entry on a regular basis, for example, monthly, or when the need arises and there is an element of record keeping in this method. Another term for this type of journal entry is 'key entry'. One could use a left hand page to record the events (descriptive writing) and use the right hand page as somewhere you return to after reflecting on those events and taking action (critical writing).

Structured Journal Writing is where there is a given format to the Journal, for example questions and answers or sectioned areas throughout the Journal which have particular headings relating to the lines of enquiry. An example of this might be that your line of enquiry is a case study on an autistic child in your class in order to learn how best to support children with autism in dance classes. Your section headings could focus on: behaviour; creativity; social interaction; learning style.

The style of your document should be personal to you. It should be a working document and supportive to your development. Over time, your document will become a dialogue with yourself, presenting an analysis of your learning supported by evidence and interpretations. Events you have experienced, previously isolated, will be seen in your document to be interconnected and the patterns and relationships which emerge will enable deeper levels of insight and introspection to take place. Consulting your document should allow you to see the development of your ideas and make you aware of the evolutionary nature of the processes of learning and developing.

To be effective the document should not only be descriptive but should:
- Analyse the process of your learning about teaching.
- Recognise new things being learned.
- Identify important issues and concepts.
- Relate theses items to your ongoing practice.

Key concepts in the creation of a reflective document are:
- Critical self-awareness – the ability to look honestly at yourself and your practice.
- Patterns – the ability to identify recurring themes in your experiences and analyse what lies behind them.
- Inquiry – the ability to look beyond the surface and question the motivations which lie behind what you do and how you react.
- Insight – the ability to identify meaning in your experiences and convey an understanding of them.
- Personal definition – the ability to identify and communicate your own values and beliefs as a teacher.
- Personal and professional growth – the ability to develop as an effective practitioner.

Examples of lines of enquiry one might take are:

- The introduction of different teaching styles into my classes.
- Adopting a more creative approach to teaching Classical Ballet.
- Integrating children with physical/sensory / learning difficulties into my classes.
- Assessing progress of my students.
- Managing behaviour more effectively.

However, I will reiterate that the Reflective Journal is a personal, working document which supports you in your professional development as a practitioner. As such you must identify those areas useful for further research in order to develop your skills, knowledge and understanding as a teacher of children and young people.

> A reflective practitioner in the arts also learns to be a vocal advocate for arts education...Your own reflective articulation encourages you to be the best you can. It keeps you rooted in the present by processing the past. It keeps you rooted in the present by having a perspective on where you are going in the future.
>
> (McCutcheon, 2006, pp. 471-472)

For the purposes of DDTAL, your Reflective Journal will be shown to the assessor and it will form the basis of a discussion of the themes, topics, issues, and learning that you have documented in the journal.

REFLECTION

1. Identify an event in a class that you can reflect on. Complete the following:

Reflection in Action – thinking on your feet.		
What happened?	What did I do about it?	Was it successful?

2. Based on Moon (1999, p.180) *Schema to guide reflective activity in professional practice towards improvement of professional practice.* Answer the following questions:

Phase 1: Develop awareness of the nature of your current practice
• What is your current work practice – how do you teach dance?

Phase 2: Clarify the new learning [on the DDTAL course]
• What is it that you have learnt which can improve your practice?

> **Phase 3: Integrate new learning and current practice**
> - How does this new knowledge relate to what you knew and did before?

> **Phase 4: Anticipate or imagine the nature of improved practice**
> - What will you do differently to improve your practice?

Bibliography

Avis, J. Fisher, R. Thompson, R. (Eds.) 2010 *Teaching in Lifelong Learning – A Guide to Theory and Practice*. Berkshire: McGraw-Hill.

Boud, D. and Keogh, R. (Eds.) 1988 *Reflection: Turning experience into learning*. London: Kogan Page.

Honey, P. and Mumford, A. 1983 *Using your learning styles*. Maidenhead: Peter Honey Publications.

Hughes, G. 2009 Talking to oneself: using autobiographical internal dialogue to critique everyday and professional practice. *Reflective Practice*, 10, 4, pp.451-463.

McCutcheon, B. 2006 *Teaching Dance as Art in Education*. USA: Human Kinetics.

Moon, J. 1999 *Reflection in learning and professional development. Theory and Practice*. Routledge: London.

Mumford, A. 1999 *Effective learning*. London: Institute of Personnel Development.

Chapter 25
Behaviour Management and Communication in Practice
Helen Linsell

Introduction: What is Behaviour Management?

"The only person whose behaviour we can control is our own"

(Glasser, undated)

Behaviour management is concerned with the ability to facilitate a positive climate for safe and effective learning, enabling all students to reach their potential and achieve their learning objectives. With regard to the education of children and young people, it is our responsibility to guide them towards a coherent understanding of how to behave appropriately in a learning environment and within a wider social context.

When confronted with behaviour that disrupts the learning process, there are numerous strategies we can utilise to manage the situation. These strategies focus predominantly on building positive relationships with our students and controlling our own actions and reactions in order to make clear decisions about how best to respond to the behaviour:

Never React, Only Respond

Challenging behaviour will often cause us to experience negative emotions such as fear, insecurity, embarrassment or anger. However, in our professional role as teachers, it is essential that our own personal thoughts and feelings do not adversely interfere with how we respond to the behaviour. Controlling our own emotions and behaviour effectively will enable us to help children and young people manage theirs.

Strategies in effective behaviour management will vary according to individuals and the contexts in which we work. We must explore different approaches in dealing with challenging behaviour, accepting that some may be more successful than others and will often depend on external factors. Over time and through our on-going experience 'on the ground', we will gain confidence in our practice and develop our own preferred behaviour management procedures.

Definitions of Challenging Behaviour:

Sorensen (undated, n.p), a practitioner within the field of mental health, describes challenging behaviour as:

- **Behaviour that we do not like.**
- **Behaviour that we think we need to respond to.**

However, Carey, argues from a psychological perspective, that defining challenging behaviour can be problematic:

> What is challenging in one context can be perceived as quite normal in another. The contextual nature of human behaviour makes it difficult to be certain what is appropriate or inappropriate.
>
> (Cary, undated, n.p.)

We all have definitions of what constitutes challenging behaviour and we make choices about the behaviour we respond to and that which we ignore. However, as teachers, it is crucial that *we do not ignore* any inappropriate behaviour. If we fail to confront behavioural issues, we are confirming that such behaviours are acceptable both in the learning environment and in a wider social context.

Setting Boundaries:

Before we confront behavioural issues, it is important to assess where our boundaries lie. It is inevitable that, when working with any group, we will experience some level of what we perceive to be challenging behaviour, but what do we consider to be **low, medium** or **severe** levels of behaviour and why? Against what criteria are we measuring these levels? Are the boundaries realistic for the specific context and young people with whom we are working? Are we making professional or personal judgements?

By identifying our own boundaries, we will become more confident in setting appropriate boundaries for our participants:

> You're doing them a favour by giving them clear boundaries. Young people want certainty from the adults in their lives.
>
> (Cowley, 2010, p. 9)

Defining boundaries will:

- Increase our confidence and demonstrate our authority as leaders, helping us to establish control of the learning situation.
- Determine clear expectations and standards for our participants.
- Provide a safe and structured learning environment (particularly important for those students coming from chaotic and disruptive backgrounds).
- Make it easier to impose sanctions; if young people understand the boundaries, they will be more accepting of the sanctions and will develop a stronger understanding of the consequences of their actions.

BUT remember…

- Be clear about the reasons behind these boundaries – young people require explanations as to why certain limits are in place.
- Be consistent in maintaining these boundaries. Some students will push boundaries but we must uphold our standards, no matter how exhausting this becomes. In the long term, our participants will appreciate this level of clarity. Being too relaxed about 'rules' or shifting the boundaries will cause confusion about what is acceptable and not-acceptable behaviour and this will allow poor behaviour to increase.

There may be times when it is appropriate and necessary to be flexible with the boundaries and find compromises. However, these decisions must be made rationally and for the right reasons. We must be sure that our students will respond positively to any shifts in the boundaries and will understand the reasons behind our decisions.

How To Set Boundaries?

The most effective way to set boundaries is through a Code of Conduct; an agreed way of working. This can be used as a point of reference for the duration of the project/workshop and can help to set targets for more challenging individuals.

A Code of Conduct should:

- Be created during the early stages of a project / workshop.
- Be devised by both participants and staff.
- Outline what is expected of the participants and what they should expect from us.
- Reflect the rights and responsibilities of ALL participants and staff.
- Establish all rules and regulations.
- Consider general and specific behaviours.
- Be clear, concise and reasonable.
- Be displayed - if possible – as a visual reminder of what has been agreed.
- Be written down and signed by participants and staff (in the form of a contract) - if appropriate.
- Be re-visited regularly throughout the learning process.

Case Study 1

Whilst promoting shared ownership over the Code of Conduct, we must guide students towards what we know, from our experience, to be an effective set of rules. It is also important to clarify which rules are non-negotiable. We should not be afraid to demand certain standards of discipline. For example, when working with young offenders, imposing a no tolerance policy around criminal activity, drugs and weapons is both relevant and necessary.

- In your own practice, consider which rules are non-negotiable and why.

Although it may not be feasible to establish a Code of Conduct for one-off sessions, outlining some simple rules and boundaries at the beginning of class will significantly reduce the risk of challenging behaviour.

First Impressions

The first time we meet our participants and the tone that we set is a vital element of effective behaviour management. Children and young people, without realising it, will judge us on this first encounter.

Key Points:

Start with a positive attitude – both verbally and non-verbally

- Smile as we greet them – perhaps even shake their hand. Consider an open posture with welcoming body language, i.e. not crossed arms.
- Start to get to know them before the session begins, i.e. their names, how they are, where they have travelled from etc. Take an interest in them as individuals.

- Be ready and energised in the space.
- Introduce ourselves and the activity with positive descriptions, i.e. "I'm really excited to meet you all and I know this project is going to be really amazing."

Set the tone of respect and equality:
- If possible, start in a circle with everyone equally positioned. Attempt to make eye-contact with every individual.
- Ensure that staff are dispersed within the circle.
- Use the term 'we' to establish a sense of company.
- Thank everyone for being there – praise them for their achievements before any activity has started whilst demonstrating good manners.

Hook them in!
- Have positive expectations and set high standards from the beginning – give them something to aim for both in terms of their behaviour and their skills.
- Highlight everything they will gain from taking part in our activity and assure them they all have the potential to achieve these goals, even if they do not yet know it.
- Be passionate and confident. If we believe in the work, they will too.

When children and young people first meet us:
- *What are we doing?* We must model the behaviour that we expect. If we are in a bad mood, stressed, using our mobile phone, chewing gum, wearing shoes in the studio, using inappropriate language, we are modelling poor behaviour so cannot expect to demand anything different from our participants.
- *What are we wearing?* Although it may seem irrelevant, children and young people will judge us by what we are wearing and this can have a significant effect on the relationship we build with them, particularly teenagers.
- *What music is playing?* Our choice of music can play a significant part in building positive rapport with our students. This may be dictated by the content and style of our activity but it is useful to consider the first piece of music they hear and how they are going to relate to it. Even if it is not something they are familiar with, is it something they can connect to?

Final Tips on SETTING UP the activity
- Risk-assess the space and remove any hazards or potential distractions – an organised and appropriate space will reduce possible disruptions.
- Have all relevant resources in the space – hair bands, plasters, paper and pens, music – this will ensure that we will not have to leave the group on their own.
- Commit to learning ALL names by the end of the first session. This will allow every individual to immediately feel respected, valued and included.

> By using someone's name, you show awareness of the individuals in your class, and you demonstrate respect for those individuals.....you are at a great disadvantage if you do not know their names.

(Cowley, 2010, p. 34)

Our Pre-Conceptions:

Certain students may already have been labelled 'difficult' or 'naughty'. However, rather than anticipate negative behaviour and judge them according to someone else's experiences and opinions, we should have high expectations and treat each individual with respect. They are more likely to respond positively to us if we ignore labels which society has placed on them.

Planning, Content and Structure:

Effective planning, appropriate lesson content and logical structure are important aspects of good teaching practice but some of these elements may help prevent challenging behaviour.

PLANNING
Be prepared to meet a wide range of needs, particularly with more difficult groups. • Assess how to split the group – who may / may not work well together? • Aim to learn as a company and in small groups – allow for 1:1 attention and observation. • If planning to work with small groups or individuals, prepare tasks for all other students so they remain engaged. • Prepare to be flexible – have alternative options. • Anticipate things which MIGHT happen and prepare students adequately, i.e. visitors, written work.
CONTENT
Ensure lessons are interesting, exciting and engaging – aim to INSPIRE students. • Challenge students but allow EVERYONE the opportunity to feel they have succeeded on some level. • Consider age groups – do not patronise students or over-estimate ability. • Include a variety of activities to develop a wide range of skills. • Have fun – if students gain pleasure from what we teach, they will remain engaged/committed.
STRUCTURE
An organised session provides a sense of stability, which may well be absent from some of their lives. • Set tasks and goals within certain timeframes. • Vary the pace and energy of different activities to keep everyone engaged. • Give clear reasons and aims for each activity. • Help students to understand the connections between activities. • Evaluate achievements at the end of the session. • Outline break times.

If possible, meet students before the activity and outline anything which may prove challenging, for example, bare feet. For more vulnerable young people, this preliminary meeting may mean the difference between them attending or not.

Avoid pandering to more difficult students by giving them what they think they want. Take risks and challenge students, open their minds to new experiences and push them to learn more advanced skills. By encouraging students out of their comfort zone in a safe and structured way, they develop the potential to achieve greater things and this will have a longer-term impact on their lives.

Recognising Challenging Behaviour

Challenging behaviour will generally appear in the form of:

- Resistance
- Disengagement
- Confrontation / Abuse – verbal and physical

These behaviours will appear as a result of a range of complex underlying issues, often linked to social, environmental, medical and psychological factors. However, although we should have an awareness of the reasons behind poor behaviour, our specific role as a teacher should concentrate on addressing the more immediate causes:

- Boredom
- Short attention spans
- Insecurity, feeling undervalued and attention seeking
- Lack of understanding and relevant skills leading to a sense of failure

Strategies

1. Encourage and influence students to take responsibility for their behaviour – guide them towards recognising their behaviour, understanding its impact on themselves and others and making independent choices about rectifying it.

2. Separate the behaviour from the individual - if we appear to be criticising and accusing the person, this may amplify the negative behaviour and result in the student losing trust in us.

> 'What they do is not the same as who they are.'
>
> (Hook and Vass, 2004, p. 44)

3. Aim to defuse rather than escalate the situation.

4. Build rapport and form positive relationships with students through a range of interpersonal skills:

Use of Language and Vocabulary	Tone and Volume of Voice	Attention to Learning Styles
Pace of delivery	Clarity and Confidence	Patience
Honesty, Sensitivity and Empathy	Humour	Assertiveness
Use of Praise and Positive Feedback	Body Language, Posture and Facial Expressions	Active Listening

HOW we communicate is equally as significant as WHAT we are communicating.

Neuro-Linguistic Programming (NLP) explores the theory that:

> you always succeed in communicating something. It just may not be what you intended. The responses you get give you valuable pointers about what to do next.
>
> (O'Connor and McDermott, 2001, p. 24)

Thus, whilst interacting with our students, we must observe their responses carefully to assess whether we are communicating successfully or being misunderstood. What might we have to do differently?

Praise and Positive Language:

> The discriminating use of praise, and the ability to remain relentlessly positive, will help you a great deal in managing behaviour.
>
> (Cowley, 2010, p. 15)

- Maximise good behaviour and reduce the need for sanctions by focusing on positive behaviour, i.e. praise students for abiding by the Code of Conduct.
- Recognise individual and group achievements. Take time to praise individuals within a group context and on a one to one basis.
- Place more attention on those displaying positive behaviour.
- Try to re-direct negative behaviour back to something positive and use 'thanks' to show your acknowledgement.
- Be specific and genuine with praise.
- Explore a range of positive words – excellent, stunning, fantastic etc.
- Use non-verbal signs as well as words, i.e. smiles, nods and thumbs up.

Further Research

Our understanding of effective behaviour management can be enhanced through the study of the following practitioners and theories:

William Glasser – *Choice Theory* and *Reality Therapy*

Concerned with human behaviour and social interaction, Glasser argued that we cannot control other people's behaviour or force them to do something we want them to do. He highlighted:

- The fundamental need for love and a sense of belonging.
- The importance of young people taking responsibility for their behaviour.
- The need to develop respectful and caring relationships with students.

Carl Rogers – *Student Centred Learning*

Rogers, a leading psychologist in the Humanist movement, argued that every individual has the ability to alter and change their own behaviour when exposed to open, caring and respectful relationships. By being accepted, understood and seen in a positive light by others, individuals gain a sense of self-worth and positive self-image, therefore increasing the potential to achieve desired goals and ambitions.

Thomas Gordon – *Group-Centred Leadership*

Gordon explored the concept of allowing individuals the freedom to express their ideas and opinions and contribute to solving problems. He emphasised the need for 'active' and 'reflective' listening – feeding back to the student about what has been understood and accepting their feelings and thoughts – and the importance of separating the behaviour from the person. He argued that this approach would lead to conflict resolution and less need for disciplinary action.

Abraham Maslow – *Hierarchy of Needs*

Psychologist, Abraham Maslow, explored the different layers of human needs that lead to reaching one's potential (see Chapter 1):

Psychological ➞ Safety ➞ Love and Belonging ➞ Esteem ➞ Self-Actualisation

Within the context of education, we must recognise that certain individuals may be lacking some of the more basic human needs (home, food, love, security, self-esteem and belonging) and this will inevitably hinder their process of learning. We should therefore be aware of how we, as teachers, can contribute to some of these needs before we can look to help them towards being better and more advanced learners.

Case Study 2

A student is sitting at the side of the space refusing to participate.
What can we do? Think through your answer before reading on.

- Ask why they are sitting out? Is there something wrong? Actively listen to the response.
- Outline clearly and politely what you want and need them to: "I would like it if you would join in because I need you to learn this phrase. Thank you".
- Explain why they need to join in: "We have to finish this section by the end of the day so we can run the piece. We can't do that without you".
- Give them an incentive "If you join in again quickly, we can move on to the duets which you really enjoy".
- Offer TIME OUT (introduced in the Code of Conduct) "Take five minutes out and then come back".
- Remind them of the Code of Conduct – no sitting down in the studio – and highlight the consequences of their behaviour, i.e. the effect on the group, might be cut from that section.
- Use humour to re-engage them.
- Remind them of earlier achievements.
- Use 'we': "Shall we do the phrase together?"
- Offer understanding and sympathy: "I know it's a really long day and it's very hot…"
- Remain calm and positive – never lose your patience.
- Set the rest of the group a task whilst dealing with the situation.

Case Study 3

A student is frustrated by an activity and starts shouting abusive language. What can we do? Think through your answer before reading on.

We must learn to recognise the early signs of anger so that we can intervene BEFORE behaviour erupts.

- Offer choices: "You can either calm down and continue with the task or take TIME OUT".
- Highlight possible consequences i.e. written warning, asked to leave, police called.
- Remain VERY calm when speaking – demonstrate opposite energy to what is being displayed.
- Be aware of spatial proximity – the student may be agitated if you enter their personal space.
- If anger is directed at you, do not take it personally.
- Advise the student to take deep breaths but accept they may need to 'let off steam' before calming down.
- Remove the student from the situation BUT consider how you ask them to leave, i.e. "I need you to leave the studio for five minutes please, thank you".
- Walk away and give the student space and time alone. Tell them you will come back.
- Ask what has caused the outburst – talk through the situation and try to show understanding.
- When the student has calmed down, remind them of the Code of Conduct.

Case Study 4

Two students are whispering and laughing, not paying attention to the session. It appears that the conversation is directed towards another student. What can we do? Think through your answer before reading on.

Any kind of bullying, no matter how subtle, MUST be dealt with. Bullying can be extremely damaging in the short and long term and must NEVER be ignored.

- Refer to the Code of Conduct: "We all agreed that whispering is very disrespectful. Please can you stop and continue with the activity, thank you".
- Avoid drawing attention to the person about whom they are whispering.
- Separate the students who are whispering and ensure they are not positioned near each other and do not work together during the session.
- Speak to the students immediately after the session. Highlight the consequences – bullying is dealt with seriously. Clarify what will happen if the behaviour continues (phoning parents, written warning, asked to leave the project).
- Facilitate a group session about bullying and respect later on in the project (if it is a long-term activity).

Sanctions, Discipline Procedures and Rewards

> Sanctions do not change behaviour
>
> (Hook and Vass, 2004, p. 30)

One of the difficulties when working with challenging groups is selecting appropriate consequences for disruptive behaviour. Each organisation and individual teacher will explore a variety of disciplinary systems but the most important factors are CONSISTENCY and CLARITY. The moment we are inconsistent or uncertain with our discipline procedures is the moment we lose trust and respect from our participants.

When a student first demonstrates challenging behaviour, we may initially respond with a disapproving comment or facial expression. This may then be followed by an informal and private conversation (facilitated by one or two members of staff) during which the student should be encouraged to reflect on how and why their behaviour is unacceptable.

By immediately addressing the behaviour in the session and informally outside of the session, the situation may successfully be resolved.

However, if the behaviour continues, it will be necessary to introduce more formal sanctions:

- Coloured cards or strikes - Detentions / Reports - Losing opportunities, i.e. theatre trip - Suspension / Expulsion from school / project	- Verbal and written warnings - Letters and phone calls to parents / workers / school / teachers - Behavioural Contract

Useful Tips:

- Be aware of how sanctions are delivered – publicly or privately.
- Do not make empty threats – be prepared to carry out sanctions.
- Buy yourself time – avoid making spontaneous decisions about sanctions.
- Offer the student a choice – follow the instruction or choose the consequence.
- Ensure that sanctions are fair – the sanction must fit the behaviour / the individual and must send the right messages to the whole group.

Rewards

Depending on age and context, rewards can be an effective method of motivating learning and promoting positive behaviour. Possible rewards:

- Positive verbal and non-verbal feedback - Letters and phone calls to parents / workers / teachers	- Stars and stickers; certificates and awards - Additional opportunities, i.e. trips out - Extra responsibility

When considering sanctions and rewards, our fundamental aim should be to help students grow into respectful adults with an intrinsic desire to learn and succeed. The ultimate reward should be the experience of learning and achieving with the most threatening sanction being the possibility of that opportunity being taken away. If we can reach this place with our students, we are not only effectively managing their behaviour but we are, more importantly, significantly influencing their lives.

Consider the ending of sessions and projects:
- Finish in an orderly fashion, not in chaos.
- Avoid running out of time.
- Try to end on a positive note.
- Review and consolidate what has been achieved.
- Prepare young people for endings – some behaviours may be triggered by a positive experience coming to an end.
- Always *reflect* on your practice. It is inevitable that we will make mistakes and these mistakes will help us grow as teachers. However, we must not forget to recognise our accomplishments.
- Trust our own skills and knowledge. Have confidence in our experience.
- Always remember why we are teaching in the first place… never lose the PASSION!

Additional Resources:

Cherry, S. 2005 *Transforming Behaviour. Pro-Social Modelling in Practice*. Devon: Willan.

Leaman, L. 2009 *Managing Very Challenging Behaviour*. London: Continuum.

Porter, L 2010 *Behaviour in Schools*. Berkshire: Open University Press.

www.behaviourmanagement.org

www.gordontraining.com

www.simplypsychology.org/carl-rogers.html

www.teachingexpertise.com

www.tes.co.uk/behaviourmanagement

REFLECTION

1. Identify an occasion where you felt challenged by a participant. How did you deal with this? How might you think about this differently?

2. What rewards might you use already or consider? What is the impact of these in your own practice? Could the use of these be improved?

3. Select one of the additional resources and research behaviour management further. For example, the *Times Educational Supplement* has a range of free to download resources – see the last resource listed above.

Bibliography

Carey, D. undated (accessed 04.08.2011): http://www.davidjcarey.com.

Cowley, S. 2010 *Getting the Buggers to Behave*. London: Continuum.

Glasser, w. undated (accessed 04.08.2011): http://www.wglasser.com.

Hook, P. and Vass, A. 2004 *Behaviour Management Pocket Book*. Hampshire: Teachers' Pocketbooks.

O'Connor, J. and McDermott, I. 2001 *Way of NLP*. London: Thorsons.

Sorenson, S. undated (accessed 04.08.2011): http://www.stuartsorenson.wordpress.com.

Chapter 26
Presenting a Detailed Lesson Plan
Lorna Sanders

Introduction

Having a well-planned lesson, appropriate to learners' needs, is essential for high quality delivery in dance. You will need to draw on all the pedagogical knowledge that you have been introduced to in previous chapters; it is not the intention here to summarise or revisit this. In a Work Plan, such as considered for Unit 1 of DDTAL, a general outline of a scheme and its progression are summarised. A lesson plan translates the indicative content into fuller detail for delivery. When is it detailed enough? When someone else can pick up your plan and deliver the lesson, or when you can pick up the plan months later and follow it, then it is likely to contain enough information. The important issue is to have considered all the necessary aspects for effective teaching and learning.

Whether a planning format is found conducive can be very individual; one size does not fit all, and in the informal sector of dance education there is no required type that is considered good practice. There are many examples of lesson plan models on the web and different institutions and organisations may have their own requirements to follow. Any suitable format from reputable and recognised sources can be appropriate and you may already be using a particular type that you find useful. What is important is that the model you select covers all the information that must be considered for the planning of effective learning. For DDTAL there is no specific preferred layout or method of presentation, (e.g. landscape, portrait, tabulated, sectioned in specific ways with particular headings). The layout is a vehicle for the content and its clarity of expression.

What is presented in this chapter is a suggested Lesson Plan Template to indicate the range and type of content, in order to guide you in respect of the areas which need to be considered. In Chapter 6, three different models were suggested which provided different stages or steps in planning and these had different terms for sectioning the content. The Lesson Plan Template here builds on Gough's model but you may also use the terminology and the stages from any of the others if they suit your purpose. The four strands of dancing, performing, creating and watching will occur in different amounts and for different purposes in lessons. Whether a lesson is focusing on technique or composition, for example, dance is a whole domain and all the strands are likely to be there in some respect. Attention should be placed on how the skills of appreciation underpin learning within dance.

The first sections of the template indicate the range of factual information required; these draw attention to the importance of the context, setting, group and their prior experience for example. Ensure you understand the difference between planning for Aims and crafting Learning Outcomes (see Chapter 6). These are frequently confused with each other but they have different purposes. For the latter, a common mistake is to write what you or the participants will *do* whereas your statement needs to lead you towards being able to assess the learning involved.

> **Case Study 1**
>
> What is problematic about the phrasing of the following Learning Outcome?
>
> *Participants will create a duet.*
>
> They will have been successful whatever the quality of the duet or whatever process was involved in the creation. We are given no information about what is important and thus the statement gives little assistance in assessing the outcome. This phrase however might have usefully indicated a Movement Theme which would help to clarify the progressive tasks on offer. (Of course, in a project where the aim is a limited one of simply to get the participants actively involved in the process, the statement might be adequate as a learning outcome in that instance).

Learning Outcomes can be process orientated and product orientated depending on the Aims and context. In other words, the associated assessment can take account of the success of **the product** (for example the choreography, or the performance technique achieved) and / or **the learning process** that has taken place along the way (for example the development of appropriate communication skills while involved in creating a group choreography; or the application and practice of sustained concentration during rehearsal for a performance).

To assess effectively, Learning Outcomes / Objectives must be clear. They can be expressed as identifying what a student should know or what they should be able to do. The latter has often been more emphasised in formal education sectors:

> objectives should be couched in behavioural language so that we can judge by the changes in student behaviour whether or not the desired learning has taken place. In other words, objectives should state clearly what a student should be able to do at the end of a successful lesson.
>
> (Fontana, 1995, p. 157)

In summary, Aims are the overarching purposes of the whole; these are translated into Learning Outcomes / Objectives which identify how the Aims are achieved and what learning is involved; the Theme of the lesson is how an individual Outcome / range of Outcomes are being addressed; and the Movement Aims are how the theme is being met in selected key movements, experiences and/or processes. Each layer of information is logically dependent on the other. Prompts are given in the Lesson Template to remind you of the differences.

However you decide to lay out the lesson, there must be a clear beginning, middle and end. Time allocations should be planned for each individual activity / task; in this way if you run over during delivery you will be better placed to judge what task to leave out or to adjust; overall section timings are useful so you can judge where you are in the whole.

If you are undertaking DDTAL, the Work Plan has already given indicative action content. In order to plan for effective delivery, there is a need to plan the break down and progressive building up of each activity into sequential tasks; for example, when teaching a phrase you can reduce it down into the smaller sections you will teach and how you will do this, and then how you will refine and rehearse it before moving on (see Chapters 1 and 3 for further information).

For each task, you need to plan for and give an indication of differentiation (for inclusion, different ability or gender for example); and construct extension tasks for the highest ability or where you might need to have additional tasks planned in case participants achieve the activity more quickly than anticipated.

Each task can be accompanied by *Teaching Points*. These articulate the important information in respect of how learning styles are addressed; key safety or technique points that must be kept in mind; or any key questions to pose, or guidance for appreciation and feedback for example. Any significant information that you want to provide as a cue to yourself, and which is worth planning in advance, can be expressed.

Case Study 2

In a lesson where the Movement Ideas include: use of space: directions – front, side, back; and travelling pathways, the following Exploration Task and associated Teaching Points are planned:

'In groups of 4-6 ask the pupils to stand in a straight line (shoulder to shoulder) and then walk across the room travelling on straight, parallel pathways.

Repeat this, changing the speed at which each dancer walks.

Teaching Point. Ask the rest of the class to observe the relationships formed between the dancers. How is this affected by the dancers' various use of time?'

A clear breakdown is given of the task (you could reconstruct it in practice and can certainly visualise what could be occurring) and the key purpose for appreciation is indicated which the observing class members are to note.

(Brown, 2010, p. 37)

Teaching styles and strategies for delivery need to be considered and identified (see Chapter 3). Remember that for each teaching style there are a range of different strategies that might be employed. For example, in a technique workshop where didactic demonstration is in use it is possible to move the front line to the back – this class management strategy ensures that each student is brought to the front from time to time. It is useful to plan the strategies that will be employed.

Include plenty of opportunity to review and reflect on understanding / learning. Remember that reinforcement and distributed practice are important (see Chapter 2). Showing and sharing can also be included throughout the lesson, as can appreciation opportunities, and not just in the concluding section of the class.

Assessment criteria, linked to the Learning Outcomes / Objectives, need to be clarified and a method for appraisal decided (See Chapter 9). Warm Up and Cool Down are essential to plan for (See Chapter 16).

For DDTAL Unit 4 you currently need to prepare three consecutive lessons. Clarify at the start of each, the prior learning that is being reiterated (always check the syllabus for up-to-date requirements).

Unit 4 - Dance Teaching in Practice

A Lesson Plan Template

Your name:	Venue / Date / Duration of session:
Type of activity: technique class; creative workshop; other activity?	**Brief description:** e.g. dance style; lesson number in the scheme of work / name of syllabus or other; links to curriculum / context / setting.
Participant profile: e.g. number in session, age, gender, special needs, prior learning / previous experience.	
Resources: ICT, music, etc.	

Lesson Plan
Long Term Aims: Overarching purposes of the lesson e.g. placing the lesson in context of the Work Plan; linking to the curriculum / programme of study / syllabus. See Chapter 6.
Learning Outcomes / Objectives: Short term purposes of learning to be achieved – e.g. overall objectives of the lesson including understandings of knowledge, physical, social, or cultural aspects. What they will learn – not what is to be done as activity. See Chapter 6.
Theme of the Lesson: Key Focus / Idea / Stimulus of the lesson. See Chapter 6.
Movement Aims: Identify the key movement experience or actions to be covered (what they will do).

Health and Safety
List relevant key issues. Identify briefly how these will be dealt with.

Lesson content	
Indicate time for each task (e.g. 5 mins)	Full details of lesson including: information on activity / task / combination / exercise; key teaching points; differentiation and / or extension tasks needed; teaching role and management strategies.
Time	**INTRODUCTION** How will you open / introduce the lesson?
Time	**WARM UP** **Task 1.** Details of Activity or Task Key Teaching Points: Differentiation / Extension: Teacher Role / Strategy:
Time	**Task 2.** Details of Activity or Task Key Teaching Points: Differentiation / Extension: Teacher Role / Strategy:
Time	**Task 3** etc.

Times allocated for each task	**MOVEMENT EXPLORATION** As in Warm Up: numbered activities / tasks: e.g. exercises, combinations, creative tasks. See Chapter 5 for developing progression. Key Teaching Points: *(for each numbered activity / task etc.)* Differentiation / Extension: *(for each numbered activity / task etc.)* Teacher Role / Strategy: *(for each numbered activity / task etc.)* Identify Learning Outcomes met:
Times allocated for each task	**DEVELOPMENT** As in Warm up: numbered activities / tasks: e.g. exercises, combinations, creative tasks performance refinement). See Chapter 5 for developing progression. Key Teaching Points: *(for each numbered activity / task etc.)* Differentiation / Extension: *(for each numbered activity / task etc.)* Teacher Role / Strategy: *(for each numbered activity / task etc.)* Identify Learning Outcomes met:
Times allocated for each task	**APPRECIATION / EVALUATION** Numbered activities / tasks: e.g. climax of lesson; final showing and sharing; feedback; final dance sequence. Key Teaching Points: Differentiation / Extension: Teacher Role / Strategy: Identify Learning Outcomes that are met:

Closing the Lesson	
Times allocated for each task	**COOL DOWN** identify activity as in warm up. **PLENARY** identify closing focus – e.g. reinforcement; how they might apply information in other sessions, homework, appraisal, etc.

Assessment
Assessment Criteria: Based on Learning Outcomes / Objectives
Methods of Assessment: assessment for learning, strategies, evidence, informal/formal what the teacher will do, what participants will do, etc.

Evaluation
Identify and explain how and where the session and the delivery achieves its aims.

REFLECTION

1. Find an old lesson plan. Rewrite it using different lesson plan templates. Find a method of presentation that is suitable for you.

2. Ask a colleague to look over your lesson plan. Ask them if they can visualise the lesson happening as they read it.

3. Ask a colleague if they would be willing to let you see a lesson plan they have created. What do you learn about the level of detail that is needed for you to be able to visualise their planned tasks?

Bibliography

Brown, G. 2010 (ed) *B.creative: A creative introduction for secondary school dance teachers and pupils.* Resource Pack. London: The Royal Ballet School, Dance Partnership and Access.

Fontana, D. 1995 *Psychology for Teachers*, [3rd edition] Basingstoke: Palgrave Macmillan.

Chapter 27
Preparing for the Viva Voce
Alysoun Tomkins

Introduction

This chapter considers how to prepare for the viva voce required for DDTAL assessment. It will also be found useful for practitioners undertaking vivas as part of other courses.

What is a viva voce? Literally, "viva voce" means by or with the living voice - i.e. by word of mouth as opposed to writing. So the viva examination is where you will discuss with the assessor your practice, which will include reflection on the observed class, the lines of enquiry in your reflective journal and will encompass your values and beliefs as a dance teacher.

Viva voce is, in the context of DDTAL, a discussion between the assessor and the student following the observation of the student's practical teaching. It differs from an oral examination where the assessor comes with prepared questions which the student answers. In universities these may occur following the submission of a dissertation or thesis or because the student is deemed to be at a borderline pass level. This is not the case with the DDTAL viva voce.

> Viva Voce is the traditional phrase [...] for an examination of knowledge through question and answer or discussion, rather than through a written paper. The content of discussion will always be relevant to what has been prepared [...] and demonstrated [...] It is usually a relaxed and pleasant kind of give-and-take conversation, rather than a quiz or a grilling.
>
> (www.trinitycollege.co.uk)

However, it is important to be aware of the overall learning outcomes of the DDTAL course (as specified on page 5 of the syllabus) as these are what you will be assessed against.

Why have it?

Put simply, you should think of it as a verbal counterpart to your written or filmed work in Units 1, 2 and 3. Your work in the previous Units demonstrated your skill at presenting your research in writing or to camera. In the viva examination you will demonstrate your ability to articulate your thoughts verbally. Being articulate about our work to both dance and non-dance colleagues is crucial in terms of being advocates for dance in both the formal and informal sectors. A very good measure of someone's understanding of a subject is their ability to explain verbally the subject to someone else.

In Chapter 24 on Reflective Journals you were encouraged to talk to yourself or use an imagined 'other' and now, in the viva, you can have those conversations with the assessor. You are expected to be a reflective practitioner applying theory to practice in learning and teaching. The purpose of the viva examination, therefore, is to demonstrate:

- Knowledge of theory and practice in learning and teaching in dance for children and young people.
- Understanding of dance teaching and facilitation of learning in different contexts.

- Verbal communication skills.
- Reflective and analytical skills.

Content of the Viva Voce

The viva assessment will take place after the assessor has observed you teaching, read your three lesson plans and looked at your reflective journal.

The assessor will have an agenda:

- Discussion of and reflection on the observed lesson and accompanying three lesson plans.
- Discussion of themes and lines of enquiry in your reflective journal.

During those discussions, the assessor may refer to the content of Units 1, 2 or 3 and the application of learning in those units to your present practice.

However, you may also come to your viva assessment with an agenda. There may be aspects of dance learning and teaching which you wish to discuss and this is perfectly acceptable and indeed, desirable.

Preparing for your viva voce assessment

In order to feel confident during the viva assessment it is advisable to prepare for it and anticipate the discussions which may occur and the topics which you may wish to introduce. Positive thinking will help you feel in control of the situation and will also increase your confidence. Try to:

- Anticipate the discussions to be had.
- Be ready to debate your points.
- Prepare thoroughly.
- Be eager and pleased to be there.
- Be excited at the challenge ahead but stay calm and focused.
- Listen carefully to the questions.
- Be passionate about your practice.
- Look forward to completing the qualification

The assessor will want to engage you in discussion so avoid answering with a simple 'yes' or 'no' to questions. Take your time to think about any questions posed and answer honestly. If you do not understand the question, ask the assessor to repeat the question, or repeat your interpretation to the assessor. If you still do not understand the question, then it is better to admit it than to try and bluff. Be prepared to justify your ideas. If the assessor challenges your idea but you feel that your case is a good one, support your arguments with examples from your practice.

If the assessor is observing a one-off workshop then the preceding and follow up sessions will be imaginary, in that they will not actually take place. The three lesson plans demonstrate your ability to plan detailed progression and it will be important to have fully imagined the sessions and what you hoped would have occurred in them so you can discuss this with the assessor.

In conclusion, consider the viva voce as an opportunity to talk about all of your learning and experiences whilst studying on the DDTAL programme. The process of learning is on-going and as such will continually inform your practice in order that it evolves and develops. The assessor will not expect you to be at the end of that learning, but rather consider that they are meeting you at a certain point in your development. It is the discussions to be had about the process of your learning that are important.

REFLECTION

Examples of questions to consider in your preparation:

Rather than just thinking about the following questions, ask someone to watch a class and then conduct a mock viva with you using some of the questions below:

- What were the aims of your session?
- What were the learning outcomes (what did you want the young people to know, understand and be able to do by the end of the session)?
- What is your evaluation of the session just taught?
- What worked well and why?
- What might you have done differently and why?
- How did the previous session prepare the young people for this one?
- Would you make any adjustments to the next session now you have taught this one?
- What do young people gain from your classes?
- How has your reflective journal helped you to develop your practice?
- How has your learning on the DDTAL programme informed your practice?

Bibliography

Trinity College London. 2010 *Diploma in Dance Teaching and Learning (Children and Young People)*. www.trinitycollege.co.uk/ddtal

Chapter 28
Rehearsing a lesson for assessment
Jo Rhodes

Introduction

This chapter takes the reader through a series of tasks in relation to the DDTAL syllabus and assessment criteria. It will also be found useful for practitioners undertaking a range of other dance teaching courses. For the purpose of this chapter the criteria, which can be found on page 31 of the syllabus, have been broken into the following sections:

- Evaluation
- Teaching and Learning
- Communication
- Adapting to Contexts

Evaluation

Firstly, let us consider the ultimate aim of the Unit 4 practical assessment. As reiterated in the grade descriptors, it is to demonstrate:

> an authoritative and engaging knowledge and understanding of autonomous
> dance learning and teaching with children and young people in specific contexts.
>
> (DDTAL syllabus, p. 32)

In order to do this it is vital to evaluate your practice and to rehearse the lesson you plan to deliver for the examination. It is crucial that it is well planned, delivered and managed and that any aspects deemed to have been ineffectual are highlighted and referenced in the viva.

Evaluation has been covered in detail in Chapter 10 so what follows is a summary to reinforce your understanding. Evaluation gives the practitioner the opportunity to reflect, review, and refine their work to maintain and improve standards. It aids in planning for the future, you learn from issues and challenges as well as what works in any given context. If self-evaluation finds an area for improvement in individual practice this should form part of a Continuing Professional Development plan. Sir Brian McMaster recommended a move towards self-assessment and peer review in '*Supporting Excellence in the Arts*' (2008). Therefore we must not only review ourselves, but also observe peers to share practice, experiences and question processes. Active learning occurs when an individual has a dialogue with themselves, as well as with others, and has experience of doing as well as observing. Recording and logging responses allow the artist to look back and make adjustments as necessary.

There are a variety of methods, with three examples listed as follows:

Video recordings

BENEFITS – you see through the eyes of the examiner and what they will see. You are able to look objectively at events and analyse them.

PITFALLS – needs to be clear, audible. Necessary permissions must be obtained. Position camera so whole space can be seen. Ensure personal interactions can be seen and heard. If watching it alone, perception of self may/ may not be challenged.

Interviewing participants / observers

BENEFITS – verbal response if done straight afterwards can express more. Directed or focused questioning can be useful.

PITFALLS – interviewees may not want to offend you. If done at a later stage, content or feedback may have been forgotten. Open questioning may not bring back required responses for reflection.

Questionnaires

BENEFITS – can be anonymous so might be more truthful, directed questions.

PITFALLS – need to be carefully designed, can give minimum amount of feedback, or rushed. May alienate some participants.

Case Study 1

Experiment with each method and log your responses in your Reflective Journal.

Questions one could ask include:
- How do participants enter the space? How are expectations set up?
- Do communication methods employed seem conducive to fostering and maintaining good relationships in the group? How?
- Do activities and the whole lesson have logical progression? How is this demonstrated?
- Are objectives made clear and are they achieved? How do you know?
- Are a variety of teaching strategies being utilised and to what effect?
- How are different learners addressed?
- Are you imparting knowledge of the art form and to what effect?

Dancers are adept and familiar with the **rehearsal** process. Just as you would not perform on stage without having rehearsed set material, you should not undertake Unit 4 assessment without having prepared and practised the planned lesson. With repetition, improvements can be made to existing plans, allowing for opportunities to adjust and refine specific strategies and develop different versions of tasks, or ways to articulate them.

UNIT 4 - DANCE TEACHING IN PRACTICE

> **Case Study 2**
>
> With your assessment class in mind record your responses to the following:
>
> 1. What improvements can be made to existing plans and why?
>   e.g. this could be a structural aspect to the lesson in that it did not logically progress in terms of skill development.
> 2. How can you adjust and refine a teaching strategy to enhance a task?
>   e.g. utilise demonstration instead of / or as well as auditory description.
> 3. Develop a different version of an activity
>   e.g. a solo task could be developed into a trio task.
> 4. Identify an instruction given in your class and consider how you could articulate it in a different way if participants do not understand the instruction.

Repetition enables the practitioner to familiarise themselves with the plans, approaches and structural aspects to the lesson(s). Thereby there is less reliance on referring to paper lesson plans as memory and recall can be used. Reproducing tasks in differing contexts demands modification of approaches and activities, enabling the practitioner to distinguish between what is effective and what is ineffective (see case study below). However, if working with the same group for the examination and the rehearsed lesson, certain tasks can be repeated, such as warm ups, but decide whether development of other sections might be useful rather than repetition of tasks. Participants who might have responded positively in the rehearsed session may become bored.

> **Case Study 3**
>
> Below are some examples of ineffective practice. In the boxes adjacent, try to analyse why these may occur and pinpoint actions.
>
> | Examples of ineffective practice | Why might this have occurred? | Action points |
> |---|---|---|
> | Participants feel excluded from the lesson | Material may be too difficult or too easy, geography of room – may not be able to see, may be peer group conflict unnoticed etc. | Ensure differentiation in tasks. Design activities and teaching style to change fronts in the room, work in circle for particular activity, look at how to organise groups, set up expectations of each other etc. |
> | Individual disengaged | | |
> | Factions appear in the room | | |
> | Injury occurs, unsafe practice | | |
> | Participants not 'on task' | | |
> | Participants do not understand | | |

Knowledge can be factual, such as knowing dance terminology, or experiential. It is up to the practitioner to discipline themselves to pick up and retain experiential knowledge, as experience without reflection is not conducive to development.

There are said to be three stages to reflection:

1. 'Thoughtful deliberation' (Tickle 1994, in Reid, 1994). This is careful and lengthy consideration about the class and strategies used within it. It can be done through your own observations or reflections but is often best done where discussion and debate are involved. It can be prior to or after the class.

2. 'Systematic, critical and creative thinking about action, with the intention of understanding its roots and processes' (Fish and Twinn 1997, in Reid, 1994). Systematic refers to regular, methodical and exact thinking. How often will you reflect on practice and in what ways? How will you interpret and understand its roots to improve practice?

3. 'Learning from experience' (Reid, 1994). Learning becomes evident when consideration is made as to what can be done next time, how has it improved practice?

Case Study 4

Look at your own observations of your rehearsed class. Try to find examples of the above stages.

Teaching and Learning

It is important to refer to Chapter 1 where teaching and learning theories were introduced. You will be applying this information in practice when you teach your live class for Unit 4. The following case study is to remind you of the content you studied there.

Case Study 5

In relation to your lesson plan consider where you have addressed the following learning styles in your warm up activities:

Activists – learn by doing!

Reflectors – like to think things through, watch others before having a go.

Theorists – like to understand reasons / concepts before doing.

Pragmatists – like to have tips and techniques before having a go.

In your practice lessons, try to identify these types of learners and note their reactions to tasks.

Understanding the ways in which children and young people learn will help you to tailor your planning of the assessed lessons. *Figure 1* on the next page provides a planning tool to fill in with reference to your assessment class.

Unit 4 - Dance Teaching in Practice

Consider Vygotsky's 'Zone of Proximal Development'. See Chapter 1 for a summary of this. Answer the questions posed in relation to pitching an appropriate level for your assessment class as well as planning the progression between classes.

Where the group / individuals are at	Where they want to be / potential / attainment levels	How to get there
Assess the context, address: • Age, gender, experience? • Specific needs? • Setting? • Purpose, aims, objective of the project?	Establish collective aims: For example: • Is it to improve technical dance skill? • To engage the community? • To engage the disengaged? • Curriculum based?	Planning: • Identify appropriate activities and structural aspects to the lesson for the group and individuals within it. • What strategies will you employ at what stages? • How will lessons progress?

Figure 1

Now you have considered where the group can progress to and how this manifests itself in planning, let us think about the teaching strategies you will use to support the group in reaching the end result. Look at Chapter 3 for details of Teaching Styles.

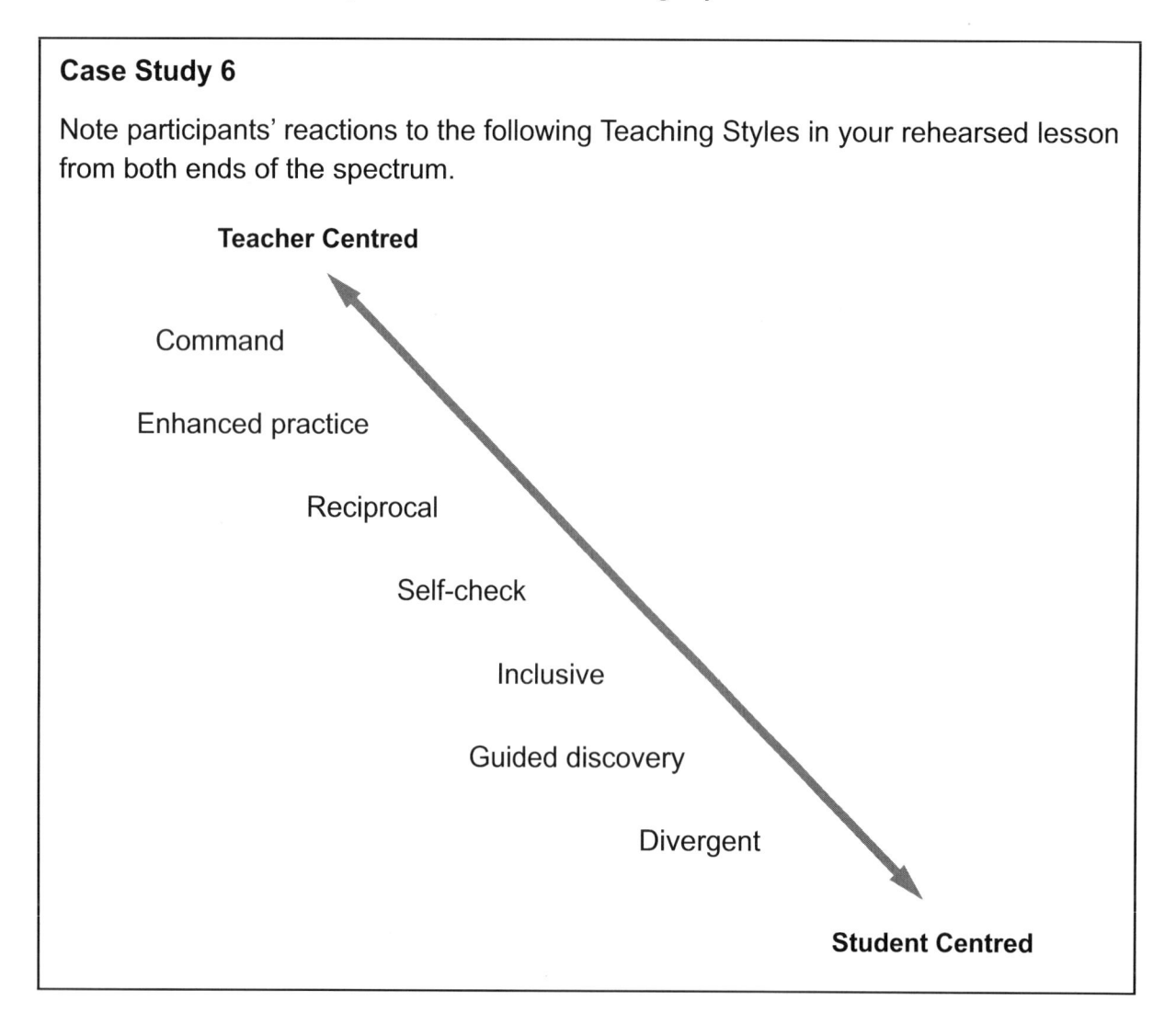

Case Study 6

Note participants' reactions to the following Teaching Styles in your rehearsed lesson from both ends of the spectrum.

Teacher Centred

- Command
- Enhanced practice
- Reciprocal
- Self-check
- Inclusive
- Guided discovery
- Divergent

Student Centred

With the evidence you have collected for the above Case Study, try to find alternative methods of doing the same activity in your planned lesson. For example:

Command – some may find this too constrictive, or alienating. How can you adapt this style to suit such participants?

Enhanced Practice – some may come 'off task'. How can you adapt this style to give support to suit such participants?

Reciprocal – some may not wish to be observed so closely by a peer. How can you adapt this style to suit such participants?

Self-Check – some may be self-conscious and not wish to participate; or they may comment on others in video sharing. How do you stop this or encourage positive feedback?

Inclusive – some may be playing safe and not be challenging themselves. When might this be appropriate? How can you adapt this style to suit such participants?

Guided Discovery – some may hide in a group context. How will you check understanding and analysis?

Divergent – some may wish to be told what to do and not enjoy free time to explore, some may become disengaged. How do you empower them to take part?

You have now contemplated, identified and observed your own strategies in your lesson. Let us now look at how others observe practice. Although practitioners' work is varied and may not answer to formal educational settings, one framework that remains useful to explore is Ofsted.

Consider the following quotation:

> Teaching is at least good and much is outstanding, with the result that the pupils are making exceptional progress. It is highly effective in inspiring pupils and ensuring that they learn extremely well [...]. Resources, including new technology, make a marked contribution to the quality of learning [...]. Teachers systematically and effectively check pupils' understanding throughout lessons, anticipating where they may need to intervene and doing so with striking impact on the quality of learning.
>
> (National New Heads Conference, 2009, n.p.)

What elements commented upon in this quotation do you find persuasive?

Using Ofsted criteria: the criteria in the checklists provided in the following pages are selected and adapted for their suitability to guiding analysis and reflection of your rehearsed class in the informal sector.

- Fill in the checklists with your assessment lesson in mind.
- Ask an observer to fill in the same checklist and compare their responses with your own to see if this matches your own perceptions of self. You could also rate each element as poor, satisfactory, good, very good, thereby addressing weaknesses.

1. Does the lesson get off to an orderly start?

- practitioner and participants arrive punctually.
- prepared for the lesson.
- suitable clothing, footwear etc.
- participants quick to focus on lesson.

- latecomers acknowledged.
- behavioural expectations are clear.

2. Are the aims and objectives of the lesson shared between practitioner and participants?

- aims and objectives are made clear and participants see the purpose of the lesson.
- links are made to the last lesson.
- lesson is drawn together at the end.
- participants are able to see how the learning will progress in future lessons.
- appropriate to context of session.

3. Does the practitioner establish good relationships with participants which promote learning?

- the practitioner is approachable.
- appropriate use of humour is used.
- participants are relaxed and confident.
- participants listen and respond to the teacher.
- praise is used very effectively.
- participants seem involved and challenged.

4. Does the practitioner use an appropriate variety of learning styles to promote participant achievement?

- learning styles are appropriate to lesson objectives and participants.
- participants are able to concentrate and contribute.
- participants are active and involved, even if injured.
- participants are able to communicate with each other. Learning is collaborative.
- the lesson is broken up into a variety of manageable activities.
- use of resources is appropriate to learners and activity.

5. Is the delivery style effective?

- the practitioner is audible.
- the tone and volume of delivery is varied.
- the pace of the lesson is appropriate to the group.
- all participants contribute.
- learning is checked throughout in a variety of ways, including questioning.
- participants are able to express their lack of understanding.
- a range of teaching roles are used (even when teaching specific skill / repertoire).
- clear instructions are given.
- work is checked, participants are supported.
- key words / terminology emphasised.

6. Does the lesson take account of differing ability of participants?

- teaching strategies allow participants to progress.
- teaching is planned and organised to ensure differentiated learning:
    → less able participants are supported;

→ more able participants are supported;

→ those with specific disabilities and difficulties have full access and are able to progress.

- tasks are thoughtfully constructed, evaluated and set.

7. Does the practitioner appear to display sound knowledge and understanding of their subject?

- the practitioner talks confidently about the subject matter.
- the practitioner is able to answer participants' questions and queries.
- participants are encouraged, inspired.
- appropriate terminology and language is used.
- the practitioner has the respect of the participants.

8. Is appropriate use made of equipment and other resources to support teaching and learning?

- practical work is carried out safely.
- any resources such as music, DVD are participant-friendly, clear and enhance learning.
- resources used effectively and when relevant.

9. Does the teaching environment promote learning?

- everyone in the studio can make eye contact, the geography of room has been considered.
- any written instructions / mindmaps etc. are clear.
- ventilation / heating is considered.
- health and safety is fully considered and adaptations successfully made.
- collaborative work is possible.
- space appropriate to dance activity.
- changing facilities pointed out.
- water is allowed and stored safely.

Communication

It is essential to consider Communication Skills in the delivery of dance. See page 31, point 2 of the DDTAL syllabus. There are things we do instinctively that impact upon others. For the purposes of the viva and for the development of your practice, Schön (1991) suggests that reflection is best in action where individuals *think what they are doing while they are doing it*. Below are examples of communication strategies and styles.

Verbal Communication

Examples of verbal communication in dance are speaking and listening skills. Consider the language that is used, is it suitable, understandable, encouraging and inclusive? Do you speak with clarity and confidence? Are you assertive in speaking? Do you ask questions to show interest, help a group or individual to develop/check understanding? Do you use motivational language? Do you empower others to be involved and progress? Do you listen carefully to what participants say?

Non-verbal communication

Body language, facial expression, posture and gesture all convey meaning. Are you confident, open and approachable? Do you make eye contact with individuals? Do you show enthusiasm and empathy via non-verbal means? Do you judge when it is more effective to encourage a participant through a gesture rather than using positive affirmations in language? Do you judge when it is more effective to resolve conflict through changing physical aspects in the room rather than through voice?

> **Case Study 7**
>
> Another useful model to look at in self-observation and reflection is Gibbs' reflective cycle, in table form below. Gibbs advocates that the emotion involved in a situation should be analysed. It is thought that if this can be made sense of, action can be put in place if it were to reoccur. With communication skills in mind, fill this in following a rehearsal lesson.
>
> See *Figure 2* below for an example that analyses an incident during an actual assessment class.

What happened? (description)	The teaching assistant present joined in unexpectedly with her socks on.
What were you thinking? (feeling)	I was thinking that I should ask her to take her socks off but thought she was just stepping in momentarily and would sit back down again afterwards. I felt that I didn't want to patronise her.
What was good / bad about the experience? (evaluation)	It was good that she was confident to assist in the development of the session with a particular individual child, as previous experience with the same school had showed a slight unwillingness of staff to participate. It was bad that she could have slipped and injured herself or fallen on a child.
How can you make sense of what happened? (analysis)	I was too focused on the participants and was unsure as to how to approach her, when firstly she was empowered enough to join in, and secondly I thought she was only joining in for a moment. I thought my focus on her was less important than my focus on the children that needed my support. Though this contravened health and safety.
What alternatives did you have? (reach a conclusion)	I could have found an opportunity when children were on task to speak with her quietly on her own and ask her to take them off. I could consider further how I can communicate with her.

CHAPTER 28 - REHEARSING A LESSON FOR ASSESSMENT

What would you do if it happened again? (construct an action plan)	I would ensure that I planned time to make it clear at the beginning that everyone must have bare feet and give reasons why. I could address her as and when appropriate to do so, on her own (preferably before the session begins so I would need to plan time and opportunity for this).

Figure 2

Adapting to Contexts

A practitioner should be able to show knowledge, understanding and competence in transferring and adapting skills across contexts. See page 31, point 3 in your DDTAL syllabus. Sometimes it can be hard to see what these adaptations are until you have observed others teaching out of your usual context. The following task enables the practitioner to relate experiences in their assessment class to discussions in their viva.

Case Study 8

Taking your lesson plan for assessment, redesign the plan from warm up to cool down for another context and explain how this would be adapted and the reasons for that adaptation. It may be with an older or younger group, a less or more experienced group, a gifted and talented group or a youth offending group for example.

Consider content, communication styles, learners' prior experience, teaching strategies etc. Will you also need to adapt any aims, objectives, assessment methods etc?

Creating an Action Plan

It is useful to write an action plan to follow in the months preceding the assessment. You do not want to be rushing around the day before trying to pull aspects together. You need to be focused on the task at hand when in the examination. The following is presented as an example to consider:

	Resources / Space	Planning	Health / safety	Reflections
In the months preceding	Look for the most appropriate space for the assessment class to take place in.	Try out certain tasks on different groups. Focus on logical development of lessons; one task leading into the next.	Consider safety aspects of the different tasks.	Be observed. Identify strengths and weaknesses in practice. Create a regular reflection strategy, addressing weaknesses in particular.

265

	Resources / Space	Planning	Health / safety	Reflections
In the weeks preceding	Source appropriate music for the group and theme of session.	Draft your completed lesson plans and try them out.	Obtain necessary media consent / emergency contact details if appropriate.	Be observed again to see if improvements have been made. Consider your Reflective Journal and ensure you are familiar with its content – see Chapter 27 for advice on preparing for the viva.
The week before	Ensure necessary equipment will be available.	Make any refinements to plans and re-print. If possible rehearse lesson.	Ensure instructions have safe practice aspects covered. Have you done a risk assessment?	Reflect on draft plans and consider adaptations. Discuss adaptations with peer or mentor.
The day before	Pack CDs, pens and any other resources required.	Ensure spare copies of lesson plan are available	Re check these aspects so you can be confident in delivering the lesson tomorrow.	Go through plan in your head, mental rehearsal. Know the preceding and follow on class.
On the day	Prepare space: remove obstacles, tape cables, consider geography of room and location of examiner / camera.	Give lesson plans to examiner.	Make health and safety your first priority when arriving at the venue. Check fire exits, location of first aid, facilities etc.	Read through plan once more. Try to recall events during the lesson in order to refer to in the viva. You may want to introduce the examiner to the group and reassure them that it is you that is being watched etc.

Figure 3

REFLECTION

1. In the reflection for *Figure 1*, what collective aims might there be in your assessed lesson that you might not have articulated fully on the plan?

2. Reflecting on the Vygotsky task further: in your rehearsed lesson, did participants reach their potential? How do you know? How did you check for learning? How will you show the assessment class in the context of a bigger work plan?

3. Look at the assessment criteria listed on page 31 of the DDTAL syllabus. (Or for the course you are studying) Under point 1, 'demonstrate effective practical teaching and learning skills within selected dance contexts', there are six detailed criteria. Take each in turn and reflect on how these are met in the three lesson plans that you will submit to the examiner.

4. Referring to the same set of assessment criteria considered in point 3 above, reflect on how these are now evidenced in your rehearsed class.

5. Using the model time line in *Figure 3* as guidance, draw up your own Action Plan with full dates and details of actions to be taken.

Bibliography

Amans, D, 2008 (Ed), *An Introduction to Community Dance Practice*. Basingstoke: Palgrave MacMillan

Bramley, I. 2002 (Ed), *Dance Teaching Essentials*. London: Dance UK.

Gibbs, G. 1988 Gibbs' Reflective Cycle, from *Learning by Doing: a guide to teaching and learning methods.* http://pdp.northampton.ac.uk/PG_Files/pg_reflect3.htm

Kassing, G. and Jay, D. 2003 *Dance Teaching Methods and Curriculum Design*. Champaign, Illinois: Human Kinetics.

Lord, M. 1993 'Reflections on the Preparation of Effective Dance Teachers'. In Fortin, S. Lord, M. Overby, L. Y. Stinson, S. W. (eds). Dance Dynamics: developing dance teachers' competencies. *Journal of Physical Education, Recreation and Dance*, Vol. 64.

McMaster, B. 2008 *Supporting Excellence in the Arts*. DCMS (January).

National New Heads Conference, 2009, *Leading Teaching and Learning*. National College for Leadership of Schools and Children's Services, www.nationalcollege.org.uk

Reid (first name unavailable), 1994. Reflective Practice. www.devon.gov.uk/reflectivepractice.pdf

Schön, D. A. 1991 *The Reflective Practitioner*. Aldershot: Arena, Ashgate [originally pub; London: Maurice Temple Smith, 1983].

Smith-Autard, J. 2004 *Dance Composition*. (5th edition) London: A & C Black.

Tickle, 1994 in http://www.scribd.com/doc/49422114/reflectivepractice.

Trinity College London. 2010 *Diploma in Dance Teaching and Learning (Children and Young People)*

Further Reading

Journals

Animated (Foundation for Community Dance)

dancematters (National Dance Teachers Association)

Dance Gazette (Royal Academy of Dance)

Research in Dance Education (Taylor and Francis Journal)

Professional Development in Education (Taylor and Francis Journal)

Theory into Practice (49, 3 – special issue: Accomplished Teaching as a Professional Resource) (Taylor and Francis Journal)

High Ability Studies (gifted and talented focus) (Taylor and Francis Journal)

Educational Review (Taylor and Francis Journal)

IADMS Bulletin for Teachers (free to download from www.iadms.org.uk)

Books

Akroyd, S. 2000 *Perspectives on Continuing Good Practice*. Ipswich: Dance East.

Amans, D. (ed) 2008 *An Introduction to Community Dance Practice*. Basingstoke: Palgrave Macmillan.

Bedell, S. (ed) 2007 *Turning the Tide – Designing and Managing a Participatory Arts Regeneration Project*. Momentum Arts. www.momentumarts.org.uk

Benjamin, A. 2002 *Making an Entrance: Theory and Practice for Disabled and Non-disabled Dancers*. London: Routledge.

Blakey, P. 1992 *The Muscle Book*. Stafford: Bibliotek Books.

Bloom, K and Shreeves, R. 1998 *Moves: a Sourcebook of Ideas*. London: Routledge.

Brinson, P. 1991 *Dance as Education: Towards a National Dance Culture*. London: Falmer Press.

Buckroyd, J. 2000 *The Student Dancer*. Alton: Dance Books.

Butler, R. J. 1996 *Sports Psychology in Action*. Oxford: Butterworth-Heineman.

Cash, M. and Wadmore, A. 1999 *The Pocket Atlas of the Moving Body*. London: Ebury Press.

Chmelar, R. D. and Fitt, S. 2002 *Diet for Dancers: A Complete Guide to Nutrition and Weight*. New Jersey: Princeton Book Co.

Clippinger, K. 2007 *Dance Anatomy and Kinesiology*. Champaign: Human Kinetics.

Davies, M. 1995 *Helping Children to Learn Through a Movement Perspective*. London: Hodder & Stoughton.

Davies, M. 2003 *Movement and Dance in Early Childhood (0-8)* (2nd edition). London: Sage Publications.

Duerden, R. and Fisher, N. 2008 *Dancing Off The Oage: Integrating Performance, Choreography, Analysis and Notation / Documentation*. Alton: Dance Books.

Dyke, S. 1999 *The Dancer's Survival Guide*. Dance UK.

Dyke, S. 2001 *Your Body Your Risk*. London: Dance UK.

Fay, M. 1997 *Mind Over Body: the development of the dancer – the role of the teacher*. London: A&C Black.

Fleming, N.D. undated *Teaching and Learning Styles: VARK Strategies*. www.vark-learn.com

Fontana, D. 1995 *Psychology for Teachers*. Basingstoke: Macmillan.

Franklin, E. 1996 *Dance Imagery for Technique and Performance*. Champaign: Human Kinetics.

Gardner, H. 2011. *Frames of mind: The Theory of Multiple Intelligences*. New York: Basic books.

Gibbons, E. 2007 *Teaching Dance: The Spectrum of Styles*. Author House.

Gough, M. 1999 *Knowing Dance, aA Guide for Creative Teaching*. London: Dance Books.

Grieg, V. *Inside Ballet Technique: Separating Anatomical Fact from Fiction in the Ballet Class*. New Jersey: Princeton Book Co.

Hall, T. 2007 *The Dance Review*. DCSF/DCMS. www.yde.org.uk/otherpublications

Hills, P. 2003 *It's Your Move!: An Inclusive Approach to Dance*. Birmingham: Questions Publishing.

Honey, P. and Mumford, A. 1986 *Using Your Learning Styles*. (revised edition) Maidenhead: Peter Honey.

Hutchinson Guest, A. and Curran, T. 2007 *Your Move, a New Approach to the Study of Movement and Dance*. Abingdon: Taylor Francis.

Jasper, L. and Siddal, J. (eds) 1999 *Managing dance: Current issues and future strategies*. Tavistock: Northcote.

Kassing, G. and Jay, D. 2003 *Dance Teaching Methods and Curriculum Design*. Champaign: Human Kinetics.

Kaufmann, K. 2005 *Inclusive Creative Movement and Dance*. Champaign: Human Kinetics.

Kimmerle M. and Côté-Laurence, P. 2003 *A Motor Learning and Development Approach*. USA: Michael J Ryan.

Kolb, D. A. 1984 *Experiential Learning – Experience as the Source of Learning and Development*. London: Prentice Hall.

Koutedakis, Y and Sharp, N, C. 1999 *The Fit and Healthy Dancer*. Oxford: Wiley Blackwell.

Lerman, L. and Borstel, J. 2003 *Liz Lerman's Critical Response Process: a method for getting useful feedback on anything you make*. US: Liz Lerman Dance Exchange. www.danceexchange.org

Lindon, J. 1993 *Child Development from Birth to Eight: A practical focus*. London: Dance Books

Lindon, J. 1996 *Understanding Children and Young People - development from 5-18 years*. London: Hodder Arnold.

Mastin, Z, 2009 *Nutrition for the Dancer*. Alton: Dance Books.

Moon, J. 2000 *Reflection in learning and professional development. Theory and Practice*. London: Routledge.

McCutchen, B. 2006 *Teaching Dance as Art in Education*. Champaign: Human Kinetics.

McFee, G. 2004 *The Concept of Dance Education*. (expanded edition) Eastbourne: Pageantry Press.

Siddall, J. 2010 *Dance In and Beyond Schools: An essential guide to dance teaching and learning*. London: Youth Dance England. www.yde.org.uk/publications

McGreevy-Nichols, S. and Scheff, H. 2005 *Building Dances*. (2nd edition) Champaign: Human Kinetics.

McGreevy-Nichols, S. Scheff, H. and Sprague, M. 2001 *Building More Dances: blueprints for putting movements together*. Champaign: Human Kinetics.

Mumford, A. 1999 *Effective Learning*. London, Chartered Institute of Personnel Development: Management Shapers.

Olsen, A. 1998 *Body stories: A guide to Experiential Anatomy*. Barrytown: Station Hill.

Peter, M. 1997 *Making Dance Special*. London: David Fulton.

Pomer, J., 2009 *Dance Composition: An Interrelated Arts Approach*. Champaign: Human Kinetics.

Ryan, A. J. and Stevens, R. 1989 *The Healthy Dancer, Dance Medicine for Dancers*. London: Dance Books.

Sexton, K. 2000 *The Dance Teacher's Survival Guide*. Alton: Dance Books.

Sherbourne, V. 1990 *Developmental Movement for Children*. Cambridge: Cambridge University Press.

Shreeves, R. 1990 *Children Dancing: A Practical Approach to Dance in the Primary School*. London: Ward Lock Educational.

Smith-Autard, J. 2002 *The Art of Dance in Education*. (2nd edition) London: A&C Black.

Smith-Autard, J. 2004 *dance composition*. (5th edition) London: A&C Black.

Smith, F. and Pocknell, L. 2007 *A Practical Guide to Teaching Dance*. UK: Association for Physical Education

Sprague, M. Scheff, H. and McGreevy-Nichols, S. 2006 *Dance About Anything*. Champaign: Human Kinetics.

Solomon, J. and Cerny Minton S. 2005 *Preventing Dance Injuries*. (2nd edition) Champaign: Human Kinetics.

Thomasen, E. and Rist, R. A. 1996 *Anatomy and Kinesiology for Ballet Teachers*. London: Dance Books.

Thornton, C. and Taylor, G. 1996 *Creative Equality: Making Equal Opportunities Work in the Arts*. Cambridge: Eastern Arts Board.

Todd, M. 1997 *The Thinking Body*. London: Dance Books

Whitley, A. 1995 *Look Before You Leap*. London: Dance UK.

Willis, P. 1990 *Moving Culture*. London: Calouste Gulbenkian Foundation.

Woolf, F. 2004 *Partnerships for Learning*. London: Arts Council England.